2 to 22 DAYS IN ITALY

THE ITINERARY PLANNER
1993 Edition

RICK STEVES

John Muir Publications
Santa Fe New Mexico

JMP travel guidebooks by Rick Steves
Asia Through the Back Door (with John Gottberg)
Europe Through the Back Door
Europe 101: History, Art, and Culture for the Traveler (with Gene Openshaw)
Kidding Around Seattle
Mona Winks: Self-Guided Tours of Europe's Top Museums (with Gene Openshaw)
2 to 22 Days in Europe
2 to 22 Days in France (with Steve Smith)
2 to 22 Days in Germany, Austria, and Switzerland
2 to 22 Days in Great Britain
2 to 22 Days in Italy
2 to 22 Days in Norway, Sweden, and Denmark
2 to 22 Days in Spain and Portugal

John Muir Publications, P.O. Box 613, Santa Fe, NM 87504

Printed in the United States of America

ISSN 1064-9328
ISBN 1-56261-089-9

Research assistance Steve Smith
Maps David C. Hoerlein
Typography Ken Wilson
Printer Banta Company
Cover Photo Leo de Wys Inc./Joachim Messerschmidt

Distributed to the book trade by
W. W. Norton & Co.
New York, New York

CONTENTS

How to Use this Book 1
Back Door Travel Philosophy 20
Itinerary 21
Italy 25
Depart U.S.A. 28
Days 1 and 2 Arrive and See Milan 29
Days 3 and 4 Milan to Italy's Riviera, the Cinque Terre 42
Day 5 Riviera to Florence via Pisa 53
Day 6 Florence 56
Day 7 Florence to Siena via San Gimignano 70
Day 8 Siena 72
Day 9 Siena to Civitá di Bagnoregio 82
Day 10 Free Day in the Hill Towns or Assisi 88
Days 11, 12, and 13 Rome 93
Day 14 Rome to Naples to Sorrento 124
Day 15 Sorrento Side Trips: Pompeii, Amalfi, Capri 136
Day 16 Amalfi Coast, Paestum, Night Train to Venice 144
Days 17 and 18 Venice 148
Days 19 and 20 The Dolomites, Italy's Alps 175
Days 21 and 22 Lake Como, Best of the Italian Lakes 184
Appendix 192
Telephone Information 192
Italy: Public Transportation 194
Train Connections 195
Index 197

Italy in 22 Days Tour Route

HOW TO USE THIS BOOK

This book is the tour guide in your pocket. It lets you be the boss by proposing in a clear step-by-step plan the best 22-day introduction to Italy. This guidebook helps you organize your time and offers hard opinions to give you maximum travel thrills per mile, minute, and dollar. It's for independent types who'd like the organization of a tour but the freedom of a do-it-yourself trip. You can follow it like the 22 Commandments, or use the information to create your own best itinerary.

Realistically, most travelers are interested in the predictable biggies—a gondola ride, the Sistine Chapel, the Leaning Tower, and more pasta. This tour covers those while mixing in a good dose of "back door intimacy"—forgotten Umbrian hill towns, a far-reaches-of-Venice pub crawl, idyllic Riviera harbors, and a cultural scavenger hunt through village Rome.

This 22 Days in Italy plan is carefully shaped and balanced to avoid tourist burn-out by excluding the mediocre and including only the most exciting places and experiences. I've been very selective. For example, there are dozens of great Italian hill towns. We'll zero in on just my favorite. The best is, of course, only my opinion. But after 20 busy years of travel writing, lecturing, tour guiding, and exploring Europe, I've developed a sixth sense of what tickles the traveler's fancy. And, just between you and me, this itinerary tickles mine.

While the trip is easiest and less expensive using Italy's impressive system of trains and public buses, it can also be done by car. I've designed the plan for those without a car, but each day's journey is adapted for car travel with explanations, options, and appropriate instructions.

The 2 to 22 Days itinerary planner series originated (and is still used) as the handbook for those who join me each summer on my "Back Door Europe" tours. And, since most large organized tours work to keep their masses ignorant while visiting many of the same places we'll cover, this book can serve as a self-defense manual for anyone taking a typical big bus tour who wants to maintain independence and flexibility.

Of course, connect-the-dots travel isn't perfect, just as color-by-numbers isn't great art. But this book is your friendly Florentine, your Roman buddy, your handbook. It's your well-thought-out and tested itinerary. I've done it—and refined it—many times on my own and with groups. Use it, take advantage of it, but don't let it rule you.

Your Trip Cost

This three-week trip by train and bus costs around $300. It costs $800 to $1,000 to fly round-trip to Milan from the U.S.A. For room, board, and sightseeing, figure about $70 a day for 22 days, totaling $1,540. (That's assuming $60 doubles with breakfast, $7 lunches, $18 dinners, $10 for sightseeing, and $5 for cappuccino and gelati. This is a feasible budget and can be done for less if necessary. The tricks are taught in my book, *Europe Through the Back Door.*) Add $300 or $400 of fun money, and you've got yourself a great Italian adventure for around $3,000. Do it!

The Layout

Read this book from cover to cover, then use it as a rack upon which to hang more ideas as your trip evolves. As you study and travel and plan and talk to people, you'll fill it with notes. It's your tool. The book is completely modular and adaptable to any Italian trip. You'll find 22 units—or days—each built with the same sections:

1. Introductory **overview** for the day.

2. Suggested hour by hour **schedule** for the day (using the 24-hour clock).

3. **Transportation** plan for train, bus, or car.

4. **Orientation,** tourist information.

5. List of **Sightseeing Highlights** (rated: ▲▲▲ Don't miss; ▲▲ Try hard to see; ▲ Worthwhile if you can make it; no pyramid—worth knowing about).

6. An easy-to-read **map** locating all recommended places.

7. **Eating and Sleeping:** how and where to find the best budget places, including addresses, telephone numbers, prices, and my favorites.
8. **Itinerary Options** for those with more or less than the suggested time, or with particular interests. This itinerary is flexible!

The back of the book includes an important Appendix with helpful extras such as a tour telephone directory and public transportation specifics. Use the Appendix.

Efficient Travel: Thinking Ahead and Using Tourist Information Offices

Many travel through Italy thinking it's a chaotic mess. Any attempt at organization is seen as futile and put off until they get to Switzerland. This is dead wrong—and expensive. Italy is a living organism that on the surface seems as orderly as spilled spaghetti, but it functions quite well. Only those who understand this and travel smart can enjoy Italy on a budget. This itinerary assumes you are a well-organized traveler who lays departure groundwork upon arrival, reads a day ahead in the itinerary, uses the telephone routinely, keeps a list of things that should be taken care of, takes full advantage of the local tourist offices, and avoids problems whenever possible before they happen.

If you expect to travel smart, you will. If you insist on being confused, your trip will be a costly mess. Do what you can to call ahead or double check hours and times when you arrive.

When to Go

Italy's best travel months are May, June, September, and October. November through April is usually pleasant weather with generally none of the sweat and stress of the tourist season. Peak season (July and August) offers the longest hours and the most exciting slate of activities—but terrible crowds and, at times, suffocating heat. August, the local holiday month, isn't as bad as many make it out to be, but big cities tend to be quiet and beach and mountain resorts are jammed. If you anticipate crowds, arrive early in the day or call hotels in advance (call from one hotel to the next; your receptionist can help you). Summer temperatures range from the 70s in Milan to the high 80s and 90s in Rome. In the winter it often drops to the 30s and 40s in Milan and the 40s and 50s in Rome.

Italy has more than its share of holidays. Each town has a local festival honoring its patron saint. February is Carnevale time in Venice. Italy closes down on these national holidays: January 1, January 6 (Epiphany), Easter Sunday and Monday, April 25 (Liberation Day), May 1 (Labor Day), August 15 (Assumption of Mary), November 1 (All Saints Day), December 8 (Immaculate Conception of Mary), December 25 and 26. For a complete listing of this year's festivals in English, write to the Italian National Tourist Office (address below).

Prices

I've priced things throughout this book in lire with rough exchange reminders at the beginning of each Eating and Sleeping section. These prices, as well as the hours, telephone numbers, and so on, are accurate as of late 1992. Italy refuses to sit still, and I have tossed timidity out the window knowing you'll understand that this book, like any guidebook, starts growing old even before it's printed. Approximate prices are given. While discounts are not listed, seniors (60 and over), students (with ISIC cards), and youths (under 18) may get substantial discounts. Lately, many senior, student, or youth discounts only work for European residents. Italy's annual inflation rate is down to about 5 percent.

Accommodations

Sleeping in Italy is expensive. Those traveling on a budget need help. Cheap hotels can be sleazy, depressing, and dangerous. Tourist information services can give no opinions on quality. A major feature of this book is its extensive listing of good value hotels with doubles ranging from $40 to $140 a night. I like places that are clean, small, central, quiet at night, traditional, inexpensive, and friendly, with firm beds and not in other guidebooks. Most places listed have six of these nine virtues. Budget travelers have a wide range of money-saving alternatives to choose from—convents, youth hostels, campgrounds, and private homes. Whenever applicable, I've listed these.

Hotels

Unless otherwise noted, hotel prices are for two people in a double room with breakfast. Those listed in this book will range from about $40 (very simple, toilet and shower down the hall) to $140 (maximum plumbing and more) for a double, with most clustering around $60. It's higher in big cities and heavily touristed cities and less off the beaten path. Three or four people can economize by requesting larger rooms. Solo travelers find that the cost of a *camera singola* is often only 20 percent less than a *camera doppia*. Most listed hotels have rooms for anywhere from one to five people.

Italy has a five-star rating system, but while the stars can give you a general idea of price range, the government no longer regulates hotel prices. Prices are pretty standard, and you normally get close to what you pay for. Shopping around earns you better location and more character but rarely a cheaper price. You'll save $10 to $20 if you ask for a room without a shower and just use the public shower down the hall (although in many cases the rooms with the extra plumbing are larger and more pleasant). A bathtub costs about $5 more than a shower. Double beds (*matrimoniale*, but hotels aren't interested in your marital status) are cheaper than twins (*camera doppia*). A few places have kept the old titles, *locanda* or *pension*. These indicate they offer budget beds. The word *albergo* means hotel.

Ancient Romans ate no breakfast at all, and the breakfast scene has improved only marginally. Except for the smallest places, a very simple continental breakfast is normally included. If you like juice and protein for breakfast, supply it yourself. I enjoy a box of juice in my hotel room and often supplement the skimpy breakfasts with a piece of fruit and a separately wrapped little piece of cheese. (A zip-lock baggie is handy for petite eaters to grab an extra breakfast roll and slice of cheese, when provided, for a fast and free light lunch.) The hotel breakfast is usually a bad value—$8 for a roll, jelly, and lots of *cafe con leche.* Budget travelers should avoid it when possible.

Rooms are safe. Still, zip cameras and money out of sight. More pillows and blankets are usually in the closet or available on request. Remember, in Italy towels and linen aren't always replaced every day—drip dry and conserve.

To reserve a hotel room from the U.S.A, write or fax (simple English is usually fine) to the address listed and identify clearly the dates you intend to be there. (A two-night stay in August would be "2 nights, 16/8/93 to 18/8/93"—European hotel jargon uses your day of departure and European system.) You may receive a letter response requesting one night's deposit. Send a $50 signed traveler's check or a bank draft in the local currency. More and more, travelers can reserve a room with a simple phone call or fax, leaving a credit card number as a deposit. You can pay with your card or by cash when you arrive, and if you don't show up, you'll be billed for one night anyway. Ideally, the hotel receptionist will hold a room for you without a deposit if you promise to arrive by midafternoon and call to reconfirm two days before arrival.

When you reserve or confirm through the TI, they often get a fee from you and a percent from the hotel. Go direct when you can. Upon arrival, the receptionist will normally ask for your passport. Hotels are legally required to register each guest with the local police. Americans are notorious for making this chore more difficult than it needs to be.

You can do this tour without making long-distance hotel reservations. Even so, when you know where you'll be tomorrow night, life on the road is easier if you telephone ahead to reserve a bed. The most highly recommended hotels in this book get lots of likable and reliable 22 Days readers and will usually hold a room with a phone call until 17:00 with no deposit. They are usually accustomed to us English-speaking monoglots. Except in July or August, I would do this entire tour calling listed places the morning of the day I plan to arrive. Use the telephone! I've listed numbers with area codes. See the Appendix for long-distance dialing instructions.

While bed and breakfasts (*affitta camere*) and youth hostels (*ostello della gioventu*) are not as common in Italy as elsewhere in Europe, I've listed quite a few through this 3-week plan. While big city hostels are normally overrun with the Let's Go crowd, small town hostels can be a wonderfully enjoyable way to save money and make friends. I know little about camping in Italy except that nearly every city is served by a campground with a handy bus connection, many travelers enjoy camping Italy, and with an appropriate "camping through Italy" guidebook it's about the cheapest way to go. Remember, buying your own groceries and cooking is far cheaper than the cheapest meals you'll find in Italian restaurants.

Eating Italian

The Italians are masters at the art of fine living. That means eating . . . long and well. Long multicourse lunches and dinners and endless hours sitting in outdoor cafés are the norm. Americans eat on their way to an evening event and complain if the check is slow in coming. For Italians, the meal is an end in itself and only rude waiters rush you. Dinners get later as you go south (19:30 in Milan, 21:00 in Rome). When you want the bill, say "Il conto?"

Even those of us who liked dorm food will find that the local cafés, cuisine, and wines become a highlight of our Italian adventure. Trust me, this is sightseeing for your palate, and even if the rest of you is sleeping in cheap hotels, your buds will want an occasional first-class splurge. You can eat well without going broke. But be careful; you're just as likely to blow a small fortune on a disappointing meal as you are to dine wonderfully for $20.

Restaurants

When restaurant hunting, choose places filled with locals, not the place with the big neon signs boasting, "We speak English and accept credit cards." Look for menus posted outside. For unexciting but basic values, look for set-price or tourist menus. Galloping gourmets order à la carte with the help of a menu translator. (The *Marling Italian Menu Master* is excellent. My Europe Through the Back Door Italian phrase book has phrases covering eating and just about everything else.)

While the full meal consists of an appetizer (antipasto, L5000 and up), a first course (*primi piatto*, pasta, or soup, L6000-9000) and a second course (*secondo piatto,* expensive meat and fish dishes, L12,000-20,000). Vegetables (*contorno*) may come with the secondo or be available for extra lire as a side dish. Restaurants normally pad the bill with a cover charge (*pane e coperto*, about L2000) and a service charge (*servizio*, 15%). These days, service is added automatically to the bill, and tipping beyond that is unnecessary.

As you can see, the lire will add up in a hurry. Light and budget eaters can get by with a primi piatto. Hungry paupers can even go with two: a minestrone and a pasta. Self-service places and a few lower-class eateries feed you without the add-ons. Family-run places operate without hired help and can offer cheaper meals. *Osteria* is normally a simple local-style restaurant.

Many modern Italian fast food places slam dunk pasta rather than hamburgers cheap and fast. Rosticceria are like delis with great cooked food to go. Pizza places (often called "Pizza Rustica") serve up fresh pizza by the weight. Two hundred grams with a soft drink makes a good cheap lunch. American-style fast food is inexpensive and often a good bet for a salad bar.

Cafés and bars offer snacks (mini-pizzas, sandwiches, cartons of milk from the cooler, plates of fried cheese and vegetables under the glass counter ready to reheat) and tables. This is my budget choice, the Italian equivalent of English pub grub. It's cheap, friendly, very local, and edible, and you can sit down.

Bar and cafeteria procedure can be frustrating. Decide what you want, check the price list on the wall, pay the cashier, give the receipt to the bartender (whose clean fingers handle no dirty lire), and tell him what you want. *Panini* is sandwich. *Da portar via* is "for the road."

Picnic

In Italy, picnicking saves lots of lire. Besides the savings, picnicking is a great way to sample local specialties. And, in the process of assembling your meal, you get to plunge into local markets with the Italians.

On days you choose to picnic, gather supplies early. You'll probably visit several small stores or market stalls to assemble a complete meal, and many close around noon. While it's fun to visit the small specialty shops, a local *alimentari* is your one-stop corner grocery store. *Supermarcatos* give you decent quality with less color, less cost, and more efficiency.

Juice lovers can get a liter of OJ for the price of a Coke or coffee. Look for "100%" on the label or suffer through a sickly sweet orange drink. Buy juice in less expensive liter boxes, and store what you don't drink in your reusable water bottle for nipping between sights. Hang onto the twist-top half-liter mineral water bottles (sold everywhere for L1000).

Remember, picnics can be an adventure in high cuisine. Be daring; try the smelly cheeses, midget pickles, ugly olives, and any UFOs the locals are excited about. Local shopkeepers are happy to sell small quantities of produce and even slice and stuff a sandwich for you. If in a busy market, a merchant may not want to weigh and sell small, three carrot-type quantities. In this case estimate generously what you think it should cost and hold out the lire in one hand, the produce in the other, and a smile on your face. He'll grab the money. A typical picnic for two might be fresh rolls, two tomatoes, three carrots, 100 grams of cheese, 100 grams of meat (100 grams = about a quarter pound, called *etto* in Italy), two apples, a liter box of juice, and a yogurt. Total cost for two—$8.

Culture Shock—Accepting Italy as a Package Deal
While we think shower curtains are logical, many Italians just cover the toilet paper and let the rest of the room shower with you. Italians give their "ones" an upswing and cross their "sevens." If you don't adapt, your "seven" will be mistaken for a sloppy "one" and you'll miss your train—and probably find a reason to be mad at the local system. Fit in! If the beds are too short, the real problem is that you are too long. Two different travelers can experience the same Italy and, depending on their attitudes, have entirely different experiences.

Transportation: Car or Train?
This itinerary goes either way. But more than in any of my other 2 to 22 Days books, this itinerary works best by train and bus. Therefore, this book is written directly to the train traveler, with notes throughout for drivers.

Each mode of transportation has pros and cons. One of the few bargains in Italy is its public transportation. Trains and buses are not only inexpensive, they are very good. City to city travel is faster, easier, and cheaper by train than by car. Trains give you the convenience and economy of doing long stretches overnight. By train I arrive relaxed and well rested—not so by car.

Parking, gas, and tolls are expensive in Italy. But drivers enjoy more control, especially in the countryside. Cars carry your luggage for you, generally from door to door—especially important for heavy packers (such as families traveling with children). And groups know that the more people you pack into a car or minibus, the cheaper it gets per person.

Train Travel in Italy
You could do this itinerary cheapest by simply buying the tickets as you go and avoiding the more expensive express trains. A second-class Rome to Venice ticket costs about $45. But Italy's train ticket system confounds even the locals, and, for convenience alone, I'd go with the Italian State Railway's BTLC "Go Anywhere" pass. It comes in first- or second-class varieties for 8, 15, 21, and

30 days and includes all of Italy's confusing express train supplements. The 21-day second-class pass costs only $220. For specifics on these contact CIT, Italian Rail's U.S.A. representative, in Los Angeles at 310/338-8615 or in New York at 212/274-0593.

There is also a "kilometric" ticket good for 20 trips or 3,000 kilometers over two months and shareable by up to five people ($156 second class or $264 first class in 1993). This pass, which doesn't cover fast train supplements, can be bought at major Italian train stations. Each journey must be recorded and stamped at a ticket window before you board the train. Children under 12 cost you only 50 percent of their mileage traveled. Children under 4 travel free. For this itinerary a Eurailpass is not worthwhile.

You'll encounter four types of trains in Italy: the *accelerato* or *locale* is the miserable milk-run train. The *diretto* is faster. The *espresso* zips very fast connecting only major cities. *Rapido* and Intercity trains are the sleek, air-conditioned top-of-the-line trains that charge a supplement (covered by the Eurail and BTLC train passes).

Italians trains are famous for their thieves. Never leave a bag unattended. There have been cases when bandits have gassed an entire car before looting the whole snoozing gang. I've noticed recently that police ride the trains and things seem more controlled. Still, for an overnight ride, I'd feel safe only in a *cuccetta* (a $15 bunk bed in a special sleeping car with an attendant who keeps track of who comes and goes while you sleep).

Avoid big city train station lines whenever you can. You can buy tickets at a travel agency. And you can plan your rail journey with fun and clever new computer train schedule terminals. Watch the locals use one and then give it a try yourself. Because of the threat of bombs, you won't find storage lockers. But each station has a *deposito* where, for L1500 a day, you can safely leave your bag.

Car Rental

Research car rental before you go. It's much cheaper to arrange car rentals for Italy in the United States through your travel agent. Rent by the week with unlimited mileage. If you'll be renting for more than three weeks, ask about leasing, which is a scheme to save on insurance and taxes. I normally rent the smallest, least expensive model. Explore your dropoff options. For this tour consider scrambling things around to do the car-friendly stuff (the Lakes and Dolomites and hill towns) by car and the cities and the south by train.

Your car rental price includes minimal insurance with a very high deductible. A CDW (Collision Damage Waiver) insurance supplement covers you for this deductible. This provides great peace of mind but is a bad value when purchased from your car rental agency. Since deductibles are horrendous, normally the entire value of the car, I usually splurge for the CDW. Ask your travel agent about money-saving alternatives to this car rental agency rip-off. The way I understand it, the roughly $10 a day you'll spend for CDW is where the car rental agency makes up for its highly competitive, unprofitably low, weekly rental rates.

Driving in Italy

Driving in Italy is frightening—a video game for keeps and you only get one quarter. All you need is your valid U.S. driver's license and a car. (According to everybody but the Italian police, international drivers' licenses are not necessary.)

Italy's freeway system is as good as our interstate system. But you'll pay about a dollar for every ten minutes of use. Savvy local drivers know which toll-free highways are actually faster and more direct than the autoroute, which should not be the automatic choice. I favor the autoroutes for the time and gas saved and because I find them safer and less nerve-racking than the smaller roads. You'll pay more to park in Italy than in a comparable American town. Garages are safe and save time and the stress of parking tickets. Always take the parking voucher with you to pay the cashier before you leave. Cars are routinely vandalized and stolen. Try to make your car look locally owned: hide the "tourist-owned" rental company decals, put a local newspaper in your back window.

Scheduling

Your overall itinerary strategy is a fun challenge. Read through this book and note the problem days when most museums are closed. (Mondays are bad in Milan, Florence, and Rome.) Many museums and sights, especially large ones, stop admitting people 30 minutes to an hour before closing time.

Sundays have the same pros and cons as they do for travelers in the U.S.A. City traffic is light. Sightseeing attractions are generally open, but shops and banks are closed. Rowdy evenings are rare on Sundays. Saturdays are virtually weekdays with earlier closing hours. Hotels in tourist areas are often booked out in August and on Fridays and Saturdays.

Plan ahead for banking, laundry, post office chores, and picnics. Mix intense and relaxed periods. Every trip needs at least a few slack days. The itinerary this book proposes is a series of two-night stands. A series of one-night stands is hectic and tiring.

To function smoothly in Italy, get comfortable with the 24-hour clock. I've used "military time" throughout this book. Everything is the same until noon. After noon just subtract 12 and you'll get the p.m. time. (So 16:30 is 4:30 p.m.)

Speed

This itinerary is fast but feasible. It's designed for the American who puts up with the shortest vacation time in the rich world and wants to see everything—but doesn't want the "if it's Tuesday it must be Tuscany" craziness. It can be done if all goes well. But all won't go well. A few slack days come in handy. I've listed many more sights than any mortal tourist could possibly see in 22 days. They are rated so you can make the difficult choices to shape your most comfortable, smooth, and rewarding trip.

Pace yourself. Assume you will return. Every traveler's touring tempo varies. Personalize this busy schedule; plug in rest days, and skip sights where and when you need to. Stretching this trip to 28 or 30 days would be luxurious. (Your boss will understand.)

Keeping Up with the News (If You Must)

To keep in touch with world and American news while traveling in Europe, read the *International Herald Tribune*, which comes out almost daily via satellite from many places in Europe. Every Tuesday the European editions of *Time* and *Newsweek* hit the stands with articles of particular interest to European travelers. Sports addicts can get their "fix" from *USA Today* newspapers. News in English will only be sold where there is enough demand—in big cities and tourist centers. If you are concerned about how some event might affect your safety as an American traveling abroad, call the U.S. consulate or embassy in the nearest big city for advice.

Receiving Mail in Italy

Mail service is miserable in Italy. And postcards get last priority. It's best to tell your loved ones you're going behind the dark side of the moon for a while or keep in touch with a few phone calls. If you must have mail stops consider a few prereserved hotels along your route or use American Express Mail Services. Most American Express offices in Italy will keep mail addressed to you for one month. (They mail out a free listing of addresses.) This service is free to anyone using an AmExCo card or traveler's checks (and available for a small fee to others). Allow 14 days for U.S. to Italy mail delivery, but don't count on it. Federal Express makes two-day deliveries, for a price.

Terrorism

As those who enjoyed their European travels in 1991 can attest, media hype about terrorism has no business affecting your travel plans. Viewed emotionally, it may seem dangerous. But statistically, while terrorism is a risk, the streets of Italy are much safer than the streets of urban America (where 8,000 people are killed every year by hand guns). Just keep the risk in perspective, and melt into Italy by traveling like a temporary local. Terrorists don't bomb the kinds of hotels listed in this book—that's where they sleep.

Recommended Guidebooks

This small book is your itinerary handbook. While you could have a fine trip relying only on this book, I'd supplement it with a guidebook or two. Guidebooks are $15 tools for $3,000 experiences. For Italy, these are my favorites:

General low budget directory-type guidebook: *Let's Go: Italy* is a worthy supplement for student low-budget train travelers, people planning to leave my recommended route, youth hostelers, and those interested in the nightlife and youth scene (which I have basically ignored). For this trip do not use *Let's Go: Europe* unless you wish you were in Fort Lauderdale.

Cultural and sightseeing guides: The tall green Michelin guides to Italy and Rome have nothing on room and board but lots on driving, the sights, customs, and culture. The little blue American Express guides to Venice, Florence, and Rome are also handy for those who like lots of information. The Cadagon guides to Italy offer an insightful look at the rich and confusing local culture. And those heading for Florence should read Irving Stone's *The Agony and the Ecstasy* for a great—if romanticized—run-down on Michelangelo, the Medici, and the turbulent times of the Renaissance.

Rick Steves's books: Finally, my books, *Europe Through the Back Door* and *Europe 101*, will give you practical skills to travel smartly and independently and information to really understand and enjoy your sightseeing. To keep this book pocket-sized, I've resisted the temptation to repeat the most applicable and important information already included in my other books; there is virtually no overlap.

Europe Through the Back Door (John Muir Publications, 1993) gives you the basic skills that make this demanding 22-day plan possible. Chapters cover choosing and using a travel agent, minimizing jet lag, packing light, driving or train travel, finding budget beds without reservations, changing money, theft and the tourist, hurdling the language barrier, health, travel photography, itinerary strategies, ugly-Americanism, laundry, and more. The book also includes special articles on my 40 favorite "Back Doors," several of which are stops on this 2- to 22-day plan.

Europe 101: Art for Travelers (co-written with Gene Openshaw, John Muir Publications, 1993), which gives you the story of Europe's people, history, and art, is heavy on Italy's ancient, Renaissance, and modern history. A little "101" background knowledge brings to life the sights you'll see.

Mona Winks: Self-Guided Tours of Europe's Top Museums (co-written with Gene Openshaw, John Muir Publications, 1993) gives you self-guided tours through Europe's most exhausting and important museums, with one-to three-hour tours of the major museums with historic highlights. Nearly half the book is devoted to Italy with tours covering Venice's St. Mark's, the Doge's Palace, and Accademia Gallery; Florence's Uffizi Gallery, Bargello, Michelangelo's *David*, and a Renaissance walk through the town center; Rome's Colosseum, Forum, Pantheon, the Vatican Museum, and St. Peter's Basilica. If you're planning on touring these sights, *Mona* will be a valued friend.

Italy is one country where a phrase book is as fun as it is necessary. My *Europe Through the Back Door* Italian phrase book (published by John Muir) is the only book of its kind, designed to help you meet the people and stretch your budget by a monoglot who for twenty years has fumbled happily through Italy struggling with all the other phrase books. This is a fun and practical communication aid so you can make accurate hotel reservations over the telephone, ask for a free taste of cantaloupe-flavored gelato, and have the man in the deli make you a sandwich.

Your bookstore should have these four books, or you can order directly from John Muir Publications using the order form in the back of this book.

For this trip, I'd buy: (1) *Let's Go: Italy*, (2) *Mona Winks* (take only applicable chapters), and (3) the ETBD Italy phrase book. (Total cost: about $40.) Read *Europe Through the Back Door* and *Europe 101* at home before departing. Except for the Michelin guides, English-language guidebooks are hard to find and very expensive in Italy.

Maps

Don't skimp on maps. Train travelers do fine with Michelin's #988 Italy map or even just the free rail pass map and local tourist office freebies. But drivers need a good map for each leg of their journey. Italian gas stations and bookstores have good maps. Get the most sightseeing value out of your maps by learning the key.

This book's maps are concise and simple, designed and drawn by David C. Hoerlein (who travels this route each year as a tour guide) to make the text easier to follow and to help you locate recommended places and get to the tourist office where you'll find a more in-depth map (usually free) of the city or region.

Tourist Information

Before your trip, send a letter to an Italian National Tourist Office telling them of your general plans and asking for information: **Italian Government Tourist Office,** 630 Fifth Avenue, #1565, New York, NY 10020, 212/245-4822; 12400 Wilshire Boulevard, #550, Los Angeles, CA 90025, tel. 310-820-0098, or 500 North Michigan Avenue, #1046, Chicago, IL 60611, tel. 312/644-0990. They'll send you the general packet, and if you ask for specifics (a publication called "General Information for Travelers to Italy," the calendars of festivals, good hikes around Lake Como, wine-tasting in Umbria, or whatever), you'll get an impressive amount of help. If you have a specific problem, they are a good source of assistance.

During your trip, your first stop in each town should be the tourist office where you'll take your turn at the informational punching bag smiling behind the desk. This person is rushed and tends to be robotic. Prepare. Have a list of questions and a proposed plan to double check with him or her. They have a wealth of material that the average "Duh, do you have a map?" tourist never taps. I have listed phone numbers throughout, and if you'll be arriving late, call ahead. Be wary of travel agencies or special information services serving fancy hotels that masquerade as tourist information offices. They are usually crooks and liars.

Send Me a Postcard, Drop Me a Line

While I do what I can to keep this book accurate and up-to-date, Italy just won't sit still. If you enjoy a successful trip with the help of this book and would like to share your discoveries (and make my job a lot easier), please send any tips, recommendations, criticisms, or corrections to Box 2009, 109 4th N., Edmonds, WA 98020. All correspondents will receive a year's subscription to our "Back Door Travel" quarterly newsletter (it's free anyway). Traveling eggheads can update this book for free or share tips by tapping into our free computer bulletin board travel information service (206-771-1902:1200 or 2400/8/N/1). Thanks, and happy travels!

Raise Your Dreams to Their Upright and Locked Position

My goal is to free you, not chain you. Please defend your spontaneity as you would your mother. Use this book to avoid time- and money-wasting mistakes, to get more intimate with Italy by traveling as a temporary local person, and as a starting point from which to shape your best possible travel experience.

If you've read this far, you're smart enough to do this tour on your own. Be confident; enjoy the hills as well as the valleys. Judging from all the positive feedback and happy postcards I get from travelers who used my other 2 to 22 Days guidebooks, it's safe to assume you're on your way to a great Italian vacation—independent, inexpensive, and with the finesse of an experienced traveler. Italy, here you come.

BACK DOOR PHILOSOPHY

AS TAUGHT IN *EUROPE THROUGH THE BACK DOOR*

Travel is intensified living—maximum thrills per minute and one of the last great sources of legal adventure. Travel is freedom. It's recess, and we need it.

Experiencing the real Europe requires catching it by surprise, going casual . . . "Through the Back Door."

Affording travel is a matter of priorities. (Make do with the old car.) You can travel—simple, safe, and comfortable—anywhere in Europe for $50 a day plus transportation costs. In many ways, spending more money only builds a thicker wall between you and what you came to see. Europe is a cultural carnival, and time after time, you'll find that its best acts are free and the best seats are the cheap ones.

A tight budget forces you to travel close to the ground, meeting and communicating with the people, not relying on service with a purchased smile. Never sacrifice sleep, nutrition, safety, or cleanliness in the name of budget. Simply enjoy the local-style alternatives to expensive hotels and restaurants.

Extroverts have more fun. If your trip is low on magic moments, kick yourself and make things happen. If you don't enjoy a place, maybe you don't know enough about it. Seek the truth. Recognize tourist traps. Give a people the benefit of your open mind. See things as different but not better or worse. Any culture has much to share.

Of course, travel, like the world, is a series of hills and valleys. Be fanatically positive and militantly optimistic. If something's not to your liking, change your liking. Travel is addicting. It can make you a happier American, as well as a citizen of the world. Our Earth is home to six billion equally important people. It's humbling to travel and find that people don't envy Americans. They like us, but with all due respect, they wouldn't trade places.

Globe-trotting destroys ethnocentricity. It helps you understand and appreciate different cultures. Travel changes people. It broadens perspectives and teaches new ways to measure quality of life. Many travelers toss aside their hometown blinders. Their prized souvenirs are the strands of different cultures they decide to knit into their own character. The world is a cultural yarn shop. And Back Door travelers are weaving the ultimate tapestry. Come on, join in!

ITINERARY

Days 1 and 2 Why not start with an urban Italian bang—in Milan. While many tourists visit Italy to find the past, Milan is today's Italy—a cultural superpower—and no Italian trip is complete without seeing it. This is a fine start for a real experience of Italy—not the poster Italy but the trend-setting, cigarettes-are-chic, industrial powerhouse Italy.

Day 3 Having conquered jet lag and one of Italy's big five cities, it's time to start your vacation. Head south for a sunny and remote chunk of the Italian Riviera called the Cinque Terre where you'll set up for two nights. You'll get plenty of museums later. This is beach time—just sun, sea, sand (well . . . pebbles), wine, and pure, dangerously unadulterated Italy.

Day 4 Take a free day to enjoy the villages, swimming, hiking, and evening ambience of one of God's great gifts to tourism, the Cinque Terre. You'll fall in love with this sunny, traffic-free alternative to the French Riviera. Evening is free. Beware the romance on the breakwater.

Day 5 From the lazy Riviera, work gradually into the epicenter of the Italian Renaissance with a stop at Pisa, an art power in its own right. After checking out Pisa's cathedral and tipsy tower, it's on to Florence. Get your artistic bearings with a Renaissance walk.

Day 6 While Florence, Europe's art capital, can't be seen in two days, if you're well organized, you can enjoy its highlights. After your break on the Riviera, your solar cells should be charged up for a look at the greatest collection anywhere of Italian Renaissance paintings and a thrilling walk through several of the greatest museums in Europe.

Day 7 Florence has the art, but two smaller towns nearby have more urban charm. San Gimignano is the quintessential hill town, with Italy's best surviving medieval skyline. Siena seems to be the pet town of every connois-

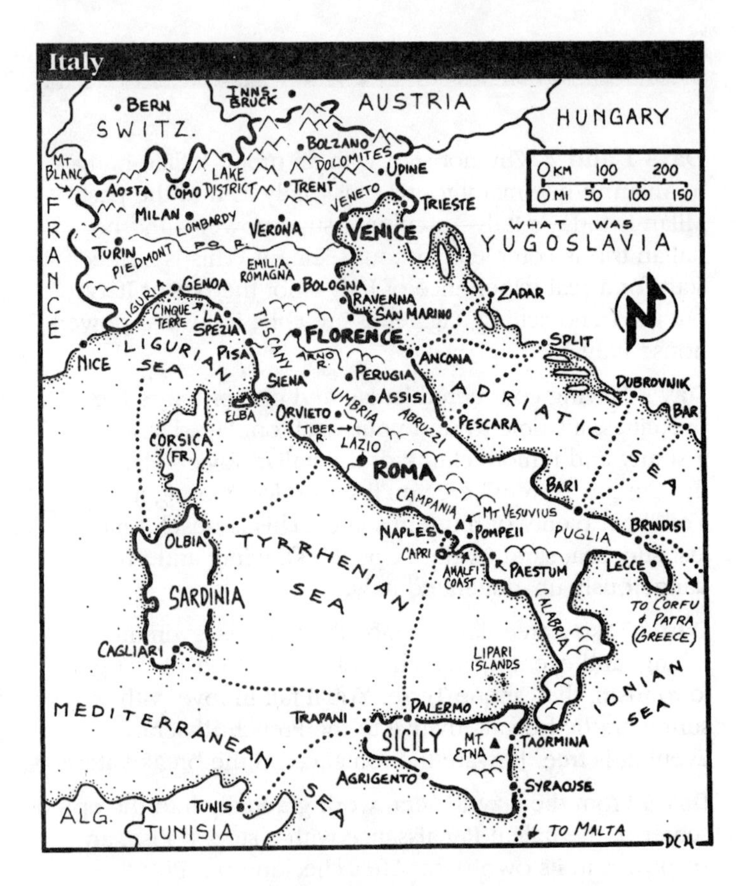

seur of Italy. In my office whenever Siena is mentioned, someone moans, "Siena? I Luuuv Siena!"

Siena is the hill town equivalent of Venice. Traffic-free red brick lanes cascade every which way. The thriving historic center offers Italy's best Gothic city experience. While Florence has the blockbuster museums, Siena has an easy-to-enjoy soul. For those who dream of a Fiat-free Italy, this is it.

Day 9 After leaving Tuscany for a stop in Umbria's most famous hill town, Orvieto, head for Italy's ultimate hill town, stranded alone on a pinnacle in a vast canyon, Cività di Bagnoregio. Spend the late afternoon and early evening immersed in the traffic-free village of Cività. Curl your toes around its Etruscan roots. Dine at the village's only restaurant, or eat "bunny" at Angelino's hotel. Later, drop into Angelino's gooey, wine- and laughter-stained Cantina.

Day 10 This is a day of slack, a good idea in any itinerary. Have an easy morning, hike up to Cività and maybe into the grand canyon that surrounds it. Or, head on over to the popular-but-still-powerful town of St. Francis, Assisi. Whatever you do, enjoy the crickets because Rome is just down your road.

Day 11 Drive your chariot into the stormy city of Julius, Peter, and Benito; set up and enjoy a short siesta. Fill the late afternoon and the cool early evening with the "Caesar shuffle"—a historic walk from the Colosseum, through the ancient Forum, and over the Capitol Hill.

Day 12 Get quirky in the morning with fascinating sights in the core of old Rome—including the incomparable (and far from quirky) Pantheon. After a self-service lunch, necessary siesta, and free afternoon, catch a taxi to Trastevere, Rome's wrong side of the Tiber River.

Day 13 Learn something about eternity by spending the morning touring the huge Vatican Museum. Of course, your reward for surviving Rome is Michelangelo's Sistine Chapel. Then, after a lunch and siesta break, tour St. Peter's, the greatest church on earth. Scale Michelangelo's 100-yard-tall dome. The early evening is for the "Dolce Vita Stroll" down the Via del Corso with Rome's beautiful people.

Day 14 Italy intensifies as you plunge deeper. Naples is a barrel full of cultural monkeys, Italy in the extreme and an essential piece in the puzzle of the country. After surviving the Vespa slalom called Naples and checking out Europe's top archaeological museum, escape to an entirely different world—the resort of Sorrento, gateway to the Amalfi coast and Italy's most stunning scenery.

Day 15 Depending on your energy you can spend today enjoying Sorrento with a quick trip to Pompeii. Or you can be more aggressive and plug in some more travel either to the Amalfi coast or over to the touristic but scenic island of Capri.

Day 16 After Italy's most hair-raising coastal joy ride, catch a one-hour train ride back 2,500 years into the days when this part of Italy was called Magna Graecia, Greater Greece. The temples of Paestum are the best bit of ancient Greece this side of Athens. Then sleep on the train, past everything you've already seen and wake up in Venice.

Days 17 and 18 Soak, all day, in this puddle of elegant decay. Venice is Europe's best-preserved big city, a car-free urban wonderland of 100 islands, laced together by 400 bridges and 2,000 alleys. After seeing the Doge's Palace and St. Mark's, you'll have time for browsing, shopping, art, or a side trip into the Lagoon. Are you ready for the famous "Back Door Stand-Up-Progressive-Venetian-Pub-Crawl-Dinner?"

Day 19 and 20 Italy's dramatic limestone rooftop, the Dolomites, offers some of the best and certainly unique mountain thrills in Europe. The weather forecast is great, and the staggering peaks can't wait. Hike, then sleep in a mountain hut.

Day 21 and 22 Round out your tour of Italy with a relaxing last stop, and commune with nature where Italy is welded to the Alps, in the Lakes District. Lago di Como offers the best mix of Italian lakes wonder and aristocratic old days romance. And it's just an hour or so from Milan where you'll complete your circle and call it a trip.

Italy has lots more to offer, but this book is called 2 to 22 Days, and we've run out of time.

Italy

- 116,000 square miles (the size of Arizona)
- 60,000,000 people (477 people per square mile)
- 800 miles tall, 100 miles wide
- about 1300 lire = US$1; 1000 lire = about $.75.
- Country telephone code: 39, international dial-out prefix: 00

Bella Italia! It has Europe's richest, craziest culture. If I had to choose just one, Italy's my favorite. If you take it on its own terms and accept the package deal, Italy is wonderful. Some people, often with considerable effort, manage to hate it. Italy bubbles with emotion, corruption, stray hairs, inflation, traffic jams, body odor, strikes, rallies, holidays, crowded squalor, and irate ranters shaking their fists at each other one minute and walking arm in arm the next. Have a talk with yourself before you cross the border. Promise yourself to relax and soak in it; it's a glorious mud puddle. Be militantly positive.

With so much history and art in Venice, Florence, and Rome, you'll need to do some reading ahead to maximize your experience. There are two Italys: the north is relatively industrial, aggressive, and "time-is-money" in its outlook. The Po River basin and the area between Milan, Genoa, and Torino have the richest farmland and constitute the industrial heartland. The south is more crowded, poor, relaxed, farm oriented, and traditional. Families here are very strong and usually live in the same house for many generations. Loyalties are to the family, city, region, soccer team, then country—in that order. The Appenine Mountains give Italy a rugged north-south spine.

Economically, Italy has had its problems, but things somehow work out. Today Italy is the Western world's seventh largest industrial power. Its people earn more per capita than the British. Italy is the world's leading wine producer. It is sixth in cheese and wool output. Tourism (as you'll find out) is also big business in Italy.

Cronyism, which complicates my work, is an integral part of the economy.

Italy, home of the Vatican, is Catholic, but the dominant religion is life—motor scooters, football, fashion, girl-watching, boy-watching, good coffee, good wine, and *la dolce far niente* (the sweetness of doing nothing). The Italian character shows itself on the streets with the skilled maniac drivers and the classy dressers who star in the ritual promenade, or *passeggiata*.

The language is fun. Be melodramatic and move your hand with your tongue. Hear the melody, get into the flow. Fake it, let the farce be with you. Italians are outgoing characters. They want to communicate, and they try harder than any other Europeans. Play with them.

Italy, a land of extremes, is also the most thief-ridden country you'll visit. Tourists suffer virtually no violent crime—but plenty of petty purse-snatchings, pickpocketings, and shortchangings. Only the sloppy will be stung. Wear your money belt! Unfortunately, you'll need to assume any gypsy woman or child on the street is after your wallet or purse.

Traditionally, Italy uses the siesta plan: people work from 8:00 or 9:00 to 13:00 and from 15:30 to 19:00, six days a week. Many businesses have adopted the government's new recommended 8:00 to 14:00 workday. In tourist areas, shops are open longer.

Sightseeing hours are always changing in Italy, and many of the hours in this book will be wrong by the time you travel. Use the local tourist offices to double check your sightseeing plans.

For extra sightseeing information, take advantage of the cheap, colorful, dry but informative city guidebooks sold on the streets all over. Also, use the information telephones you'll find in most historic buildings. Just set the dial on English, pop in your coins, and listen. The narration is often accompanied by a mini-slide show. Many dark interiors can be brilliantly lit for a coin. Whenever possible, let there be light.

Some important Italian churches require modest dress: no shorts or bare shoulders on men or women. With a little imagination (except at the Vatican), those caught by surprise can improvise something—a tablecloth for your knees and maps for your shoulders. I wear a super light-weight pair of long pants for my hot and muggy big city Italian sightseeing.

While no longer a cheap country, Italy is still a hit with shoppers. Glassware (Venice), gold, silver, leather, and prints (Florence), and high fashion (Rome) are good souvenirs.

Many tourists are mind-boggled by the huge prices: 16,000 lire for dinner! 42,000 for the room! 126,000 for the taxi ride! That's still real money—it's just spoken of in much smaller units than a dollar. Since there are roughly L1300 in a dollar, figure Italian prices by covering the last three zeros with your finger and taking about 75 percent of the remaining figure. That L16,000 dinner costs $12 in U.S. money; the L42,000 room, $32; and the taxi ride . . . oh-oh!

Beware of the "slow count." After you buy something, you may get your change back very slowly, one bill at a time. The salesperson (or bank teller) hopes you are confused by all the zeros and will gather up your money and say *grazie* before he or she finishes the count. Always do your own rough figuring beforehand and understand the transaction. Only the sloppy are ripped off.

La dolce far niente is a big part of Italy. Zero in on the fine points. Don't dwell on the problems. Accept Italy as Italy. Savor your cappuccino, dangle your feet over a canal (if it smells, breathe with your mouth), and imagine what it was like centuries ago. Ramble through the rubble of Rome and mentally resurrect those ancient stones. Look into the famous sculpted eyes of Michelangelo's *David*, and understand Renaissance man's assertion of himself. Sit silently on a hilltop rooftop. Get chummy with the winds of the past. Write a poem over a glass of local wine in a sun-splashed, wave-dashed Riviera village. If you fall off your moral horse, call it a cultural experience. Italy is for romantics.

DEPART U.S.A.

Call 72 hours before departure to confirm your ticket (those who don't can be bumped with no recourse if the flight is overbooked). Call again before going to the airport to confirm that your departure time is as scheduled. Expect delays. Bring something to do—a book, a journal, nail clippers, some hand work—to make any waits easy on yourself. Cultivate an attitude that as long as you land safely on the day you hope to, the flight is a great success.

To Minimize Jet Lag

- Leave well rested. Pretend you're leaving a day earlier than you really are. Be completely packed and ready to go so you can enjoy a peaceful last day. Leave healthy and rested. Jet lag can bring a budding cold into full bloom.
- During the flight, minimize stress to your system by eating lightly and avoiding alcohol, caffeine, and sugar. Every chance I get I say, "Two orange juices, no ice please." Take walks.
- After boarding the plane, set your watch ahead to European time: start adjusting mentally before you land.
- Sleep through the in-flight movie, or at least close your eyes and fake it. While they don't work for me, many travelers love their inflatable U-shaped neck pillows.
- On the day you arrive, keep yourself awake until a reasonable local bedtime. Jet lag hates fresh air, daylight, and exercise (a long evening city walk).
- You'll probably wake up with the birds and wired the next morning. Fighting it is futile. Enjoy a pinch-me-I'm-in-Italy sunrise walk.

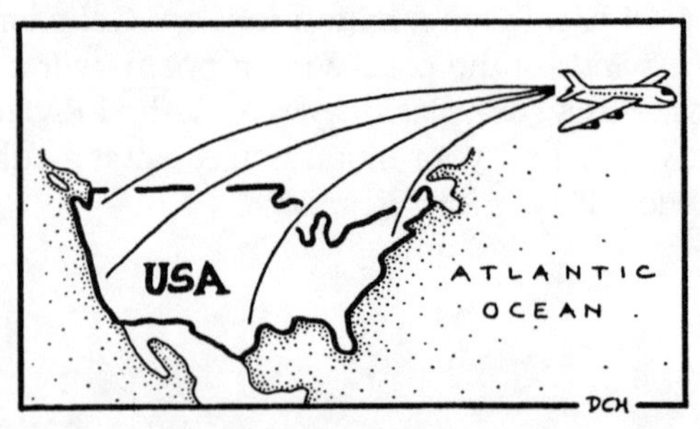

DAYS 1 and 2

ARRIVE AND SEE MILAN

We'll get over jet lag and break in to Italy by staying put in Milan. While Milan is nobody's idea of an easy starting point, it is Italy's city of today. It's a great way to introduce yourself to Italy—not to the tour-poster Italy but to the trend-setting, industrial powerhouse Italy. The city is well organized. As long as you have and use good information, it's completely manageable and an exciting kick-off to any 22-day Italian adventure.

Suggested Schedule

Day 1

Arrive, get oriented in Milan.
If time allows, take a downtown browse, familiarizing yourself with the Galleria and climbing to the top of the Duomo. This will free up time for museumgoing tomorrow.

Day 2

9:00	Browsing, elegant shops, Milan history museum.
10:30	La Scalata, coffee break in Galleria.
11:30	Duomo, see inside, climb to rooftop.
13:00	Buy picnic on Via Speronari, eat in Piazza Mercanti or in Fortezza courtyard.
15:00	Choose among Brera Art Gallery, Sforza Castle (Michelangelo), Last Supper, Science and Industry Museum, depending on your interests.

Note: Many top Milan sights are closed on Monday.

Landing in Milan

When flying to Europe, because you're spending six to nine hours crossing six to nine time zones, you usually land the next day. Most international flights land at Milan's surprisingly cozy Malpensa airport, 30 miles northwest of the city.

Malpensa airport seems to be designed to help you overcome your fears of Italy. Customs guards fan you through. Even the sniffing dog seems friendly. The airport bank has fine rates (Banco di Milano, open daily until 20:00, no limit). Visit the bus/train information and ticket office (direct buses to the Milan station, L10,000, depart at 20 and 50 minutes past each hour; convenient chance to buy train tickets and check departure times for train trips from Milan; buy a telephone card and confirm your hotel). Taxis for the 30-mile ride into Milan cost $100. If you're picking up a rental car, you're in the countryside, an ideal place to get used to driving in a new car in a new country.

Like Malpensa, Milan's second airport, Linate (5 miles to the east) is well served by regular shuttle buses from Piazza Luigi di Savoia at the central station. For flight information for either airport, call 02/74852200.

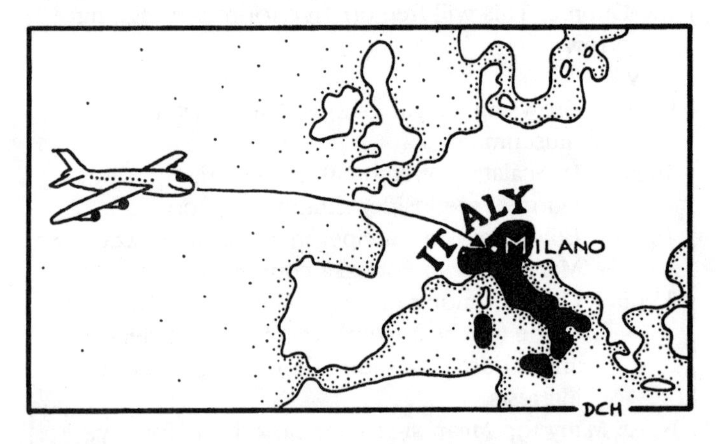

Milan

They say that for every church in Rome, there's a bank in Milan. Italy's second city and the capital of Lombardy, Milan (population 2 million) is a city of hardworking, fashion-conscious, time-is-money people. Milan is a melting pot of people and history. Its industriousness may come from the Teutonic blood of the Lombards or from the region's Austrian heritage. Milan is Italy's industrial, banking, TV, publishing, and convention capital. The economic success of modern Italy can be blamed on this city of publicists and power lunches.

It's an ugly city with a recently bombed out feeling (WW II). Its huge financial buildings are as manicured as its parks are shaggy. As if to make up for its harsh concrete shell, the people and the windows are works of art. Milan is an international fashion capital, the city that gave us the term "millinery." Even the cheese is gift wrapped.

Three hundred years before Christ the Romans called this place Mediolanum or "the central place." By the fourth century A.D. it was the capital of the western half of the Roman Empire. It was from here that Emperor Constantine issued the Edict of Milan, legalizing Christianity. After some barbarian darkness, medieval Milan rose to regional prominence under the Visconti and Sforza families. By the time of the Renaissance it was called "the New Athens" and was enough of a cultural leader for Leonardo to call it home. Then came four hundred years of foreign domination (Spain, Austria, France, more Austria). Milan was a center of the 1848 revolution against Austria and helped lead Italy to unification in 1861.

Mussolini left a heavy Fascist touch on the city's architecture (such as the central train station). His excesses also led to the serious WW II bombing of Milan. But Milan rose again. The 1959 Pirelli Tower (the skinny sleek skyscraper in front of the station) was a trendsetter in its day. Today the city has a nearly traffic-free center, a great transit system, banks everywhere, and a city gardening budget that apparently went bankrupt last year.

While many tourists come to Italy for the past, Milan is today's Italy, and no Italian trip is complete without seeing it. By the way, August is rudely hot and muggy. Locals who can, vacate, leaving the city just about dead. Those visiting in August will find many shops closed and nightlife pretty quiet. Mondays are closed days for many museums.

While Milan's public relations expertise has made it a fashion and finance winner, it's not big on the tourist circuit. But it has plenty to see, it's no more expensive than other Italian cities, and its organization is more Milanese than Italian. Our motto for Milan: don't worry, be clever.

Orientation

Driving is bad enough in Milan to make the L35,000 a day you'll pay in a downtown garage a blessing. If you're driving, do Milan (and maybe even Lake Como) before or after you rent. If you have a car, ask about the city's suburban Parcheggi, affordable and safe suburban parking lots.

Milan's public transportation is great, especially the clean, spacious, fast and easy three-line Metro. Transit tickets (L1000 at any newsstand) are good for one subway ride followed by 75 minutes of bus or tram travel. The L3500 all-day or *diurno* pass is a handy option (sold at major stations and some newsstands). I've keyed all our sightseeing into the subway system. While most sights are within a few blocks of each other, Milan is an exhausting city to walk in, and the well-marked buses can be useful. (While the kiosks all sell the L5000 Milan city transit map, the City Transit information offices, next to the TI in the station and at the Duomo Metro station, often have a free ATM map showing all bus lines.)

In Milan, I'm constantly disoriented. Go slow, use the map. Before exiting the subway, note the street markings. You'll notice the street plan is a series of rings that used to be medieval walls. Be on guard. Milan's thieves target tourists. At the station and around the Duomo, gypsy beggars are actually gypsy thieves.

Tourist Information: There are two central offices (at the central station and next to the Duomo, to the right as you face it). Both are open from 8:00 to 20:00, 9:00 to 17:00 with a lunch break on Sundays (tel. 02/809662). Stop by to confirm your sightseeing plans, pick up a map (the overall map is handy with sketches of sights, but the "Welcome to Milan" map lists more streets; ask for the ATM bus system map), the classy *Museums in Milan* booklet, a listing of museum hours, and the *What's On in Milan* monthly.

Avoid the long lines at the station ticket office. The handiest Milan travel agency is CIT in Galleria Vittorio Emanuele (great for buying train tickets, tel. 02/866661). American Express is right in the center (up Via Verdi from La Scala, Via Brera 3, tel. 02/85571, Monday-Friday, 9:00-5:30) and holds mail.

The Romans would still find Milan a good "central place." It's a train hub with departures at least hourly to Rome (5 hours), Florence (3 hours), Venice (3 hours), and Genoa (2 hours). Telephone code: 02.

Milan Metro

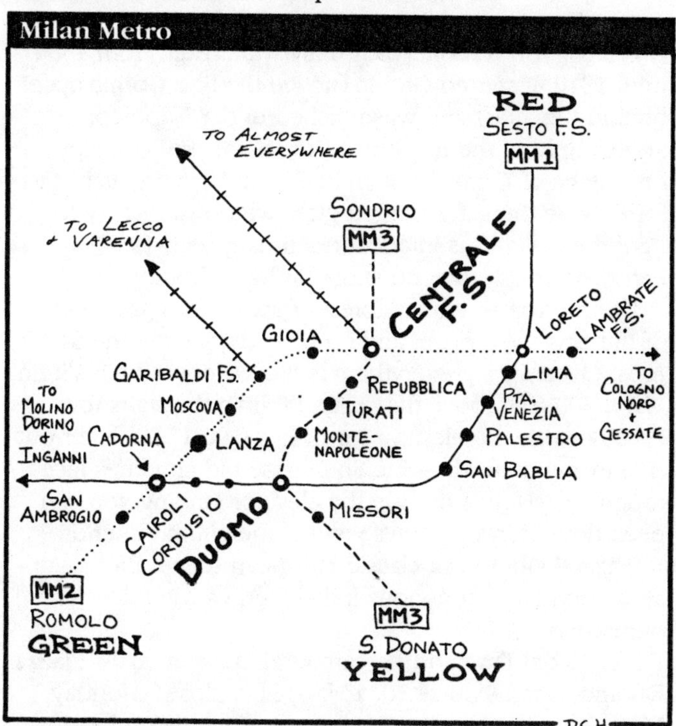

Sightseeing Highlights—Milan

I've assessed these sights assuming you have been or will be going to Rome and Florence (in other words, the city's art is relatively mediocre). However, Milan has unique and noteworthy sightseeing, well worth a carefully planned day. Plan your strategy noting efficient use of the metro and, if you're maximizing your time, noting which places stay open through the siesta. The museums that are good for you (city-run museums covering obscure history and matters of local pride) are free and closed the last Monday of the month. The famous things that all tourists do are generally expensive (L5000 to L10,000). I've listed things loosely in walking order.

▲▲ **Duomo**—Milan's cathedral, the city's centerpiece, is the third-largest church in Europe (after the Vatican's and Sevilla's). At 480 feet long and 280 feet wide, with fifty-two 150-foot-tall sequoia pillars inside and over 2,000 statues, the place can seat 40,000 worshipers. If you do two laps, you've done your daily walk. Built from 1386 until 1810, it started Gothic (notice the fine Gothic apse behind the altar) and was finished under Napoleon. It's an example of the flamboyant or "flamelike" overripe final stage of Gothic, but architectural harmony is not its forte. Note the giant stained-glass windows that try to light the cavernous interior (open daily 7:00-19:00; enforced dress code: no shorts or bare shoulders).

The rooftop is a fancy forest of spires with great views of the city, the square, and on clear days, even the Swiss Alps. Overlooking everything is the 13-foot-tall gilt Virgin Mary, 300 feet above the ground (climb the stairs for L3000 or ride the elevator for L5000, 9:00-17:30, enter outside from the north—clue, in Europe old churches face roughly east). Just outside the elevator landing you can peek down for a pigeon's view of the church interior.

Piazza Duomo is a classic European scene. Professionals scurry, label-conscious kids loiter, young thieves peruse.

Museo del Duomo (the cathedral museum at 14 Piazza Duomo, open 9:30-12:30, 15:00-18:00, closed Monday, L5000) is a scrapbook of 600 years of cathedral history offering a close look at the stained glass, statues, and gargoyles.

Within a block of Piazza Duomo are a few interesting glimpses of old Milan. The center of medieval Milan was a small square just opposite the church, the Piazza Mercanti. It's a strangely peaceful place today. The church of Santa Maria presso San Satiro (just off Via

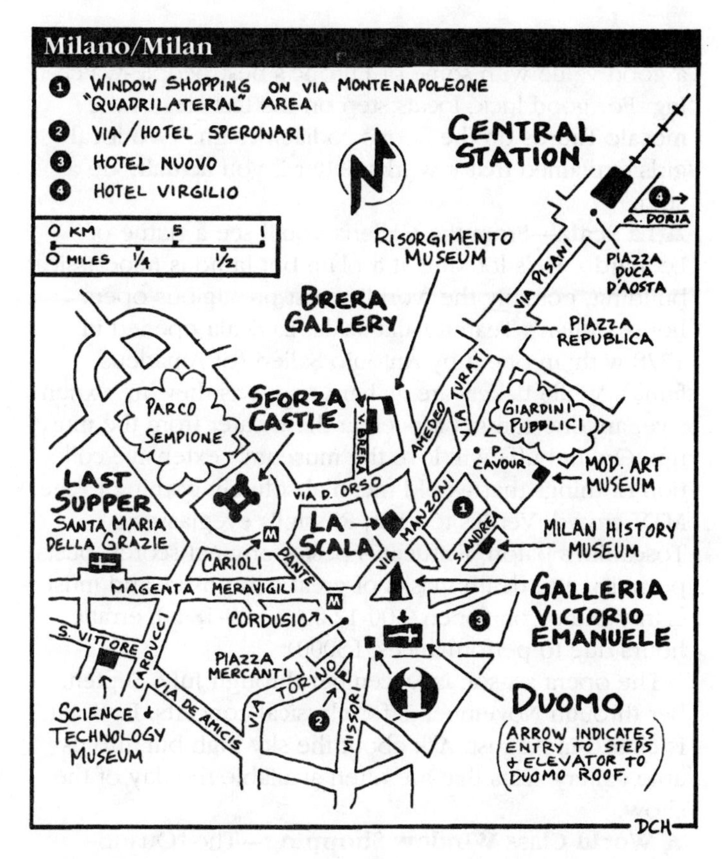

Torino, a few yards past Via Speronari) was the scene of a temper tantrum in 1242 when a losing gambler vented his anger by hitting the baby Jesus in the Madonna and Child altarpiece. "Miraculously," blood spouted out and the beautiful little church has been on the pilgrimage trail ever since. For the 750th anniversary the pope has offered special indulgences (good through March 1993) to those who worship here. Even if the offer has expired, it's worth a visit to see the illusion of depth (trompe l'oeil) that Bramante painted behind the altar.

▲▲ Galleria Vittorio Emanuele—Milan is also symbolized by its great four-story-high, glass-domed arcade. Sadly, just a day before its 1878 grand opening, the designer fell from the top to his death. This is the place to spend too much money for a coffee and turn that into a good value with some of Europe's best people-watching. For good luck, locals step on the testicles of the mosaic Taurus on the floor's zodiac design. Two local girls explained that it works better if you actually do a spin.

▲ **La Scala**—From the Galleria you'll see a statue of Leonardo. He's looking at a plain but famous neoclassical building, possibly the world's most prestigious opera house, Milan's Teatrale alla Scala. La Scala opened in 1778 with an opera by Antonio Salieri (of Amadeus fame). While tickets are as hard to get as they are expensive, anyone can get a peek at the theater from the museum. Opera buffs will love the museum's extensive collection of things that would mean absolutely nothing to the MTV crowd: Verdi's top hat; Rossini's eyeglasses; Toscanini's baton; Fettucini's pesto; original scores, busts, portraits, and death masks of great composers and musicians; and so on (open 9:00-12:00, 14:00-18:00, erratic hours due to performances, L5000).

The opera season is December through July. September through November is for classical concerts. La Scala is closed in August. Ask about the sky-high but affordable gallery seats that are often available the day of the show.

▲ **World-Class Window-Shopping**—The "Quadrilateral," as the elegant high fashion shopping area around Via Montenapoleone is called, is worth a wander. In this land where cigarettes are still chic, the people-watching is as fun as the window-shopping.

The Museums of Milan and of Contemporary History (both at Via Sant'Andrea 6) are free and offer a quick walk through wall-sized pages of Milan's past, including the especially interesting 1914 to 1945 period (9:30-17:30, often with a lunch break).

▲ **The Brera Art Gallery**, Milan's top collection of paintings, is without a doubt world class. But you'll see better in Rome and Florence. Established in 1809 to house Napoleon's looted art, the gallery's highlights include works by the Bellini brothers, Caravaggio (*Supper* *at Emmaus*), Raphael (*Wedding of the Madonna*), and Mantegna's textbook example of feetfirst foreshortening (*The Dead Christ*). Even if you don't go into the gallery, see Napoleon nude (by Canova) in the courtyard and wander through the art school on the ground floor (cheapest cup of coffee in town from the machine down the hall, open 9:00-17:30, Sunday 9:00-12:30, closed Monday, L8000).

▲ **The Resorgimento museum** is an interesting (if you speak Italian or luck out as I did with a talkative English-speaking guard) story of Italy's road to unity: from Napoleon (1796) to the victory in Rome (1870). Near the entry the Laboratorio Didattico is a workshop filled with original old uniforms (just around the corner from the Brera Gallery at Via Borgonuovo 23, open 9:30-17:30, free).

▲ **Sforza Castle (Castello Sforzesco)**—This immense, much bombed and rebuilt brick fortress is exhausting at first sight. It can only be described as heavy. But its courtyard has a great lawn for picnics and siestas, and its free museum is filled with interesting medieval armor, furniture, early Lombard art, and, most important, Michelangelo's unfinished Rondanini Pietà. Michelangelo died while still working on this work, which hints at the elongation of the mannerist style that would follow. This is a rare opportunity to enjoy a Michelangelo with no crowds (9:30-17:30, closed last Tuesdays of the month, free).

▲ **Leonardo da Vinci's *Last Supper* (Cenacolo)** is in the refectory of the church of Santa Maria delle Grazie. The Renaissance masterpiece captures the emotional moment when Jesus says to his disciples, "One of you will betray me," and each of the twelve wonders nervously, "Lord, is it I?" Notice Judas with his thirty pieces of silver looking pretty guilty. This ill-fated masterpiece suffers from Leonardo's experimental use of oil rather than the normal fresco technique. Deterioration began within six years of its completion. The church was bombed in WW II but the *Last Supper* survived. It's undergoing extensive restoration. Most of the original paint is gone. (9:00-13:15, L10,000 and still behind scaffolding! May be closed Monday.)

▲ **National "Leonardo da Vinci" Science and Technology Museum** (Museo Nazionale della Scienze e della Tecnica)—The spirit of Leonardo lives here in Italy's top science and technology museum. Most tourists visit for the hall of Leonardo designs illustrated in wooden models, but Leonardo's mind is just as easy to appreciate by paging through a coffee table edition of his notebooks in any bookstore. The rest of this immense collection of industrial cleverness is fascinating, with plenty of push-button action (unfortunately, no English descriptions): trains, the evolution of radios, old musical instruments, computers, batteries, telephones, chunks of the first trans-Atlantic cable, and on and on. (Via San Vittore 21, bus #50 to the Duomo, 9:30-16:50, closed Monday, L8000.)

There is much more to see in Milan. Its many thousand-year-old churches make it clear that Milan was an important beacon in the Dark Ages. Local guidebooks and the tourist information office can point you in the right direction if you have more time in Milan. For evening action check out the arty, student-oriented Brera area in the old center and Milan's formerly Bohemian, now gentrified "Little Venice," the Navigli neighborhood. Specifics change so fast, it is best to rely on entertainment information in periodicals from the TI.

Sleeping in Milan (about L1300 = US$1)

If you've got some extra money or don't mind a little big city grunge, Milan has plenty of simple, central, and reasonable accommodations. Prices are the same throughout the year; none include breakfasts, which, if available, are a lousy value (eat down the street in a café). Most places listed charge L20,000 extra for rooms with a private shower. Those without have access (usually free) to a shower on the corridor. I have listed only places that should have no traffic noise problems. All are within a few minutes' walk of Milan's fine subway system. Anytime but summer, the city can be completely jammed by conventions. Summer is usually wide open. Hotels cater more to business travelers than to tourists. I've limited recommendations to two areas: in the center near the Duomo and near the station.

Rooms in the Center: The Duomo (cathedral) area is my favorite place to feel the pulse of Milano. It's an area thick with people-watching, reasonable eateries, and the major sightseeing attractions but just four stops on the Metro from the central train station.

Hotel Speronari (L55,000-77,000 doubles, L38,000-53,000 singles, the cheaper rooms can use a shower down the hall for L5000, ideally located on a pedestrian street off Via Torino, one block off the far end of the Piazza Duomo at Via Speronari 4, 20123 Milano, tel. 02/86461125, fax 72003178, English spoken) could be run by your eccentric aunt, or her children. A porcelain lion welcomes you into a bright world of red carpets, old Pepsi posters on the wall, and mirrors everywhere. The rooms are cozy, if cheaply decorated.

Hotel Nuovo (forty L60,000 doubles with showers down the hall, through two blocks of shopping arcades immediately behind the Duomo on the quiet, ugly Piazza Beccaria 6, 20122 Milano, tel. 02/8646444, fax 72001752) is a rare one-star hotel in the center. The price and locale are great. The interior is quiet and clean but depressing with cracked and peely yellow paint throughout.

Rooms near the Station: With Milan's fine Metro, you can get anywhere in town in a flash. For pure convenience and price, this is a handy, if dreary, area. The area between the station and Corso Buenos Aires has a seedy, prostitutes-after-dark problem. Most of these listings are on the fringe of decency. Corso Buenos Aires is a bustling main shopping and people-watching drag. These are listed in order of closeness to the station. All are within two subway stops or a fifteen-minute walk of the station. The last three are on or near the less seedy but noisier main drag, Corso Buenos Aires.

Hotel Virgilio (L70,000-106,000, just four blocks from the station, down Via Andria Doria, then left to Via P.L. da Palestrina 30, 20124 Milano, tel. 02/6691337, fax 66982587), run carefully by the English-speaking Genchi family, is the best splurge. A chandeliered lobby sets the tone throughout. Especially with the few doubles without showers, this is the best hotel value so close to the station. Consider **Hotel Emilia** (L68,000-L96,000, with a garage, around the corner to the right as you're leaving at Via Ponte Seveso 38, tel. 02/6897498) as a last resort . . . well "resort" is not a good word.

"The Best" Hotel (L80,000, all with showers and telephones, a ten-minute walk from the station near the Lima Metro stop at Via B. Marcello 83, 20124 Milano, tel. 02/29404757) actually is the best in its price range. It's run by friendly and English-speaking Luciana and Peter and has a homey lounge and rooms overlooking either a garden or a square that is an open-air market on Tuesdays and Saturdays (otherwise, just an ugly car park). In a sad battle of self-congratulatory names, the **Hotel Paradiso** next door (L60,000-80,000, Via B. Marcello 85, tel. 02/2049448) is sleepable but fails miserably to live up to its name.

Hotel Casa Mia (L50,000-70,000, just a stone's throw from the Piazza della Repubblica Metro stop, on Viale Vittorio Veneto 30, tel. 02/6575249) is a simple, quiet, hardworking family affair rare in downtown Milan.

Hotel Serena (L100,000, 30 yards off Corso Buenos Aires near the Lima Metro stop, at Via Boscovich 59, tel. 02/29522152) is plain and quiet, with bright new showers in all but a couple of the cheaper rooms. The nearby **Albergo Nettuno** (L50,000-68,000, Via Tadino 27, tel. 02/29404481, no English spoken) is dark and plain with neon lights, old wood floors, and only its price to brag about.

Hotel Cristoforo Colombo (L154,000, at Metro: Porta Venezia, Corso Buenos Aires 3, 20124 Milano, tel. 02/29406214, fax 29516096) is my token normal hotel recommendation complete with uniformed bellhops, TVs, and the works.

Eating in Milan

This is a fast-food city. But fast food in a fashion capital isn't a burger and fries. The bars, delis, rosticceria, and self-services cater to people with plenty of taste and more money than time.

You'll find delightful eateries all over town. Notice the fine (and free) munchies that appear late in the afternoon in many bars. An L2000 cappuccino can (if you're either likable or discreet) become a light meal. For a low-stress affordable lunch near the Duomo, eat at **Ciao**, a shiny modern self-serve on the second floor in the center across from the TI (open 12:00-15:00, 18:30-23.30, closed Saturday). For a more challenging adventure in eating Milanese, hit the colorful shops on Via Speronari (off Via Torino, a block southwest of Piazza Duomo). **Peck**, nearby on Via G. Cantu, off Via Dante, is a classy rosticceria (closed Sunday, Monday morning, and 13:00-15:00).

Other self-serve restaurants near the Duomo are **Brek** (Corso Italia 3), **Amico** (Via Orefici, closed Monday), and **La Piazza** (Piazza Duomo 17). Near the station, try Brek (Via Lepetit 20). Both Breks are closed on Sunday.

DAYS 3 and 4

MILAN TO ITALY'S RIVIERA, THE CINQUE TERRE

Having conquered jet lag and one of Italy's big cities, it's time to start your vacation. Head south for the Cinque Terre, a sunny and remote chunk of the Italian Riviera, where you'll set up for two nights. You'll get plenty of museums later, this is beach time—just sun, sea, sand (well, pebbles), wine, and pure unadulterated Italy. Give yourself an entirely free day to enjoy the villages, swimming, hiking, and evening romance of one of God's great gifts to tourism, the Cinque Terre.

Suggested Schedule	
Day 3	
9:00	Depart Milan.
13:00	Arrive in La Spezia, catch little train into Cinque Terre.
14:00	Check into hotel, free time.
Day 4	
No schedule—you're on holiday.	

Transportation: Milan to the Cinque Terre (130 miles)

By train there are hourly departures from Milan making the 3- to 4-hour trip to La Spezia (sometimes changing in Genoa). In La Spezia's station, the milk-run beach town Cinque Terre train schedule is posted at window #5. If you have time to kill, call and reconfirm your hotel. Then take the L1200 half-hour train ride into the Cinque Terre town of your choice.

Drivers will speed south by autostrada from Milan, skirt Genoa, and drive along some of Italy's most scenic and impressive freeway toward the port of La Spezia. The road via Parma is faster but less scenic.

It's now reasonable to snake your car down the treacherous little road into the Cinque Terre and park above the town. This is risky in August and on Saturday or

Sunday when Italian day trippers clog and jam the region. Vernazza has several parking lots above the town. To drive into the Cinque Terre, leave the autostrada at Uscita Brugnato just west of La Spezia.

You can also park your car near the train station in La Spezia. Any spot with white lines and no sign should be okay. Look for diagonal parking spots in front of the station or on the streets below. Be patient, spots do open up. Confirm that it's okay and leave nothing inside to steal.

Transportation along the Cinque Terre

While you can hike or catch the irregular boats, the easy way to zip from town to village is by train. These *locale* trains (that's Italian for "milk run") are so tiny they don't even register on the Thomas Cook train timetable. But they go nearly hourly, are very cheap, and arrive either on time or late. To orient yourself, remember that directions are either "*per* (to) *Genoa*" or "*per La Spezia*," and virtually any train that stops at one of the five villages will stop at all of them. The five towns are just a few minutes apart by train. This schedule is as stable as a mink in heat. Any station and most restaurants post the up-to-date schedule. Since a one-town hop costs the same as a five-town hop (L1600) and every ticket is good all day with stopovers, save money by exploring the region in one direction on one ticket.

Cinque Terre Train Schedule

Trains leaving La Spezia for the Cinque Terre villages: 1:40, 4:31, 5:29, 6:38, 7:24, 7:45, 9:03, 10:37, 11:20, 12:22, 13:03, 13:33, 14:17, 15:00, 15:34, 17:05, 17:35, 18:12, 18:53, 19:10, 19:50, 21:18, 22:35, 23:10.

Trains leaving Vernazza for La Spezia: 1:13, 4:59, 5:18, 6:04, 6:44, 7:13, 8:33, 8:58, 9:56, 10:44, 11:37, 12:11, 13:01, 13:52, 14:23, 15:43, 17:10, 18:12, 19:06, 19:33, 19:43, 20:42, 21:36, 22:23, 22:52.

This chart shows hiking time between the five villages of the Cinque Terre, as numbered on the map above. (Thinking of towns as numbers simplifies your beach life.)

Sightseeing Highlights—Cinque Terre

Riomaggiore—town #1: The most substantial nonresort town of the group, Riomaggiore is a disappointment from the station. But walk through the tunnel (right as you exit the station) or follow the road, straight up and to the right, and you land in a fascinating tangle of pastel homes leaning on each other as if someone stole their crutches. The Bar Central makes homemade gelati. Its beach is just a few black pebbles, but that's enough to give the gang at Mama Rosa's a place for a midnight dip. A stairway (in front of the station, to the right of the Station bar) leads down to a dark and potentially peaceful pile of sunbathing rocks under the station.

From the Riomaggiore station, the wide-enough-for-a-baby-stroller Via dell' Amore affords a film-gobbling fifteen-minute promenade around the coast to Manarola. (This has been closed by a washed out section for a few years, but walkers routinely climb over or around the fences and enjoy the hike anyway.)

Manarola—town #2: Like town #1, #2 is attached to its station by a 200-yard-long tunnel. Manarola is tiny and rugged, a tumble of buildings bunny-hopping down its ravine to the tiny harbor that somebody, sometime must have called the "Devil's Caldron." An uppity crowd seems to hang out on the congested waterfront of Manarola. This is a good place to buy your picnic before walking to the beaches of town #3, Corniglia (stores close from 13:00-17:00). As you leave, the low trail is a scenic dead end. Take the high one from the harbor-front. This is a more rugged walk that any fit person could enjoy.

Corniglia—town #3: A zigzag series of stairs that looks worse than it is leads up to the only town of the five not on the water. For that reason, Corniglia is the most remote and rarely visited, with a windy belvedere, a few restaurants, and a handful of often empty private rooms for rent.

Unfortunately, much of the rocky, man-made Corniglia beach has washed away and is almost nonexistent when the surf's up. It has a couple of buoys to swim to and is cleaner and less crowded than the beach at town #5. The beach bar has showers, drinks, and snacks. Between the station and the beach you'll pass a bungalow village filled with Italians doing the Cinque Terre in 14 days.

Vernazza—town #4: With the closest thing to a natural harbor, overseen by a ruined castle and an old church, and only the occasional noisy slurping of the train up the mountain to remind you these are the 1990s, Vernazza is my Cinque Terre home base.

The action is at the harbor, where you'll find a kids' beach with showers, plenty of sunning rocks, outdoor restaurants, a bar hanging on the edge of the castle (great for evening drinks), the tiny town soccer field, and the busiest foosball game in Italy.

The hike from #3 to #4 is the wildest of the coast. The trail from Vernazza to #5 is a scenic, up-and-down-a-lot, hour. The hourly boat service connects #4 and #5 in the summer (L4000, L6000 round-trip). A five-minute hike in either direction from Vernazza gives you a classic village photo stop.

In the evening, wander down the main (and only) street to the harbor to join the visiting Italians in a sing-along. Have a gelato, a cappuccino, or a glass of the local Cinque Terre wine at a waterfront café or on the castle bar's patio that overlooks the breakwater at sunset (follow the rope railing above the tiny soccer field, notice the photo of rough seas just above the door inside). Stay up as late as you like because tomorrow you're actually on holiday—nothing is scheduled!

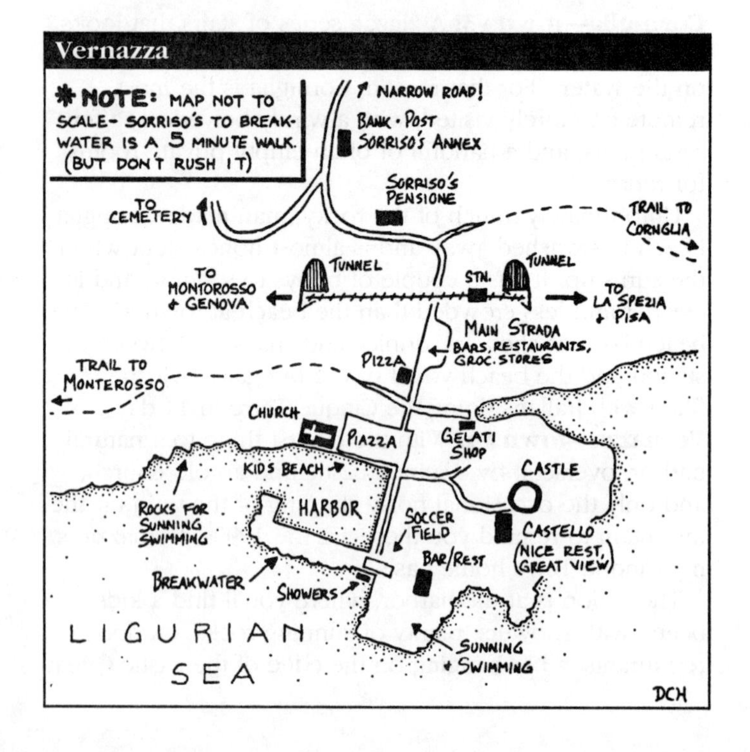

The expensive **Castello** (Castle) restaurant serves good food just under the castle with Vernazza twinkling below you. The town's only gelati shop is good, and most harborside bars will let you take your glass on a breakwater stroll. The pizza bar on the main street serves a great blend of crust, sauce, cheese, and spice—by the L3500 slice. Grocery stores are open from 7:30 to 13:00 and 17:00 to 19:00.

Monterosso al Mare—town #5: This is a resort with cars, hotels, rentable beach umbrellas, and crowds. Still, if you walk east of the station (left as you face the water) to the section through the tunnel, it has its charm. If you want a sandy beach, this is the only place you'll find it. Adventurers may want to rent a rowboat or paddleboat and find their own private cove. There are several between #4 and #5. One has its own little waterfall. (Tourist office, 10:00-12:00 and 17:00-19:00, closed Sunday afternoon, tel. 0187/81 75 06.)

Helpful Hints

Pack your beach and swim gear, wear your walking shoes, and catch the train to Riomaggiore (town #1). Walk the cliff-hanging Via dell' Amore to Manarola (town #2) and buy food for a picnic, then hike to Corniglia (town #3) for a rocky remnant of a washed away beach. From the beach there's a train to zip you home to Vernazza (town #4). Or train all the way to Monterosso (town #5) for a real beach (and real tourism), then hike or catch the boat back. Make a point to take full advantage of the trains.

If you're into la dolce far niente and don't want to hike, you could enjoy the blast of cool train tunnel air that announces the arrival of every Cinque Terre train and go directly to Monterosso al Mare or Corniglia to maximize beach time.

If you're a hiker, hike from Riomaggiore all the way to Monterosso al Mare, where a sandy "front door"-style beach awaits. Each beach has showers that probably work better than your hotel's. (Bring soap and shampoo.)

If you like sweet wine, the local Sciachetre wine is expensive but delicious. While ten kilos of grapes will give you seven liters of local wine, it yields only 1.5 liters of Sciachetre. The local white wine flows cheap and easy throughout the region.

Sit on the Vernazza breakwater, wine or whatever in hand, and get mushy. Do the church lights look like three ladies on a beach and a very interested man? Can a mountain slurp spaghetti trains? Do we have to move on tomorrow?

Sleeping and Eating in the Cinque Terre (about L1300 = US$1)

While the Cinque Terre is unknown to the international mobs that ravage the Spanish and French coasts, plenty of Italians come here, so room-finding can be tricky. August and summer Fridays and Saturdays are tight. August weekends are miserable. If you're trying to avoid my readers, stay away from Sorriso's and Moma Rosa's. But the area is worth planning ahead for. If you arrive without a room and the hotels are full, ask anyone on the street or in the local bars for *affitta camere* (rooms in private homes). If you go direct, it's usually easy to talk the price down. The hotels, enjoying more demand than they can handle, are high-priced and don't try very hard. With some luck, you can get a more comfortable room with a magnificent view for half the price in a private home. Off-season, you can just drop in and ask around. At Easter and in July and August, call long in advance and reconfirm a day before your arrival.

Sleeping in Vernazza: Vernazza, the essence of the Cinque Terre, is my favorite town. There is just one real pension, but three restaurants have about a dozen simple rooms each. There must be 40 private homes that rent rooms, mostly through the local restaurants and pensions. If you arrange a private room directly, you'll save L10,000 or so.

Pension Sorriso (L60,000 per person including dinner and breakfast, on Monday, Tuesday, or Wednesday the dinner is not obligatory and you can get a double with breakfast for L65,000, you can ask for simply B&B at other times, 19018 Vernazza, Cinque Terre, La Spezia, just up the street from the train station, tel. 0187/81 22 24, English spoken, train noise is a problem for some in the front rooms, the annex up the street is quieter and more comfortable, closed November to March) is the only real pension in town, and Sr. Sorriso knows it. He's a bit jaded but having a tough time retiring. Don't expect an exuberant welcome. Sr. Sorriso and his nephew, Giovanni, will hold a room for you without a deposit, if you call and reconfirm a few days before your arrival with another call. If you like sweet wine, you'll love his Sciachetre (shock-ee-tra).

Trattoria Gianni (L60,000-75,000 doubles, no breakfast, good modern showers, Piazza Marconi, 5, 19018 Vernazza, tel. 0187/81 22 28) has 14 simple, comfortable doubles up lots of stairs near the castle, where it's very quiet and the views are Mediterranean blue. The restaurant/reception is right on the harbor square. Their pension business is kept very simple.

Locanda Barbara is run by Giacomo at the Taverna da Capitano (L55,000 tiny doubles, L65,000 big doubles, no breakfast, Piazza Marconi 20, tel. 0187/81 22 01), which is also on the harbor square. His rooms are on the top floors of what seems like a vacant city hall, with lots of stairs. The cheap doubles have low sloping ceilings and small windows with wide harbor views.

Trattoria da Sandro (L50,000 doubles, no breakfast, Via Roma 62, tel. 0187/81 22 23) has a line on seven rooms scattered just below the train station in the back alleys of Vernazza. These are off the water a few hundred yards but more *tipico.*

Sleeping in Riomaggiore: Riomaggiore is a bit more substantial than Vernazza, with less magic. But it's an easier place to find a bed. Unfortunately, the accommodations are in the less colorful, concrete part of town near the station. A short walk through the tunnel puts you in the heart of Riomaggiore.

Youth Hostel Mama Rosa (L15,000 beds, price guaranteed through 1993, Piazza Unita 2, 20 yards in front of the station on the right past the "sporting club" in an unmarked building, tel. 0187/92 00 50, rarely answered, most just show up without a reservation) is a splash of Mother Theresa and a dash of John Belushi (a little more of the latter), offering you the only cheap dorm on the Cinque Terre. Run by Rosa Ricci, an almost too effervescent and friendly character who welcomes backpackers at the train station (whether they know they're staying with her or not), her husband, Carmine, and their English-speaking son, Silvio, this informal hostel is a chaotic but manageable jumble with the ambience of a YMCA locker room filled with bunk beds. The five coed rooms with 4 to 10 beds each are plain and basic, but a family atmosphere rages, with a self-serve kitchen, laundry facilities, showers, free "beauty soap," and Silvio's 20 unnamed cats (available as bed partners upon request). This is one of those rare places where perfect strangers become good friends with the slurp of a spaghetti and wine supersedes the concept of ownership. The Mama Rosa spaghetti feed gives you all you can eat for L5000. She also offers a discount for meals at the neighboring Vecchio Rio restaurant. Mama Rosa has access to several nearby double rooms (camera doppio) in private homes (L40,000 each).

Affitta Camere "da Mario" (L50,000 doubles, no breakfast, just to the left of the Riomaggiore station, yellow Zimmer sign, tel. 0187/92 06 92, call in a reservation) is the best place for anyone needing privacy and quiet (apart from the hourly thunder of the train). Federica and Angela have five very comfortable rooms. (Don't let Mama Rosa lasso you if you're heading their way.) For a stay in the characteristic center of Riomaggiore, ask at the Central Bar.

Eating in Riomaggiore: The place to feast quite inexpensively on great seafood is the **Vecchio Rio** restaurant (L15,000 meals, 50 yards in front of the train station, tel. 0187/920173, closed Wednesday except in summer). Pesto lovers should order their pasta "pesto grande."

Sleeping in Manarola: Marina Piccola has fine rooms right on the water (L85,000 doubles, no breakfast, tel. 0187/92 01 03) so they figure a personal touch is unnecessary.

The **Albergo ca' d'Andrean** (L85,000 doubles with showers, breakfast extra, Via A. Discovolo 25, tel. 0187/920 040) is quiet, comfortable, and modern, with a cool garden complete with orange trees right up the hill almost to the church. This is your best normal hotel deal in the Cinque Terre.

Casa Capellini (L45,000 doubles, no breakfast, Via Antonio Discovolo 6, tel. 0187/92 08 23), farther up the street (take a hard right just off the church square, then two doors down the hill on your right), is the best private home I found. Run by a bouncy elderly woman, with a prize-winning village-Mediterranean-vineyards-church bell tower view from its terrace, a self-service kitchenette, and modern facilities down the hall, this place is worth the language hassles.

Eating in Manarola: Il Porticiolo near the water on the main street or **Trattoria da Billy** with the best view in town up in the residential area are both reasonable for the overpriced area.

Sleeping elsewhere in or near the Cinque Terre: Some enjoy staying in Monterosso al Mare, the most beach-resorty and least friendly of the five Cinque Terre towns. There are plenty of hotels, rentable beach umbrellas, shops, and cars. This is the forbidden city, and if you want to sleep here (**Pensione al Carugio**, tel. 0187/81 74 53, and the **Hotel Marina**, Via Buranco 40, tel. 817242 or 817613), may you meet in hell all the hitchhikers you never picked up.

Nearby Lerici is a pleasant town with several reasonable harborside hotels and a daily boat connection to Vernazza. Boat in, train and bus home. The youth hostel in the funky beach town of Finale Ligure, down the coast on the other side of Genoa, is a friendly, deluxe castle (tel. 019/690515). When all else fails, you can stay in a noisy bigger town like La Spezia. **Hotel Terminus** (L46,000-55,000 doubles, no breakfast, Via Paleocapa 21, next to the station, tel. 0187/37204) has an elegant, arcaded old lobby used by old locals to watch soccer, worn-out carpets, yellow walls, old plumbing, and basic rooms. **Albergo Parma** (L40,000-50,000 doubles, without breakfast, Via Fiume 143, 19100 La Spezia, tel. 0187/74 30 10), brighter but lacking the character, is located just below the station, down the stairs.

DAY 5
RIVIERA TO FLORENCE VIA PISA

From the lazy Riviera, work gradually into the epicenter of the Italian Renaissance with a stop at Pisa, an art power in its own right. After checking out Pisa's cathedral and tipsy tower, it's on to Florence, the city of Michelangelo and Leonardo. Get your artistic bearings with a Renaissance walk.

Suggested Schedule	
9:00	Train to La Spezia, and on to Pisa.
10:30	Tour the Piazza of Miracles—the Church and Leaning Tower.
12:00	Picnic on the grass.
14:00	On to Florence.
17:00	Tour the Uffizi Gallery, home of Italy's best paintings.
19:00	Follow the Renaissance Ramble walk through central Florence.

Transportation: Cinque Terre to Pisa to Florence (90 miles)

By train you'll find hourly connections from La Spezia to Pisa (one hour) and from Pisa to Florence (90 minutes). Even the fastest trains stop in Pisa, and you'll very likely be changing trains here whether you plan to stop or not.

Getting from the station to the tower is easy: bus #1 leaves from the bus circle to the right of the station every ten minutes. Buy your ticket from the magazine kiosk in the station's main hall or from the yellow machine just outside to the left (push *corsa semplice*) outside the Tourist Information door (9:30-13:00, 15:00-19:00 daily, tel. 050/56 04 64). Some milk-run trains stop at San Rossore station and some buses stop at Piazza Manin (each just a short walk from the Leaning Tower).

Drivers will see the Leaning Tower as they approach Pisa from the north. There's a large parking lot right at the sights, just outside the wall on the north end of town, so those coming in by freeway don't actually have to drive into Pisa.

The drive from Pisa to Florence is a rare case when the nonautostrada highway (free, more direct, and at least as fast) is a better deal than the autostrada. (If you do take the autoroute, take the Firenze Nord-Al Mare exit, where you'll see a modern church dedicated to the workers who lost their lives building this autostrada. It's worth a look.) In Florence, follow signs to Centro and Fortezza di Basso. After driving and trying to park in Florence, you'll understand why Leonardo never invented the car. Cars flatten the charm of Florence. Get near the centro and park where you can.

Parking (and driving) is a problem in Florence. Garages are expensive (around L30,000 a day; the cheapest and biggest garage is at Borgo Ognissanti 96 near the Amerigo Vespucci bridge). You can try Piazza del Carmine for a free spot if you're staying across the river. (When the new under-the-station car park is complete, it will be best for those staying in that area.) White lines are free, blue are not. I once got towed here—an expensive lesson.

Pisa

Pisa was a regional superpower in her medieval heyday (eleventh, twelfth, and thirteenth centuries), rivaling Florence and Genoa. Its Mediterranean empire, which included Corsica and Sardinia, helped make it a wealthy republic. But the Pisa fleet was beat (1284, by Genoa) and its port silted up, leaving it high and dry with only its Piazza of Miracles (and its university) keeping it on the map.

Pisa's three important sights, the cathedral, baptistery, and bell tower, float regally on a lush, picnic-perfect lawn—the best grass in Italy, with the most expensive public toilets (L1000) to match. Even as the church was being built, the Piazza del Duomo was nicknamed the Campo dei Miracoli or "Field of Miracles" for the grandness of the undertaking. The style throughout is Pisa's very own "Pisan Romanesque."

▲▲ **The famous Leaning Tower** is a textbook example of the town's unique Pisan Romanesque architecture. The 294 tilted steps to the top are now closed. The tower was leaning even before its completion. Notice how the architect, for lack of a better solution, kinked up the top section.

▲▲ **The huge "Pisan Romanesque" cathedral** with its richly carved pulpit by Giovanni Pisano (open 7:45-12:45, 15:00 or 15:30-18:45, free) is more important artistically than its more famous tipsy bell tower. The baptistery (biggest in Italy, in front of the church, same hours but L5000) with a pulpit by Nicolo Pisano (1260) which inspired Renaissance art to follow is interesting for its great acoustics; if you ask nicely and leave a tip, the doorman uses its echo power to sing haunting harmonies with himself. Notice, even the baptistery leans about five feet.

Pisa, of course, is much more than the Campo dei Miracoli. The cemetery bordering the cathedral square is not worth the L5000 admission, even if its "Holy Land dirt" does turn a body into a skeleton in a day. Its untouristed and interesting old town centers along the Arno between the Duomo and the station. But for most, Pisa is just a cliché that needs to be seen and a chance to see the Pisano pulpits. For more Pisan art, see the Museo dell' Opera del Duomo (behind the tower) and the Museo Nazionale di San Matteo (on the river near Piazza Mazzini).

Florence

See tomorrow.

DAY 6
FLORENCE

Florence is a treasure chest of artistic and cultural wonders from the birthplace of our modern world. Since our time here is limited, we'll get intimate with Tuscany later in Siena. For us, Florence is a "supermarket sweep," and the groceries are the best art in Europe. And Florentine art goes beyond paintings and statues—there's food, fashion, handicrafts, and Italy's best gelato.

Suggested Schedule	
9:00	San Marco for Fra Angelico's art.
10:00	*David* in the Accademia.
11:00	Bargello for the best sculpture.
13:00	Lunch at Vivoli's? Siesta in hotel or at Boboli Gardens.
16:00	Climb Giotto's cathedral bell tower for a Florence view.
17:00	Shopping or visit Museo dell' Duomo.
20:00	Dinner in Oltrarno.
Note:	Florence's top museums are closed on Monday.

Orientation

The Florence we're interested in lies mostly on the north bank of the Arno River. Everything is within a 20-minute walk from the train station, cathedral, or Ponte Vecchio (Old Bridge). Some of the best hotels and restaurants are on the more colorful, less awesome Oltrarno (south bank). Orient yourself by the red-tiled dome of the cathedral (the Duomo) and its tall bell tower (Giotto's Tower). This is the center of historic Florence.

Florence's Tourist Offices are normally overcrowded, underinformed, and understaffed. If the line is not too long, pick up a map, and the *Florence Today* booklet with current museum hours, events, and entertainment listings. You may find small temporary information booths around the town supplementing the main Informazione Turistica at the train station (open daily in summer 8:30-21:00, tel. 055/28 28 93). There's often a small information booth across from the baptistery. While the tourist information people dawdle, Florence has particularly hardworking gypsy thief gangs.

Florence requires organization, especially for a blitz tour. There's so much to see. Local guidebooks are cheap and give you a decent commentary to the sights and a map. Remember, many museums call it a day at 14:00 and stop selling tickets 30 minutes before that. Most are closed Monday and at 13:00 on Sunday. Churches usually close from 12:30 to 15:00 or 16:00. Hours can change at a peon's whim. No one knows exactly what's going on tomorrow. Street addresses throw visitors a curve by listing businesses in red and residences in black or blue. *Pensioni* are usually black but can be either. Taxis are expensive. Buses are cheap. An L800 ticket lets you ride anywhere for 70 minutes.

If you arrive early enough, see everyone's essential sight, *David*, right off. In Italy, a masterpiece seen and enjoyed is worth two tomorrow; you never know when a place will unexpectedly close for a holiday, strike, or restoration. Late afternoon is the best time to enjoy the popular Uffizi Gallery without its crowds. Telephone code: 055. Tourist Medical Service: tel. 475411.

Sightseeing Highlights—Florence

▲▲▲ A Florentine Renaissance Walk—For a walk through the core of Renaissance Florence, start at the Accademia (home of Michelangelo's *David*) and cut through the heart of the city to the Ponte Vecchio on the Arno River. (A 10-page, self-guided tour of this walk is outlined in my museum guidebook, *Mona Winks.*) From the Accademia, walk to the cathedral (Duomo). Check out the famous doors and the interior of the baptistery. Consider climbing Giotto's Tower. Continue toward the river on Florence's great pedestrian mall, Via de' Calzaioli, which was part of the original grid plan given the city by the ancient Romans. Down a few blocks, notice the statues on the exterior of the Orsanmichele Church. Via de' Calzaioli connects the cathedral with the

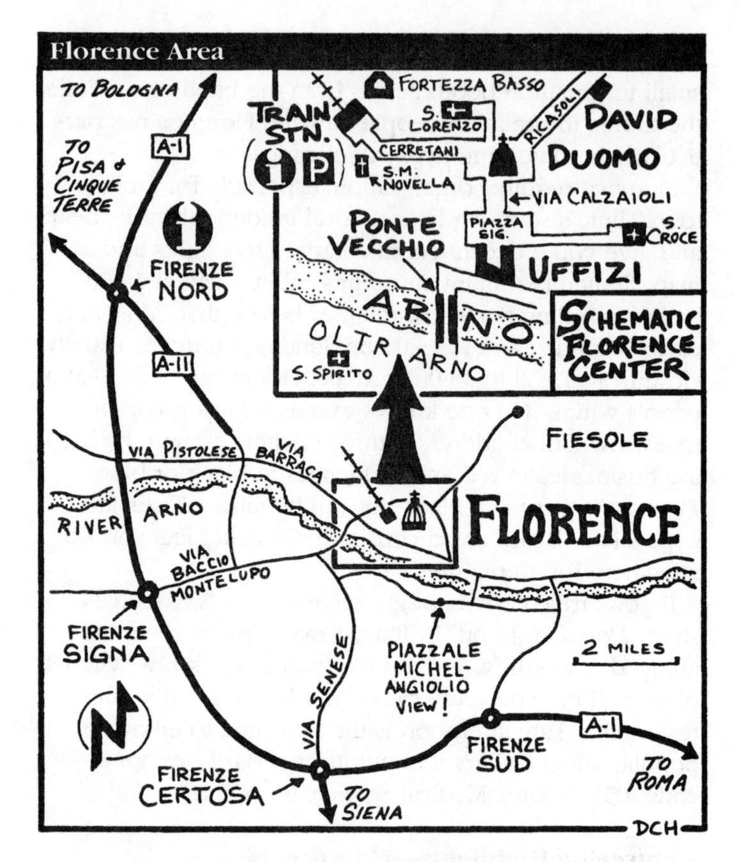

central square (Piazza della Signoria), the city palace (Palazzo Vecchio), and the great Uffizi Gallery.

After you walk past the statues of the great men of the Renaissance in the Uffizi courtyard, you'll get to the Arno River and the Ponte Vecchio. Your introductory walk will be over, and you'll know what sights to concentrate on tomorrow. You still have half a day to see a lifetime of art and history—or just to shop, people-watch, and enjoy Europe's greatest ice cream.

▲▲▲ The Accademia (Galleria dell' Accademia)— This museum houses Michelangelo's *David* and his powerful (unfinished) *Prisoners.* Eavesdrop as tour guides explain these masterpieces. More than any other work of art, when you look into the eyes of *David,* you're looking into the eyes of Renaissance man. This was a radical break with the past. Man is now a confident individual, no longer a plaything of the supernatural. And life is now more than just a preparation for what happens after you die. The Renaissance was the merging of art and science. In a humanist vein, *David*'s looking at the crude giant of medieval darkness and thinking, "I can take this guy." Back on a religious track (and, speaking of veins), notice how big and overdeveloped *David*'s right hand is. This is symbolic of the hand of God, which powered *David* to slay the giant—and, of course, Florence to rise above its crude neighboring city-states.

There's also a lovely Botticelli painting. The newly opened second floor is worth a quick look for its beautiful pre-Renaissance paintings. (Via Ricasoli 60, open 9:00-14:00, Sunday 9:00-13:00, closed Monday, L10,000.)

There's an extensive book and poster shop across the street. Walk around behind the Accademia to the Piazza Santissima Annunziata, with its lovely Renaissance harmony, and the Hospital of the Innocents (Spedale degli Innocenti, not worth going inside) by Brunelleschi with terra-cotta medallions by Della Robbia. Built in the 1420s, it is considered the first Renaissance building.

▲▲ Museum of San Marco—One block north of the Accademia on Piazza San Marco, this museum houses the greatest collection anywhere of dreamy medieval frescoes and paintings by the early Renaissance master, Fra Angelico. You'll see why he thought of painting as a form of prayer and couldn't paint a crucifix without shedding tears. Each of the monks' cells has a Fra Angelico fresco. Don't miss the cell of Savonarola, the charismatic monk who threw out the Medici, turned Florence into a theocracy, sponsored "bonfires of the vanities" (burning books, paintings, and so on), and was finally burned when Florence decided to change channels. (Open 9:00-14:00, Sunday 9:00-13:00, closed Monday, L6000.)

▲▲ The Duomo—Florence's mediocre Gothic cathedral has the third longest nave in Christendom (open 10:00-12:30, 15:00-18:00, sometimes with no lunch break, daily, free). The church's neo-Gothic facade is from the 1870s

and is covered with pink, green, and white Tuscan marble. Since all of its great art is stored in the Museo dell' Opera del Duomo, behind the church, the best thing about the inside is the shade. But it's capped by Brunelleschi's magnificent dome—the first Renaissance dome and the model for domes to follow. When planning St. Peter's in Rome, Michelangelo said, "I can build a dome bigger but not more beautiful than the dome of Florence." You can climb to the top, but climbing **Giotto's Tower** (Campanile, open daily 9:00-19:30, until 18:00 off-season, L4000) next to it is 50 less steps, faster, not so crowded, and offers a better view (including the dome).

▲▲ **Museo dell' Opera del Duomo**—The underrated cathedral museum, just behind the church at #9, has masterpieces by Donatello (a gruesome wood carving of Mary Magdalene clothed in her matted hair and the *cantoria*, the delightful choir loft bursting with happy children), Luca Della Robbia (another choir loft, lined with the dreamy faces of musicians praising the Lord), a late Michelangelo Pietà (Nicodemus, on top, is a self-portrait), Brunelleschi's models for his dome, and the original restored panels of Ghiberti's doors to the baptistery. Great if you like sculpture. To get the most out of your sightseeing hours, remember that this is one of the few museums in Florence that stays open late. (Open in summer, 9:00-18:00, often until 19:30, closed Sunday, L4000.)
▲ **The Baptistery**—Michelangelo said its bronze doors were fit to be the gates of paradise. Check out the gleaming copies of Ghiberti's bronze doors facing the Duomo and the famous competition doors around to the right. Making a breakthrough in perspective, Ghiberti used mathematical laws to create the illusion of 3-D on a 2-D surface. Go inside Florence's oldest building, sit and savor the medieval mosaic ceiling. Notice Hell. Compare that to the "new, improved" art of the Renaissance. (Open 13:00-18:00, Sunday 9:00-13:00, free. Bronze doors always "open"; original panels are in the cathedral museum.)
▲ **Orsanmichele**—Mirroring Florentine values, this was a combination church-granary. The best L500 deal in Florence is the light machine, for its glorious tabernacle. Notice the spouts for grain to pour through the pillars inside. You can go upstairs through the building behind it and over a sky bridge for the temporary exhibit and a fine city view (free). Also study the sculpture on its outside walls. You can see man literally stepping out in the great Renaissance sculptor Donatello's *St. George*. (On Via Calzaioli, 8:00-12:00, 15:00-18:00, free.) The original Orsanmichele statues will soon be stationed upstairs.
▲ **Palazzo Vecchio**—The interior of the fortified palace, which was once the home of the Medici family, is worthwhile only if you're a real Florentine art and history fan. (Open 9:00-19:00, Sunday 8:00-13:00, closed Saturday.

L8000. Handy public W.C. on the ground floor.) Until 1873, Michelangelo's *David* stood at the entrance, where the copy is today. The huge statues in the square are only important as the whipping boys of art critics and as pigeon roosts. The important art is in the nearby Loggia dei Lanzi. Notice the bronze statue of Perseus (with the head of Medusa) by Cellini. The plaque on the pavement in front of the palace marks the spot where Savonarola went to blazes.

▲▲▲ Uffizi Gallery—The greatest collection of Italian painting anywhere is a must, with plenty of works by Giotto, Leonardo, Raphael, Caravaggio, Rubens, Titian, and Michelangelo and a roomful of Botticellis including his *Birth of Venus.* There are no tours, so buy a book on the street before entering (or follow *Mona Winks*). The museum is nowhere near as big as it is great: few tourists spend more than two hours inside. The paintings are displayed (behind obnoxious reflective glass) on one comfortable floor in chronological order from the thirteenth through the seventeenth century.

Essential stops are the Gothic altarpieces by Giotto and Cimabue (narrative, prerealism, no real concern with believable depth); Uccello's *Battle of San Romano*, an early study in perspective; Fra Lippi's cuddly Madonnas; the Botticelli room filled with masterpieces including the small *La Calumnia* showing the *glasnost* of Renaissance free thinking being clubbed back into the darker age of Savonarola; two minor works by Leonardo; the octagonal classical sculpture room with Praxitiles' *Venus de Medici*, considered the epitome of beauty in Elizabethan Europe; view of the Arno through two dirty panes of glass; Michelangelo's only easel painting, the round Holy Family; Raphael's *Madonna of the Goldfinch*; Titian's *Venus of Urbino*; and an interesting view of the palace and cathedral from the terrace at the end. (Open 9:00-19:00, Sunday 9:00-13:00, closed Monday, last ticket sold 45 minutes before closing, L10,000. While many camp out early, I go very late to avoid the crowds and heat.)

Enjoy the Uffizi square, full of artists and souvenir stalls. The surrounding statues of the earthshaking Florentines of 500 years ago remind us that the Florentine Renaissance was much more than just the visual arts.

▲▲▲ Bargello (Museo Nazionale)—The city's underrated and greatest sculpture museum is behind the Palazzo Vecchio (a four-minute walk from the Uffizi) in a former prison that looks like a mini-Palazzo Vecchio. It has Donatello's *David*, the very influential first male nude to be sculpted in a thousand years, works by Michelangelo, and much more. (At Via del Proconsolo 4; open 9:00-14:00, Sunday 9:00-13:00, closed Monday, L6000.) Dante's house, just across the street and around the corner, is interesting only to his Italian-speaking fans.

Medici Chapel (Cappelle dei Medici)—This chapel is drenched in incredibly lavish High Renaissance architecture and sculpture by Michelangelo. (Behind San Lorenzo on Piazza Madonna, open 9:00-14:00, Sunday 9:00-13:00, closed Monday, L9000.) It's surrounded by a lively market scene that, for some reason, I find more interesting.

Museo di Storia della Scienza (Science Museum)—This is a fascinating collection of Renaissance and later clocks, telescopes, maps, and ingenious gadgets. A highlight for many is Galileo's finger in a little shrinelike bottle. English guidebooklets are available. It's friendly, comfortably cool, never crowded, and just downstream from the Uffizi. (At Piazza dei Giudici 1; open Monday, Wednesday and Friday 9:30-13:00 and 14:00-17:00, L10,000.)

Michelangelo's Home, Casa Buonarroti—Fans will enjoy Michelangelo's house at Via Ghibellina 70 (open 9:30-12:30, closed Tuesday, L5000).

The Pitti Palace—Across the river, it has the giant Galleria Palatina collection with works of the masters (especially Raphael), plus the enjoyable Galleria d'Arte Moderna (upstairs) and the huge semi-landscaped Boboli Gardens—a cool refuge from the city heat. (Five museums; open 9:00-14:00, Sunday 9:00-13:00, closed Monday, L8000, L11,000 if there's a special exhibit.)

▲ Brancacci Chapel—For the best look at the early Renaissance master Masaccio, see his newly restored frescoes here (cross the Ponte Vecchio and turn left a few blocks to Piazza del Carmine, 10:00-17:00, closed Tuesday, L5000).

▲ **Piazzale Michelangelo**—Across the river overlooking the city (look for the huge David), this square is worth the half-hour hike or the drive for the view. After dark, it's packed with local school kids sharing slices of watermelon with their dates and cars. Just beyond it is the strikingly beautiful, crowd-free, Romanesque San Miniato church. (Bus 13 from the station.)

▲▲ **Gelato**—Gelato is a great Florentine edible art form. Italy's best ice cream is in Florence. Every year I repeat my taste test. And every year Vivoli's (on Via Stinche, see map, closed Mondays and for the last three weeks in August) wins. Festival del Gelato, and Perche Non! just off the pedestrian street running from the Duomo to the Uffizi are almost as good. That's one souvenir that can't break and won't clutter your luggage. Vivoli's rice (*riso*) is my favorite.

Shopping: Florence is a great shopping town. Busy street scenes and markets abound, especially near San Lorenzo, on the Ponte Vecchio, and near Santa Croce. Leather, gold, silver, art prints, and tacky plaster "mini-Davids" are most popular. Check out the leather school in the Santa Croce church, to the right of the altar (10:00-18:00).

Sleeping in Florence (about L1300 = US$1)

Even in crowded and overpriced Florence, with a little information and a phone call ahead, you can find a simple, cheery, and comfortable double for around L50,000 to L65,000. For L100,000, you'll get roof garden elegance. If you're staying for three or more nights, ask for a discount. The technically optional and definitely overpriced breakfast can be used as a bargaining chip. Most prices I've listed include L10,000 for each breakfast. In practice, most places require it, but if it's not too busy, it doesn't hurt to ask. While the hottest months, July and August, are less crowded, and prices don't seem very firm, most hotels claim they are full every day from mid-March to mid-October. Call ahead. I repeat, call ahead. Places will happily hold a room until early afternoon. If they say they're full, mention you're using this book. Use the crowded station room-finding service only if you lose this book.

Near the Station: While there are scads of inexpensive (one-star) pensioni near the station (Via Fiume and Via Faenza), I'd choose something on or near Piazza Santa Maria Novella (behind the church, which is directly in front of the station) or on neighboring Via della Scala.

Casa Rabatti (L50,000-55,000 doubles or L25,000-35,000 per bed in shared quad or quint for travelers with this book, no breakfast, Via San Zanobi 48, 50129 Florence, doorbell left of door, tel. 055/21 23 93, no English spoken) is the ultimate if you always wanted to be a part of a Florentine family. Simple, clean, very friendly, four blocks northeast of the station, this is my best rock-bottom listing.

Hotel Enza (L56,000-65,000 doubles, no breakfast, Via San Zanobi 45 black, 50129 Florence, tel. 055/49 09 90) is clean, cheery, halfway between the station and *David* and warmly run by English-speaking Eugenia.

Let's Go and Arthur Frommer (the basic English-language guides to Florence) each rave about the same places two blocks from the station on Via Faenza. The street is filled with English-speaking tourists and good L50,000 to L60,000 doubles. No. 56 is a slumber mill, filled with these heavily recommended English-speaking places. **Albergo Azzi** (L50,000 doubles, L22,000 per bed in shared quads and quints, L5000 more with breakfast, Via Faenza 56, tel. 055/21 38 06), very accommodating, with a small terrace, is better than a hostel, and will hold a room until 16:00. In the same building but not quite as good, you'll find **Merlini** (cheapest and friendliest, tel. 055/21 28 48), **Paola** (tel. 055/21 36 82), **Armonia** (tel. 055/21 11 46), and **Anna** (tel. 055/239 8322).

Hotel Pensione Elite (L75,000 doubles, with modern showers but no breakfast, Via della Scala 12, second floor, a block off Piazza S. Maria Novella, and just two blocks from the station, tel. 215 395) has none of the backpacking flavor of Via Faenze and is a good basic value; run warmly by Maurizio.

Casa Cristina (L75,000 doubles, with this book, L50,000 per person with dinner, Via Bonifacio Lupi 14, just off the ring road near Piazza della Liberta, right side of courtyard, second floor, tel. 055/49 67 30) is farther away, a brisk ten-minute walk from the station and center. It's elegant, spotless, and offers free, easy parking on its quiet street. Richly and traditionally decorated and run by Mr. Holtz, this place is a rare value in Florence.

Pensione Sole (L50,000-60,000, no breakfast, Via del Sole 8, 3rd floor, no lift, tel. 055/239 6094) is a clean, cozy, family-run (Anna, Michele, and Maurito) place with kids, caged birds, and a few bright rooms. It's well located, just off S.M. Novella toward Ponte Vecchio, but there are lots of stairs.

Hotel Loggiato dei Serviti (L180,000 with everything, Piazza SS. Annunziata 3, Firenze, tel. 055/28 95 92, fax 055/28 95 95, guarantee reservations with AmExCo cards), with about the most prestigious address in Florence, right on the most Renaissance square in town, has done a fine job of giving you Renaissance romance with a place to plug in your hair dryer. Stone stairways (and an Otis elevator) lead you under open beam ceilings through this sixteenth-century monastery's elegantly appointed public rooms. The cells, with air-conditioning, TVs, mini-bars, and telephones, wouldn't be recognized by their original inhabitants. Stepping out onto the square into a traffic-free Brunelleschi world is a splurge-worthy treat.

Rooms in Oltrarno, over, on or near the river: Across the river in the Oltrarno area, between the Pitti Palace and the Ponte Vecchio, you'll still find small traditional craft shops, neighborly piazzas hiding a few offbeat art treasures, family eateries, two distinctive, clean, friendly, moderately priced hotels, and three decent hostels. Each of these places is only a few minutes walk from the Ponte Vecchio.

Pensione Sorelle Bandini (L83,000-95,000 doubles with breakfast, Piazza Santo Spirito 9, 50125 Firenze, tel. 055/21 53 08), a ramshackle 500-year-old palace on a perfectly Florentine square, two blocks from the Pitti Palace, has cavernous rooms, museum warehouse interiors, a musty youthfulness, and a balcony lounge-loggia with a classic view. Mimmo, Monica, or Sr. Romeo will hold a room until 16:00 with a phone call.

Hotel La Scaletta (L83,000-L105,000 doubles with breakfast, Via Guicciardini, 13 black, 50125 Firenze, straight up the street from the Ponte Vecchio—strange numbering, keep going, it's next to the AmExCo—tel. 055/28 30 28, fax 055/28 95 62, call first, 22 Days readers are their preferred customers) is more elegant, friendlier, and cleaner, with a dark, cool, labyrinthine floor plan and lots of Old World lounges. Owner Barbara and her children, Manfredo and Diana, speak English and elevate this well-worn and relaxing refuge with brute charm. Your journal becomes poetry when written on the highest terrace of La Scaletta's panoramic roof garden. Lucky winter travelers get Manfredo's Cena, a complete local-style dinner at an unbeatable price.

Also in Oltrarno are some of the best rock-bottom budget deals in town. **Institute Gould** (L50,000 doubles, with or without private shower, L20,000 beds in shared 2- to 4-bed rooms, 49 Via dei Serragli, tel. 055/21 25 76, office open Monday-Friday 9:00-13:00 and 15:00-19:00, Saturday 9:00-12:00, closed Sunday) is a Protestant church-run place with 72 beds in 24 rooms. The facilities, whether in the room or down the hall, are modern and clean. They'll hold a room until noon with a phone call. Since you must arrive during their office hours, there's no way to check in on Sundays.

Pensionato Pio X-Artigianelli (L15,000 beds in 2- to 10-bed rooms, L3000 extra if you want a single or a private shower, Via dei Serragli 106, tel. 055/22 50 44) is Catholic run and a little friendlier and more freewheeling and ramshackle, with 35 beds in 15 rooms, cheap meals served, and a 23:30 curfew.

Ostello Santa Monaca (L15,000 beds, L2500 for sheets, without breakfast, 6 Via Santa Monaca, a few blocks past Ponte Alla Carraia, tel. 055/26 83 38 or 055/239 6704), your last resort, with over 100 beds in 8- to 20-bed dorms, takes no reservations. Sign up for available beds from 9:30 to 13:00 or when it reopens after

16:00. You can leave bags (without valuables) there until it opens after siesta. This or the classy IYHF hostel (tel. 055/601 4151) on the outskirts of Florence should be a last alternative.

Pensione Bretagna (L85,000-105,000 doubles, west of the Ponte Vecchio, just past Ponte San Trinita, at Lungarno Corsini 6, 50123 Firenze, tel. 055/28 96 18, English spoken) is a classy/stuffy, Old World, elegant place for similar tourists. Imagine breakfast under a painted, chandeliered ceiling with an Arno view. To reserve, call first and follow up with a bank draft in lire for the first night. Or call in the morning, and they'll hold a room until noon.

Soggiorno Cestelli (L70,000-75,000, Borgo SS. Apostoli 25, 50123 Florence, tel. 055/214213), in the old center, one block off the river, is the closest thing to living in a Botticelli painting a budget traveler will find in Florence. Luciano and his aunt rent 4 doubles and 3 singles and serve breakfast in the room. They like, but don't allow, children in their pint-sized palace. The rooms are huge, many with grand matrimonial beds, tassels on the hutches, candelabra, and hardwood floors framing rich old carpets. Their room #2 is the best deal in Florence.

Eating in Florence

Places across the river: There are several good and colorful restaurants in Oltrarno near Piazza Santo Spirito. **Trattoria Casalinga** (from Pitti Palace follow Via Michelozzi to Santo Spirito, just off Piazza Santo Spirito at 9 Via dei Michelozzi, tel. 218624) is an inexpensive and popular standby, famous for its home cooking. Good values but more expensive are **Trattoria Sabitino** at Borgo S. Frediano and **Osteria del Cinghiale Bianco** at Borgo S. Jacopo 43 (closed Tuesday and Wednesday).

Trattoria Oreste (right on Piazza S. Spirito at 16), with a renowned cook and on-the-piazza ambience, may have the best L30,000 dinner in the area. The **Ricchi** bar on the same square has some of the best homemade gelati in Firenze and a particularly pleasant interior. The best places change, and I'd just wander in a colorful neighborhood and eat where you see locals eating.

Eateries near Santa Maria Novella: Trattoria il Contadino (Via Palazzuolo 69 red, a few blocks south of the train station, 12:00-14:30 and 18:00-21:30, closed Sunday, tel. 2382673) offers one L14,000 hearty family-style fixed-price menu with a bustling working-class-budget Yankee traveler atmosphere.

Pinnochio's (at the end of S.M. Novella turn right to Via della Scala 16 (tel. 218418) serves a good L17,000 tourist menu. Try the Bistecca Florentina.

Il Latini is an internationally famous but popular with the locals traditional Florentine eatery. You'll share a large table under hanging hams. There's no menu. The wine's already on the table. Just order as you go. This isn't cheap, but it can provide a memorable entire evening's experience, not to mention a wonderful dinner (Via del Palchetti 4, just off Moro between S.M. Novella and the river).

Places for a quick lunch near the sights: I keep lunch in Florence fast and simple, eating in one of countless self-service places, Pizza Rusticas (holes in the wall that sell cheap delicious pizza by weight), or just picnicking (juice, yogurt, cheese, roll: L8000). Behind the Duomo, Snack (15 Pronconsolo) serves decent cheap lunches. For a reasonably priced pizza with a Medici-style view try the pizzeria on Piazza della Signori (upper left corner as you face the Palazzo Vecchio). Try the local Chianti Classico.

DAY 7

FLORENCE TO SIENA VIA SAN GIMIGNANO

Florence has the art, but two smaller towns nearby have more urban charm. San Gimignano is the quintessential hill town, with Italy's best surviving medieval skyline. Siena seems to be every Italy connoisseur's pet town. In my office whenever Siena is mentioned, someone moans, "Siena? I Luuuv Siena!"

Suggested Schedule

9:00	Sightseeing or shopping in Florence.
11:00	Depart Florence for San Gimignano.
12:00	Browse the town, don't trip on the tourists.
13:00	Climb the castle for a picnic with a view.
15:00	Bus or drive to Siena. Set up in the old town. Practice medieval loitering on the main square.

Transportation: Florence to San Gimignano to Siena (45 miles)

From Florence, bus to San Gimignano (regular departures, 75 minutes, change in Poggibonsi) or catch the train to Poggibonsi where buses make the frequent 20-minute ride into San Gimignano. Climb through the gate and up the traffic-free town's cobbled main drag to the Piazza del Cisterna (with its 13th-century well) and the Piazza del Duomo. Buses go regularly from San Gimignano to Siena, Volterra, and Florence.

There's absolutely no driving within the walled town of San Gimignano. But a car park awaits you just a few steps from the town gate.

Transportation in Siena: From Siena's train station, buy a bus ticket from the yellow machine near the exit (L800), cross the street, and board any orange city bus (confirm that it's going to either Piazza Matteotti or Piazza Gramsci). Your hotel is probably within 300 yards of Piazza Matteotti.

While most trains take longer and require a change, rapido SITA buses go regularly from downtown Florence to Siena's San Domenico nonstop by autostrada (L8300, 70 minutes). Buy your ticket before boarding at the biglietteria (ticket office). SITA bus riders will be dropped at San Domenico church, a seven-minute walk from the center square. To walk to the center, walk to the left of the church following the yellow signs to Il Campo.

Drivers find a parking place by following the Centro, then Stadio, signs (stadium, soccer ball). The soccer ball signs take you to the tour bus lot. Park at any white striped car stall on the nearby streets or pay L15,000 a day to park in the stadium, just across from the huge brick church, San Domenico.

San Gimignano

The epitome of a Tuscan hill town with fourteen medieval towers (out of an original 72!) still standing, San Gimignano is a perfectly preserved tourist trap so easy to visit and visually pleasing that it's a good stop. Remember, in the thirteenth century, back in the days of Romeo and Juliet, towns were run by feuding noble families. And they'd periodically battle things out from the protective bases of their respective family towers. Skylines like San Gimignano's were the norm in medieval Tuscany. Florence had literally hundreds of towers.

While the basic three-star sight here is the town itself, the Collegiata (on Piazza del Duomo), a Romanesque church filled with fine Renaissance frescoes, and the Rocco (castle, free entry, a short climb behind the church, with a fine view) are important stops. You can also climb San Gimignano's tallest tower, the 180-foot-tall Torre Grossa above the Palazzo del Popolo.

Market day is Thursday (8:00-13:00), but for local merchants, every day is a sales frenzy.

San Gimignano streets are clogged mainly by day-trippers. But its hotels are expensive. The tourist office has a list of private homes that rent rooms. The town's friendly, well-run youth hostel (Ostello della Gioventu, Via delle Fonti 1, tel. 0577/941991) welcomes nonmembers. (Tourist Information, 9:30-12:30, 14:30-18:30 daily, in the old center on the Piazza Duomo, tel. 0577/940008).

DAY 8
SIENA

It seems that 700 years ago a bird dropped a Gothic egg on a hill and rich old buildings and traffic-free red brick lanes oozed every which way. Things hardened, and to this day the sad bird has let nobody change a thing. Siena's thriving historic center offers Italy's best Gothic city experience. While Florence has the blockbuster museums, Siena has an easy-to-enjoy soul. For those who dream of a Fiat-free Italy, this is it. Siena is the hill town equivalent of Venice.

Suggested Schedule	
9:00	San Domenico, Duomo, Baptistery, Duomo museum with view point.
11:00	Shopping, old town browsing, picnic or pizza on Il Campo.
13:00	Siesta, or Pinacoteca art gallery.
15:00	City Hall museum, climb tower.
17:00	Cruise with the town down Via Banchi di Sopra.

Orientation

While most people do Siena, just 30 miles south of Florence, as a day trip, it's best experienced after dark. (In fact, it makes more sense to do Florence as a day trip from Siena.) Take time to savor the first European city to eliminate automobile traffic (1966), and then, just to be silly, wonder what would happen if they did it in your city.

Seven hundred years ago, Siena was a major military power in a class with Florence, Venice, and Genoa. The town was weakened by a disastrous plague in 1348; her bitter rival, Florence, finally did her in and made a point to keep Siena a nonthreatening backwater. Siena's loss became our sightseeing gain, as its political and economic irrelevance pickled it Gothic.

Siena lounges atop a hill, stretching its three legs out from Il Campo. This main square is the historic meeting point of Siena's neighborhoods. The entire center is pedestrians only, no buses and no cars. Get in a walking frame of mind. Nearly everything I mention is within a ten-minute walk from the square. Pick up the excellent topographical town map (free at the TI), but the key is to

Siena

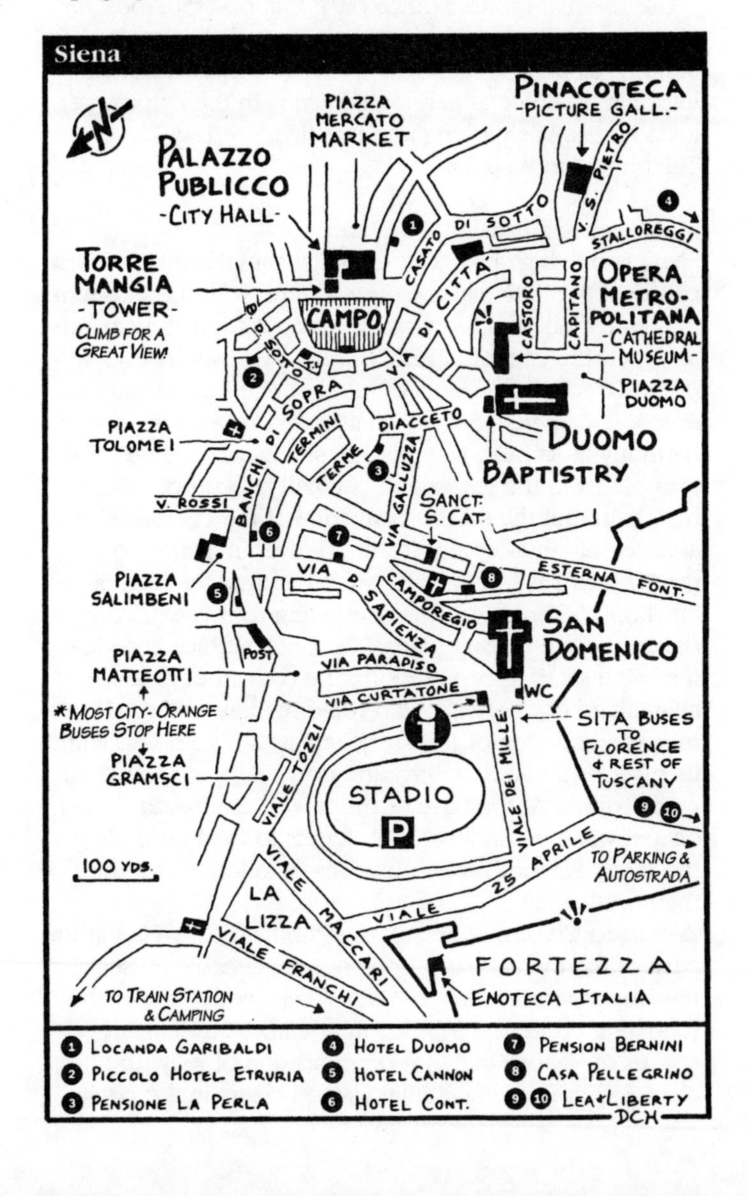

simply navigate by landmarks, following the excellent system of signs on every street corner. All landmarks are signposted. The average visitor sticks to the San Domenico–Il Campo axis. There's a handy public W.C. just off Il Campo at Via Citta.

Use the main tourist office on Il Campo (#56, look for the yellow Weschel/Change sign, open daily except Sunday, 8:30-19:30, tel. 0577/280551). The small hotel information office at San Domenico is in the employ of local hotels. For parking and bus tips, see Day 7. Telephone code: 0577.

Sightseeing Highlights—Siena

Siena is one big sight. The essential actual sights are basically just two little clusters: the square, with the museum in the city hall and its tower; and the cathedral, its baptistery, and the cathedral's museum with its surprise view point. Check these sights off, and you're free to wander.

▲▲▲ Il Campo—Siena's great central piazza is urban harmony at its best. Like a stage set, its gently tilted floor fans out from the tower and city hall backdrop. Notice how beautiful the square is in spite of the complete absence of landscaping. It's the perfect invitation to loiter. Built in 1347, Il Campo was located at the historic junction of Siena's various competing districts, or contrada, on the old market place. The brick surface is divided into nine sections representing the council of nine merchants and city bigwigs who ruled medieval Siena. Don't miss the Fountain of Joy at the square's high point, with its pigeons gingerly tightroping down slippery snouts to grab a drink. At the base of the tower, the Piazza's chapel was built in 1348 as a thanks to God for ending the Black Plague (none too soon—it killed over a third of the population).

▲ Museo Civico—The Palazzo Pubblico (City Hall at the base of the tower) has a fine and manageable museum housing a good sample of Sienese art, you'll see, in the following order, the Sala Risorgimento with dramatic scenes of Victor Emmanuel's unification of Italy, the chapel with impressive inlaid wood chairs in the choir, the Sala del Mappamondo with Simone Martini's *Maesta* (Enthroned Virgin) facing the faded Guidoriccio da Fogliano (a mercenary providing a more concrete form of protection). Next is the Sala della Pace, which has two interesting frescoes showing "the Effects of Good and Bad Government." Notice the whistle while you work happiness of the utopian community ruled by the utopian government (in the best-preserved fresco) and the fate of a community ruled by politicians with more typical values (in a terrible state of repair). Later you'll see the gruesome *Slaughter of the Innocents* (daily 9:30-19:30, winter closing at 13:45, L6000).

▲ **Torre del Mangia (the city tower)**—Siena centers itself around its city hall, not its church. It was a proud republic and its "declaration of independence" is the tallest secular medieval tower in Italy, the tall-as-a-football-field Torre del Mangia (named after a watchman who did more eating than watching; his statue is in the courtyard). Its 300 steps get pretty skinny at the top, but the reward is one of Italy's best views. (10:00-18:00 or 19:00, L4000, limit of 30 towerists at a time, so there may be a lineup.)

The Palio—The feisty spirit of each of Siena's 17 districts lives on. These neighborhoods celebrate, worship, and compete together. Each even has its own historical museum. Contrada pride is evident any time of year in the colorful neighborhood banners but most evident twice a year (around July 2 and August 16) when they have their world-famous Palio di Siena. Ten of the seventeen neighborhoods compete (chosen by lot), hurling themselves with medieval abandon into several days of trial races and traditional revelry. On the big day, Il Campo is stuffed to the brim with locals and tourists as the horses charge wildly around the square in this literally no-holds-barred race. Of course, the winning neighborhood is the scene of grand celebrations afterward. The grand prize: proving your contrada is numero uno. You'll see sketches and posters all over town depicting the Palio. The TI has a free scrapbook-quality Palio brochure with English explanations.

▲▲ **The Duomo**—Siena's cathedral is as baroque as Gothic gets. The striped facade is piled with statues and ornamentation, and the interior is decorated from top to bottom. Even the floors are covered with fine inlaid art. This is the *panforte* of Italian churches, and your special treats are a Donatello statue of St. John the Baptist (in a chapel on the left side) and a couple of Michelangelo statues (on each side of the Piccolomini altar). Above it all peer the heads of 172 popes. This is one busy interior, the antithesis of San Domenico. The artistic highlight is Pisano's pulpit. The library (L2000) has a Roman copy of the Greek Three Graces statue, fine frescoes, and illustrated medieval books. (7:30-19:30, closing an hour early in the off-season, modest dress required, free.)

▲ **Baptistery**—Siena is so hilly that there wasn't enough flat ground to build a big church on. What to do? Build a big church and prop up the overhanging edge with the baptistery. This dark and quietly tucked away cave of art is worth a look for the bronze carvings of Donatello and Ghiberti on the baptismal font and for its cool tranquillity.

▲▲ **The Opera Metropolitana (cathedral museum)**—Siena's most enjoyable museum, on the Campo side of the church (look for the yellow signs), was built to house the cathedral's art. The ground floor is filled with the cathedral's original Gothic sculpture by Pisano. Upstairs to the left awaits a private audience with Duccio's *Maesta* (Enthroned Virgin). Pull up a chair and study this medieval masterpiece. Opposite is what was the flip side of the *Maesta*, with 26 panels, the medieval equivalent of pages, showing scenes from the passion of Christ. After more art, you'll find a little sign directing you to the "panorama." It's a long spiral climb. From the first landing, take the skinnier second spiral for Siena's surprise view. Look back over the Duomo, then consider this: when rival republic Florence began its grand cathedral, Siena decided to outdo it by building a church that would be the biggest in all Christendom. The existing cathedral would be used as a transept. You're atop what would have been the entry. The wall below you that connects the Duomo with the museum of the cathedral was as far as Siena got before the terrible plague killed the city's ability to finish the project. Were it completed, you'd be looking straight down the nave. (9:00-19:30, closing at 18:30 in shoulder months, and 13:30 in off-season, L5000.)

Church of San Domenico—This huge brick church is a landmark for those arriving by bus and is worth a quick look. The simple, bland interior fits the austere philosophy of the Dominicans. Walk up the steps in the rear of the church for a look at various paintings from the life of Saint Catherine, patron saint of Siena and, since 1939, of all Italy. Halfway up the church on the right, you'll find her head. (8:30-13:00, 16:00-19:00, free.)

Sanctuary of Saint Catherine—A few downhill blocks toward the center from San Domenico you'll see signs to the Santuario di Santa Caterina. Step into this cool and peaceful place, the site of Catherine's home. Siena remembers its favorite hometown girl, a simple unschooled but almost mystically devout girl who, in the mid-1300s, helped get the pope to return from France to Rome. Pilgrims have come here since 1464. Wander around to enjoy art depicting scenes from her life. Her room is downstairs. (9:00-12:30 and 15:30-18:00, free.)

▲ The Pinacoteca (National Picture Gallery)—Siena was a power in Gothic art. But the average tourist, wrapped up in a love affair with the Renaissance, hardly notices. This museum takes you on a walk through Siena's art, chronologically from the twelfth through the fifteenth century. For the casual sightseer, the Sienese art in the museums, in the city hall, and at the cathedral is probably adequate. But art fans will thoroughly enjoy tracing the evolution of Siena's delicate and elegant art. (Walk out the Via Citta to the Piazza di Postieria and make a left on San Pietro, 8:30-19:00, closes at 14:00 on Mondays and 13:00 on Sundays, L8000.)

Enoteca Italiana (Italian wine exhibition)—For a chance to sample Italy's best wine for a fair price, walk past San Domenico and continue straight, with the stadium on your right, to the Fortezza. On the right, in the corner of the parking lot, the Enoteca sign marks a passageway that leads through the wall and into the exhibit. The rooms downstairs contain 750 different elegantly displayed bottles of Italian wine. Upstairs, indoors or out, you can enjoy a glass of your choice for L2000. (Open daily 15:00 until midnight, free.)

Sleeping in Siena (about L1300 = US$1)

Since most visitors day-trip in from Florence, finding a room is not tough (unless you arrive during Easter or for the Palio in early July and mid-August). While tour groups turn the town into a Gothic amusement park in midsummer, evening and off-season Siena is basically yours, with your pick of the following hotels.

Nearly all listed hotels lie between Il Campo and the church of San Domenico (the intercity bus stop) and Piazza Matteotti (where the bus from the train station drops you). Call ahead as it seems Siena's few budget places are listed in all the budget guidebooks. Most places serve no breakfast and are accustomed to holding telephone reservations until 17:00, if you can get the message across in Italian.

Near Il Campo: Each of these first listings is just a horse wreck away from one of Italy's most wonderful civic spaces.

Locanda Garibaldi (L50,000, showers down the hall, one cheaper windowless room, half a block downhill off the square to the right of the tower at Via Giovanni Dupre 18, tel. 0577/284204, fax . . . what's that?) is a dying breed. This very Italian, modest restaurant-albergo combines a busy restaurant with eight doubles upstairs. The friendly owners are either playing cards or busy with the restaurant. This is a fine place for dinner.

Piccolo Hotel Etruria (L50,000-75,000, with back to the tower, leave Il Campo to the right, Via Donzelle 1-3, tel. 0577/288088) is a good bet for a real hotel with all the comforts just off the square. The cheaper showers-down-the-hall rooms are in an annex across the street. **Albergo Tre Donzelle** (L50,000-60,000, Via Donzelle 5, tel. 0577/280358) is a plain, institutional, but decent place next door that only makes sense if you think of Il Campo as your terrace.

Pension La Perla (L65,000, a block off the square opposite the tower on Piazza Independenza at Via della Therme 25, tel. 47144) is a funky jumbled place with basic rooms in a laissez-faire environment, run by friendly English-speaking Paolo. All rooms have private facilities; upper floors are best.

Hotel Duomo (L130,000, facing the tower trot right from Il Campo, follow Via Citta, which becomes Via Stalloreggi, to #34 Via Stalloreggi, tel. 289088, fax 583035) is the best in-the-old-town splurge, a truly classy place with spacious elegant rooms. Try for a balcony, ideally in room 62.

A few blocks up Via Banchi di Sopra are **Hotel Cannon d'Oro** (L80,000, Via Montanini 28, tel. 44321, fax 280868) and the dreary, long ago elegant, today just giant **Hotel Continentale** (L60,000-85,000, Via Branchi di Sopra 85, tel. 41451) with rooms so big and lamps so dim you'll dream of the moon in your room.

Closer to the bus stop and San Domenico Church: These hotels are still only a ten-minute walk from Il Campo but ideal for those arriving by car or wanting to minimize lugging luggage. Most enjoy fine views of the old town and cathedral (which sits floodlit before me as I type).

Pension Bernini (L50,000, from San Domenico follow the signs to Il Campo, you'll pass Via Sapienza 15, tel. 0577/289047) is the place to stay if you want to join a Sienese family in a modest, clean home with a few immaculate and comfortable rooms. The bathrooms are down the hall, the upholstery is lively, and the welcome is warm. Even if you normally require private plumbing, the spectacular view from the garden terrace and the friendly owner, Nadia, will make the inconvenience seem petty. Picnic for dinner on the terrace.

Casa Pelligrino (L40,000-50,000 doubles, cheap singles, triples, and quads, substantial financial penance for one-night stays; from San Domenico, walk downhill toward the view, turn left down Via Camporegio; make a

U-turn at the little chapel down the brick steps and you'll see the sign, Via Camporegio 37, tel. 0577/44177) is ideal unless nuns make you nervous or you plan on staying out past the 23:00 curfew. This quasi-hotel (not a convent) is run with a firm but angelic smile by sisters who offer clean, quiet, view rooms for a steal. Bright lamps, quaint balconies, fine views, grand public rooms, top security, and a friendly atmosphere make this the best deal for the lira in town. The checkout time is a strict 10:00, but they have a deposito for luggage.

For a Sienese villa experience in a classy residential neighborhood with English spoken and easy parking on the street, a few blocks past the San Domenico bus stop, consider **Albergo Lea** (L90,000 with breakfast, Viale XXIV Maggio 10, tel. 283207), **Hotel Chiusarelli** (L95,000 without breakfast, across from the stadium at Viale Curtone 9, tel. 280562), and, if you're traveling with rich relatives who want sterility near the action, the **Hotel Villa Liberty** (L130,000 with breakfast, facing the fortress at Viale V. Veneto 11, tel. 0577/44966).

The tourist office has a long list of private homes renting out rooms for around L25,000 per person. Many are filled with students and others require a stay of several days, but some are central and a fine value. Siena's **Guidoriccio youth hostel** (L18,000 beds with breakfast, cheap meals, bus #15 from Piazza Gramsci or the train station to Via Fiorentina 89 in the Stellino neighborhood, tel. 52212) has 120 cheap beds, but, given the hassle of the bus ride and the charm of downtown Siena at night, I'd skip it.

Eating in Siena

Restaurants are reasonable by Florentine and Venetian standards. Don't hesitate to pay a bit more to eat pizza on Il Campo (Pizzeria Spadaforte, tel. 0577/281123, closed Giovedi, is good). The ambience is a classic European experience. For an authentic Sienese dining experience at a fair price, dine at the **Locanda Garibaldi** (just down Via Giovanni Dupre a few steps from the square, see accommodations listing). For a peasant's dessert, take your last glass of Chianti (borrow the *bicchiere for dieci minuti*) with a chunk of bread to the square, lean against a pillar and sip Siena Classico. Picnics any time of day are royal on the Campo.

Siena's claim to caloric fame is its **Panforte**, a rich chewy concoction of nuts, honey, and candied fruits that even fruitcake haters are impressed by (although locals I met prefer a white cookie called Riccerelli). All over town Prodotti Tipici shops sell Sienese specialties. A handy one on Il Campo (right of tower) usually has samples to taste. Don't miss the evening passagiata along Via Vanchi Sopra with gelato in hand (Ninnin's at Piazza Salembini has fine gelato).

DAY 9

SIENA TO CIVITÀ DI BAGNOREGIO

San Gimignano and Siena are Tuscany's star hill towns. Now head south for Umbria's most famous, Orvieto. Then, by early evening, you'll be in Italy's ultimate hill town, stranded alone on a pinnacle in a vast canyon—Cività di Bagnoregio.

Suggested Schedule	
9:00	Leave Siena.
11:00	Orvieto, sightseeing and lunch.
14:30	On to Bagnoregio.
16:00	Set up at Angelino's.
17:00	Evening walk through Cività.
20:00	Dinner in town or at Angelino's.

Transportation: Siena to Cività di Bagnoregio (60 miles)

For exploring the hill towns, the bus is often faster than the train. From Siena to Orvieto is a 2- to 3-hour train trip (change in Chiusi, departures at 6:25, 8:20, 11:18, 13:20 and 15:16). From Orvieto to Bagnoregio is a cheap 40-minute bus ride (at 6:25, 7:50, 9:10, 12:40, 13:55, 14:30, 15:45, and 18:35 from Orvieto's Piazza Cahen and from its train station daily except Sunday, buy tickets on the bus). From Bagnoregio, walk out of town past the old arch (follow Viterbo signs), turn left at the pyramid monument and right (follow Montefiascone sign) at the first fork to get to hotel Al Boschetto.

Driving out of Siena, follow the green autostrada signs south toward Roma. Drive south to Orvieto, then leave the freeway, pass under hill-capping Orvieto (on your right, signs to Lago di Bolsena, on Viale I Maggio), take the first left, direction: Bagnoregio, winding up past great Orvieto views, the Orvieto Classico vineyard, through Canale, and through fields of giant shredded wheat and farms to Bagnoregio, where the locals (or rusty old signs) will direct you to Angelino Catarcia's Al Boschetto, just outside town. Just before Bagnoregio, follow the signs left to Lubriano and pull into the first little square by the church on your right for a breathtaking view of Cività. Then return to the Bagnoregio road.

Orvieto Area

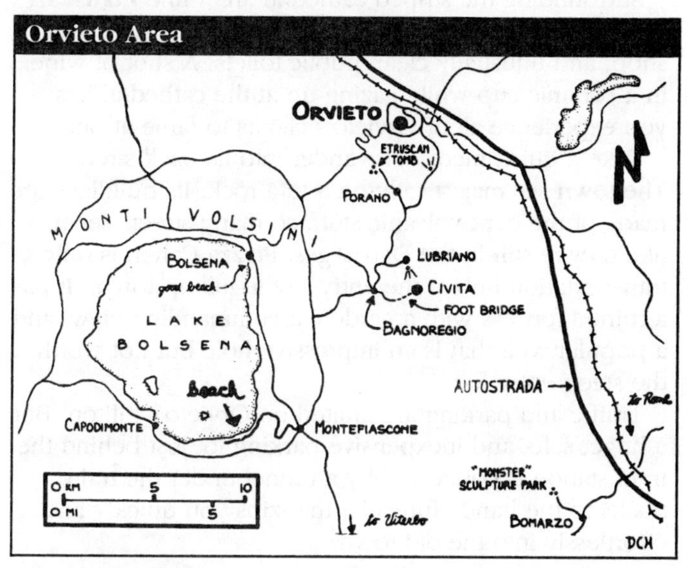

▲▲ Orvieto

Umbria's grand hill town is no secret but still worth a quick look. Just off the freeway, with three popular gimmicks (its ceramics, cathedral, and Classico wine), it's loaded with tourists by day—quiet by night.

From the train station (check your bag and your connection) ride the funicular (every 15 minutes, the L1300 ticket includes the connecting mini-bus transfer from the top, Piazza Cahen, to the cathedral square, Piazza Duomo, where you'll find the TI, and everything that matters). The Tourist Information (#24 Piazza Duomo, tel. 0763/41772, 10:00-14:00, 16:00-19:00, lunch starts at 13:00 on Saturday and at noon on Sunday) has a good free map.

The **Orvieto cathedral** has Italy's most striking facade. It's a fascinating mass of mosaics and sculpture that deserves some study. The rest of the church seems to be there only to keep it from falling down, but in a chapel next to the altar, you'll find some great Signorelli frescoes (7:00-13:00, 15:00 to 20:00, earlier in off-season).

Surrounding the striped cathedral are a fine **Etruscan museum** (9:00-13:30, 15:00-19:00, L3000), a great gelati shop, and unusually clean public toilets. A shot of wine in a ceramic cup while gazing up at the cathedral lets you experience all of Orvieto's claims to fame at once.

Take a quick medieval wander into its back streets. The town sits majestically on a tufa rock. Its buildings are made of the dark volcanic stuff, so many streets seem like they're still in the Dark Ages. Piazza Cahen is only a transportation hub at the entry to the hilltop town. It has a ruined fortress with a garden, a commanding view, and a popular well that is an impressive hole but not worth the steep entry fee.

Traffic and parking are limited on Orvieto's hilltop. But a huge, safe, and inexpensive parking lot just behind the train station is connected by a tunnel under the train tracks to the handy funicular that zips you quickly and effortlessly into the old town.

Sleeping in Orvieto

While you should do what you can to enjoy a true back-door experience sleeping in Bagnoregio, many will end up spending the night in Orvieto. While it's touristy, it's far more relaxed and affordable than Florence or Rome. Some even side-trip from Orvieto into Roma. Here are three places in the old town and one near the station.

Hotel Corso (L75,000, on the main street up from the funicular toward the Duomo at Via Cavour 343, tel. 0763/42020) is small, clean, friendly, with comfy modern rooms.

Hotel Duomo (L43,000-70,000, from the Duomo, turn left past the Gelati to Via di Maurizio 7, tel. 0763/41887) is a funky, brightly colored Old World place with simple, ugly rooms and a great location.

Albergo Posta (L50,000-70,000 doubles, Via Luca Signorelli 18, Orvieto, tel. 0763/41909) is in the center of the hill town, two minutes' walk from the cathedral. It's a big, old, formerly elegant, but well-cared-for-in-its-decline building with a breezy garden, a grand old lobby, and spacious, clean, plain rooms.

Albergo Picchio (L40,000-60,000 doubles, Via G. Salvatori 17, 05019 Orvieto Scalo, tel. 0763/90246) is a shiny, modern, concrete-and-marble place, more comfortable and family run but with less character. It's in the lower, ugly part of town, 300 yards from the train station.

▲▲▲ Civitá di Bagnoregio

Yellow signs direct you down the spine of long and skinny Bagnoregio to its older neighbor, Civitá (a pleasant 45-minute walk from Angelino's). You can drive through Bagnoregio and park at the base of the steep donkey path up to the traffic-free, 2,500-year-old, canyon-swamped pinnacle town of Civitá di Bagnoregio.

Civitá is terminally ill. Only 15 residents remain, as bit by bit it's being purchased by rich big-city Italians who will escape to their villas here.

Apart from its permanent (and aging) residents and those who have weekend villas here, there is a group of Americans, mostly Seattle-ites, introduced to the town through the small University of Washington architecture program, who have bought into the rare magic of Civitá. When it is in session, fifteen students live with residents and study Italian culture and architecture.

Al Forno (green door on main square, tel. 0761/793586, open daily), run by the Paolucci family, is the only res-

Civitá di Bagnoregio

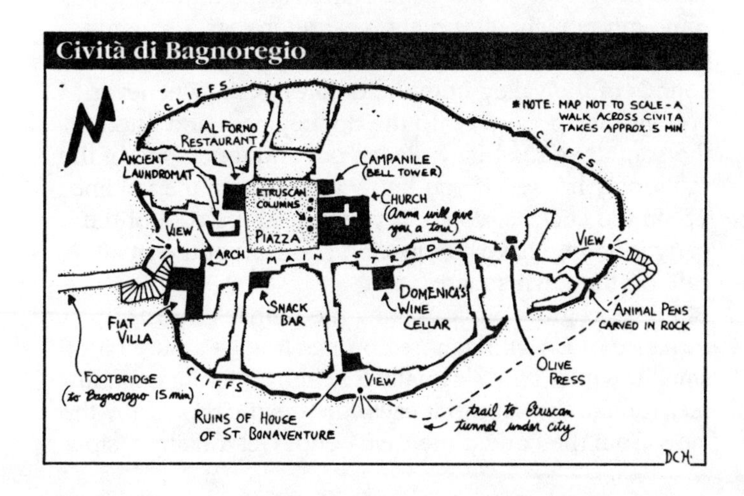

taurant in town and happy to serve just pasta and wine to budget travelers.

At the church on the main square, Anna will give you a tour (tip her and buy your postcards from her). Around the corner, on the main street, is a cool and friendly wine cellar with a dirt floor and stump chairs, where Domenica serves local wine—L1000 a glass and worth it only for the atmosphere. Step down into her cellar and note the traditional wine-making gear and the provisions for rolling huge kegs up the stairs. Tap the kegs in the cool bottom level to see which are full. Most village towns are connected to cellars like this which often go back to Etruscan times.

Down the street is Victoria's Antico Mulino (L1000), an atmospheric room of old olive presses. Just down the way, Maria will show you through her garden with a fine view (Maria's Giardino). Continuing through the town, the main drag peters out and a trail leads you down and around to the right to a tunnel that has cut through the hill under the town, also since Etruscan times. Slowly the town is being bought up by wealthy big city Italians. The "Marchesa," who married into the Fiat family, owns the house at the town gate—complete with Cività's only hot tub, for now.

Evenings on the town square are a bite of Italy. The same people sit on the same church steps under the same moon night after night, year after year. I love my cool late evenings in Cività. Listen to the midnight sounds of the valley from the donkey path. Whenever you visit, stop halfway up the donkey path and listen to the sounds of rural Italy. Reach out and touch one of the monopoly houses. If you know how to turn the volume up on the crickets, do so. If you visit in the cool of the early morning, have cappuccino and rolls at the small café on the town square.

▲ **Bagnoregio**—While lacking the pinnacle-town romance of Cività, Bagnoregio rings true as a pure bit of small-town Italy. It's actually a healthy, vibrant community (unlike the suburb it calls "the dead city"). Enjoy the view from the park at the Cività end. Get a haircut, sip a coffee on the square, walk down to the old laundry (ask, *Dovê la lavandaria vecchia?*).

Sleeping and Eating near Civitá (about L1300 = US$1)
When you leave the tourist crush, life as a traveler in Italy becomes easy and prices tumble. You should have no trouble finding rooms in small town Italy.

Just outside Bagnoregio, you'll find **Al Boschetto**. The Catarcia family speaks no English; they don't need to. Have an English-speaking Italian call for you from Venice or Florence (L70,000 doubles, Strada Monterado, Bagnoregio [Viterbo], Italy, tel. 0761/79 23 69). Most rooms have private showers (no curtains; slippery floors, be careful not to flood the place; sing in search of your shower's resonant frequency).

The Catarcia family (Angelino, his wife Perina, sons Gianfranco and Dominico, and their wives, Giuseppina and Rosella, and the grandchildren) is wonderful, and, if you so desire, the boys will take you down deep into the gooey, fragrant bowels of the cantina. Music and vino kill the language barrier in the wine cellar. Maybe Angelino or his sons will teach you their theme song, "Trinka, Trinka, Trinka." The lyrics are easy (see previous sentence). Warning: Angelino is Bacchus squared, and he's taught his boys well. Descend at your own risk. There are no rules unless the female participants set them. If you are lucky enough to eat dinner at Al Boschetto (L20,000, bunny is the house specialty), ask to try the *dolce* (sweet) dessert wine. Everything at Angelino's is deliciously homegrown—figs, fruit, wine, rabbit, pasta. This is traditional rural Italian cuisine at its best.

Hotel Fidanza (L75,000 doubles, Via Fidanza 25, Bagnoregio [Viterbo], tel. 0761/793444 or 793445) is new, comfortable, normal, and right in Bagnoregio town. Rooms 206 and 207 have views of Civitá.

Hostaria del Ponte (tel. 0761/793565, closed Monday) is a new fancy restaurant at the foot of the donkey path below Civitá. Note that there may be a mini-bus shuttle service connecting the donkey path to Civitá with Bagnoregio and Al Boschetto in 1993.

DAY 10

FREE DAY IN THE HILL TOWNS OR ASSISI

This is a day of slack, which is a good idea halfway through any itinerary. If you're on schedule and interested in savoring small-town Italy, it doesn't get any better than Bagnoregio, Cività, and Al Boschetto. Ideally, have an easy morning: hike up to Cività and maybe into the grand canyon that surrounds it. Get a haircut or do some laundry in Bagnoregio. And enjoy some more of the cooking that puts Al Boschetto on the map among locals as a great place for hearty traditional rural Italian cooking.

If you have a car, it's easy to go to Lake Bolzano for a swim, to Canale to tour the winery, to Purano to tour the Etruscan tomb.

If you figure you'll need more than three days in and around Rome, leave early and be set up in the Eternal City by 11:00.

If you'd like a different look at the hill towns of central Italy, cut east to see Assisi. The Bagnoregio-Assisi drive takes ninety minutes (follow signs for Todi, then Perugia). Train travelers often use the town of Chuisi as a home base. The region's trains (to Siena, Orvieto, Assisi) go through or change at this hub and there are several reasonable pensioni near the station.

Sightseeing Options around Orvieto and Bagnoregio

▲ **Etruscan Tomb**—Driving from Bagnoregio toward Orvieto, stop just past Purano to tour an Etruscan tomb. Follow the yellow road signs, reading Tomba Etrusca, to Giovanni's farm (a sight in itself). If the farmer is home (which is iffy), he'll take you out back and down into the lantern-lit, 2,500-year-old tomb discovered 100 years ago by his grandfather. His Italian explanation is fun. Tip him L5000. (He's normally there from 9:00 to 12:00 and 15:00 to 17:00, but the Orvieto TI can call to confirm this for you. Ask for Sr. Giovanni at Purano's Castello Robelli.)

How about a Swim?—For a fun and refreshing side trip, take a dip in Lake Bolsena, which is nestled within an extinct volcano, 30 minutes by car from Bagnoregio.

Ristorante Il Faro, directly below the town of Montefiascone, offers good meals on a leafy terrace overlooking the beach. Nearby in Bomarzo is the gimmicky monster park (Parco di Mostri), filled with stone giants and dragons. Built about two centuries ago, it proves that Italy has a long and distinguished tradition of tacky.

Tour a Winery?—Orvieto Classico wine is justly famous. For a homey peek into a local winery, visit Tanuta Le Velette where Julia Bottai and her English-speaking son, Corrado, welcome those who'd like a look at their winery and a taste of the final product (tel. 0763/29090 or 29144, daily 8:00-12:00 and 14:00-17:00, closed Sunday). You'll see their sign five minutes past Orvieto at the top of the switchbacks on the Bagnoregio road.

Hill Towns of Tuscany and Umbria—Whatever you do, rip yourself out of the Venice-Florence-Rome syndrome. There's so much more to Italy! Experience the slumber of Umbria, the texture of Tuscany, and the lazy towns of Lazio. Seek out and savor uncharted hill towns. For starters, the accompanying map lists a few of my favorites. Perugia is big and reeks with history. Cortona is

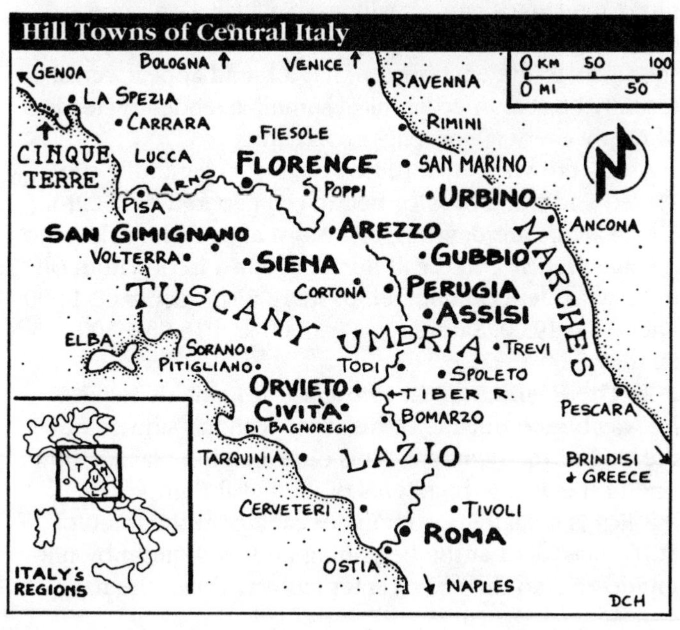

Hill Towns of Central Italy

smaller with a fine youth hostel (tel. 0575/601392). Todi is nearly untouristed. Pienza (Renaissance planned town) and Montepulciano (dramatic setting) are also worth the hill town lover's energy and time. Sorano and Pitigliano have almost no tourism.

Assisi

Around the year 1200, a simple monk from Assisi challenged the decadence of church government and society in general with a powerful message of nonmaterialism, simplicity, and a slow down and smell God's roses lifestyle. Like Jesus, Francis taught by example. A huge monastic order grew out of his teachings, which were gradually embraced (and some would say co-opted) by the church. Catholicism's purest example of Christ-like simplicity is now glorified in beautiful churches. In 1939, Italy made Francis its patron saint.

Any pilgrimage site will be commercialized and the legacy of St. Francis is Assisi's basic industry. In the summer, the town bursts with splash-in-the-pan Francis fans and Franciscan knickknacks. Those able to see past the tacky monk mementos can actually have a "travel on purpose" experience. Francis's message of love and simplicity and sensitivity to the environment has a broad appeal. Assisi recently hosted an ecumenical summit attended by leaders of nearly every major religion on earth.

Assisi, crowned by a ruined castle, is beautifully preserved and has a basilica nearly wallpapered by Giotto. Most visitors are day-trippers. Assisi after dark is closer to a place Francis could call home. (Tourist information on the Piazza del Comune, tel. 075/812 534, open 8:00-14:00 and 15:00-19:00, Saturday 9:00-13:00 and 16:00-19:00, Sunday 9:00-13:00.)

▲▲ The Basilica of St. Francis—At Francis's request, he was buried outside of his town with the sinners on the "hill of the damned." This once humble place is now one of the artistic highlights of medieval Europe. The basilica is actually two churches built over the tomb of St. Francis. Start at the beginning and the bottom by hiking down into the crypt (enter halfway down the nave of the lower church). The lower church is more appropriately Franciscan, subdued and Romanesque, offering a great look at Romanesque painting or fresco. Most important is the Cappella di San Martino (first chapel on the left as you enter the lower nave), which was designed and decorated completely by the Sienese master Simone Martini. Also important is the Madonna, Child, Angels, and St. Francis by Cimabue in the south transept.

The upper church, Gothic and therefore lighter, is designed to glorify the saint. It's basically a gallery of frescoes by Giotto showing 28 scenes from the life of St. Francis. Follow the great events of Francis's life starting at the altar and working around clockwise. The cycle culminates in the scene of St. Francis receiving the stigmata (the signs of the Crucifixion, awarded to only the most pious). Giotto was considered the first modern painter. Note the realism and depth he strives for as Italy is about to bring Europe out of the Dark Ages. In the north transept of the upper church is Cimabue's powerful Crucifixion. (The church is free, open 7:00-19:00, sometimes closed for lunch or mass, strictly enforced modest dress code, English tours daily except Sunday at 10:00 and 15:00, or tag quietly along with an English-speaking pilgrimage group, which will invariably have an English-speaking Franciscan explaining the basilica.)

Visit the bookshop in the courtyard. A short biography of St. Francis makes a walk through the back streets of Assisi, up to the ruined castle, or through the nearby countryside more of a walk with the saint.

From the basilica, Via San Francesco leads up to the town center, the Piazza della Comune, where you'll find a Roman forum, the temple of Minerva, a Romanesque tower, banks, the post office, the Pinacoteca (art gallery), and the tourist information office.

The Rocca Maggiore (big castle) offers a good look at a fourteenth-century fortification and a fine view of Assisi and the Tuscan countryside. For a picnic with the same birds and views that inspired St. Francis, leave all the tourists and hike to the smaller castle above St. Clare's church. The Church of St. Clare (Basilica de Santa Chiara) is interesting mostly for pilgrims.

Towering above the buildings below Assisi, near the train station, is a huge baroque church, Santa Maria degli Angeli (St. Mary of the Angels). It was built around the tiny chapel, Porziuncola. As you enter, notice the sketch on the door showing the original little chapel with the monk huts around it and Assisi before it had its huge basilica. Francis lived here after he founded the Franciscan Order in 1208. And this was where he consecrated St. Clare as the Bride of Christ. Clare, St. Francis's partner in poverty, founded the Order of the Poor Clares.

Buses connect Assisi's train station with the old town center (two per hour, 5 km). The town accommodates large numbers of pilgrims on religious holidays. Any other time, finding a room should be easy. The tourist office (Piazza del Comune 12, tel. 075/812534, open 8:00-14:00 and 15:00-19:00) can find you a room.

Sleeping in Assisi

Albergo Italia (L36,000, L48,000, and L60,000 doubles depending on the plumbing, just off the Piazza del Comune's fountain at Vicolo della Fortezza, tel. 075/812625) is clean and simple. Some of its 13 rooms overlook the town square.

Hotel Belvedere (two L50,000 doubles and plenty of L90,000 doubles with showers, two blocks from Piazza Santa Chiara and St. Clare's church at Via Borgo Aretino 13, tel. 075/812460) offers comfortable rooms, good views, and a friendly English-speaking management.

St. Anthony's Guest House (10 Via Galeazzo), run by Franciscan Sisters of the Atonement from New York, offers reasonable beds and a fine view.

Francis probably would have bedded down with the peasants in Assisi's new **Ostello della Pace** (L15,000 beds in 4- to 6-bed rooms, a 10-minute walk below town at San Pietro Campagna, tel. 075/816767).

DAYS 11, 12, and 13

ROME

Rome is magnificent. Your ears will ring, your nose will turn your hankie black, you'll be run down or pick-pocketed if you're careless enough, and you'll be frustrated by chaos that only an Italian can understand. But Rome is required. If your hotel provides a comfortable refuge; if you pace yourself, accept, and even partake in, the siesta plan; if you're well organized for sightseeing; and if you protect yourself and your valuables with extra caution and discretion, you'll do fine. You'll see the

Suggested Schedule

Day 11

8:00	Leave Cività (or Assisi) for Rome.
11:00	Get hotel, lunch, siesta.
15:00	Walk through ancient Rome: Colosseum, Forum, Capitoline Hill.
20:00	Dinner in Campo dei Fiori.

Day 12

9:00	Pantheon.
10:00	Curious sights near Pantheon.
12:00	Self-service or picnic lunch, siesta.
15:00	Afternoon options: Ostia, E.U.R., Villa Borghese, shopping.
18:00	Take the "Floodlit Rome Hike": Campo dei Fiori, Piazza Navona, Trevi Fountain, Spanish Steps, subway home (last ride, 23:30).

Day 13

9:00	Vatican Museum, Sistine Chapel, postal chores.
12:00	Picnic in Via Andrea Doria Market. Catch Vatican bus to St. Peter's.
14:00	St. Peter's Basilica, crypt.
16:00	Climb the dome for a fine panoroma.
18:00	The "Dolce Vita stroll" down the Via del Corso. Nocturnal museums on Capitoline hill?

sights and leave satisfied. You may even fall in love with the Eternal City.

Transportation: Bagnoregio–Orvieto–Rome (90 miles)

Buses leave Bagnoregio for Orvieto at 6:55, 10:00, 13:00, 14:20, and 17:20 (confirm these times with the schedule posted in the Bagnoregio bus shelter, when you arrive). Trains make the 90-minute Orvieto–Rome trip nearly hourly.

Drivers will wind for 30 minutes back to Orvieto where the autostrada zips you to the edge of Rome in an hour. That's where things get tricky.

Greater Rome is circled by the Grande Raccordo Anulare. This ring road has spokes that lead you into the center. Entering from the north, take the Via Salaria and work your way doggedly into the Roman thick-of-things. (You may want to follow a taxi to your hotel.) Avoid driving in Rome during rush hour. Drive defensively: Roman cars stay in their lanes like rocks in an avalanche.

Parking in Rome is dangerous: choose a well-lighted busy street or a safe neighborhood. Get advice at your hotel. My favorite hotel is next to the Italian "Pentagon," guarded by machine gunners. You'll pay about L25,000 a day in a garage. In many cases, it's well worth it. Consider this. Your car is a worthless headache in Rome. Avoid a pile of stress and save money by parking it at the huge, new, easy, and relatively safe lot behind the Orvieto station (drive around about a half mile south), and catch the train to Rome (10-hour-long, L11,000 rides a day). The town of Orte, closer to Rome, has easy parking and more frequent trains into Rome (hourly 40-minute, L6000 rides). Note: If you plan to leave Al Boschetto early, get them to leave the *chiave* (kee-ah-vee) in the door or you're locked in.

Orientation—Rome

Rome at its peak meant civilization itself. Everything was either civilized (part of the Roman Empire, Latin- or Greek-speaking) or barbarian. Today, Rome is Italy's

leading city, the capital of Catholicism, and a splendid . . . "junkpile" is not quite the right word . . . of Western Civilization. As you wander, you'll find its buildings, people, cats, laundry, and traffic endlessly entertaining. And then, of course, there are its magnificent sights.

The ancient city had a million people. Tear it down to size by tackling just the core. It's easy, though hot, on foot. The best of the classical sights stand in a line from the Colosseum to the Pantheon.

In medieval times, the population dipped as low as 50,000, and many of those were thieves. The medieval city lies between the Pantheon and the river. The nightlife and ritzy shopping twinkle near here, on or near the Via del Corso, Rome's main drag. The Vatican City is a compact world of its own, as is the seedy/colorful wrong-side-of-the-river Trastevere neighborhood—village Rome at its best. Baroque Rome is an overleaf that embellishes many great squares throughout the town with fountains and church facades. The modern sprawl of Rome is of no interest to us. Our Rome is the old

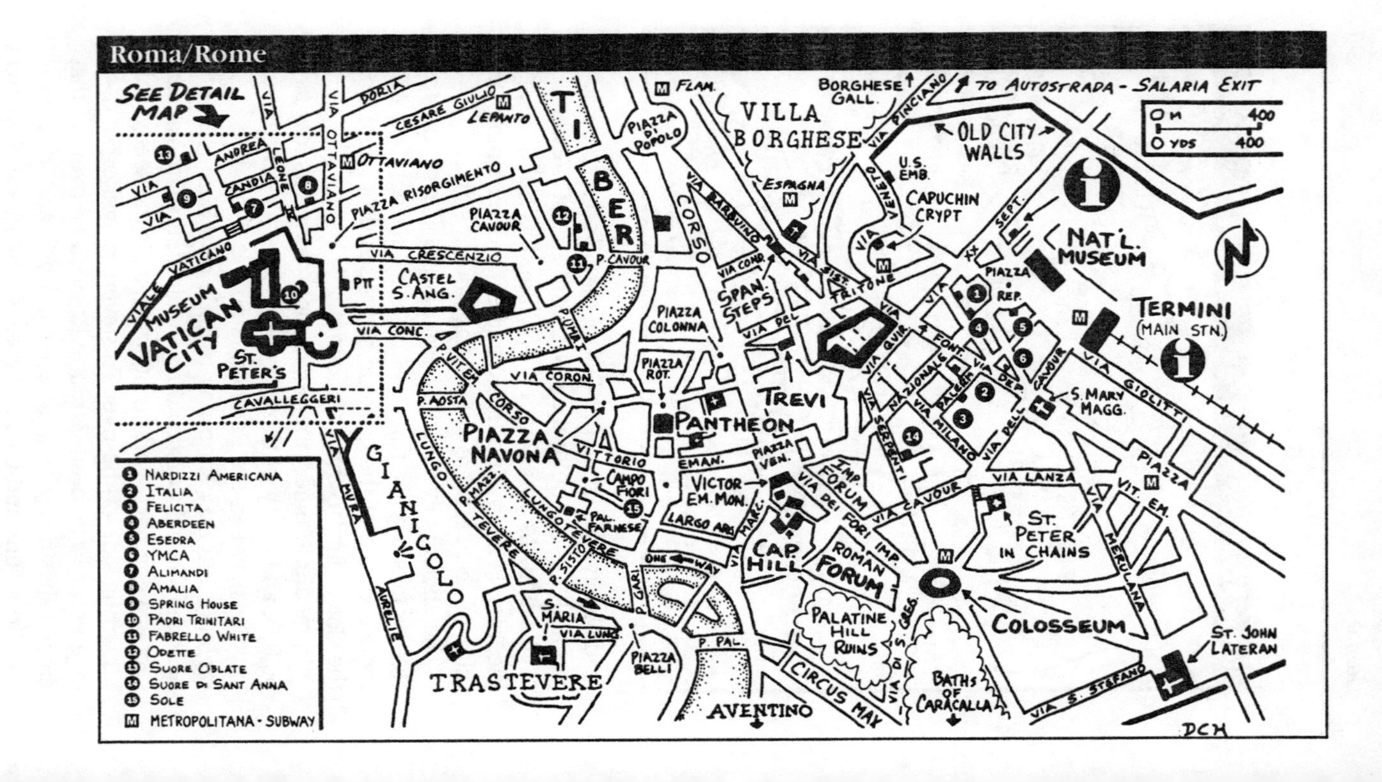
SEE DETAIL MAP
VILLA BORGHESE
BORGHESE GALL.
TO AUTOSTRADA - SALARIA EXIT
0 M 400
0 YDS 400
OLD CITY WALLS
U.S. EMB.
CAPUCHIN CRYPT
NAT'L. MUSEUM
TERMINI (MAIN STN.)
VATICAN CITY
MUSEUM
ST. PETER'S
CASTEL S. ANG.
TIBER
PIAZZA DI POPOLO
PIAZZA RISORGIMENTO
PIAZZA CAVOUR
PIAZZA COLONNA
SPAN. STEPS
TREVI
PANTHEON
PIAZZA NAVONA
CAMPO FIORI
PAL. FARNESE
VICTOR EM. MON.
CAP. HILL
IMP. FORUM
ROMAN FORUM
PALATINE HILL RUINS
COLOSSEUM
ST. PETER IN CHAINS
S. MARY MAGG.
ST. JOHN LATERAN
BATHS OF CARACALLA
CIRCUS MAX
AVENTINO
TRASTEVERE
GIANICOLO
S. MARIA
PIAZZA BELLI
CORSO
VIA CONC.
VIA CRESCENZIO
CAVALLEGGERI
VIALE VATICANO
VIA OTTAVIANO
VIA NAZIONALE
VIA CAVOUR
VIA LANZA
VIA MERULANA
VIA GIOLITTI
VIA DEI FORI IMP.
LUNGOTEVERE
ONE WAY
1 NARDIZZI AMERICANA
2 ITALIA
3 FELICITA
4 ABERDEEN
5 ESEDRA
6 YMCA
7 ALIMANDI
8 AMALIA
9 SPRING HOUSE
10 PADRI TRINITARI
11 FABRELLO WHITE
12 ODETTE
13 SUORE OBLATE
14 SUORE DI SANT ANNA
15 SOLE
M METROPOLITANA - SUBWAY
DCH

core—basically within the triangle formed by the train station, Colosseum, and Vatican.

Tourist Information: The Ente Provinciale Per il Turismo (EPT) has three offices (open 8:15-19:15, except Sunday): at the airport, in the train station (very crowded, only one open Sunday, tel. 06/487 1270), and the central office (5 Via Parigi, a 5-minute walk out the front of the station, near Piazza della Republica's huge fountain, less crowded and more helpful, air-conditioned, with comfortable sofas and a desk to plan on, tel. 06/488 3748 or 488 1851). Get the free EPT city map with bus lines and the monthly *Carnet di Roma* periodical guide. (My recommended hotels, Nardizzi and Alimandi, have promised to carry the EPT map, which for many travelers is the only reason to hassle with the TI.)

Rome's attractions have a mysterious system of rotating opening hours: some stay open longer than listed, others invent new earlier closing times. Confirming sightseeing plans each morning with a quick telephone call asking, "Are you open today?" (Aperto oggi?) or "What time do you close?" (A che ora chiuso?) can save major frustrations. I have included telephone numbers for this purpose.

The Termini station has many tourist services: a late-hours bank, a day hotel, luggage lockers, a bright, cheery self-service restaurant (La Piazza), the bus station, 24-hour thievery, and a subway stop. Handy multilingual charts make locations very clear. Telephone code: 06.

Transportation in Rome

Even if you're crazy enough to drive into Rome, sightsee on foot or by city bus. This plan groups most of your sightseeing into neighborhoods, so you'll be on foot a lot. Still, use public transportation whenever you can. It's logical, inexpensive, and part of your Roman experience.

Bus routes are charted on the EPT map and are clearly listed at the stops. Bus 64 is particularly useful, connecting the station, Victor Emmanuel monument (near the Forum), and the Vatican. Ride it for a city overview and to watch pickpockets in action. Buy tickets at *tabac* shops or at major bus stops but not on board (L800,

Rome's Termini Station

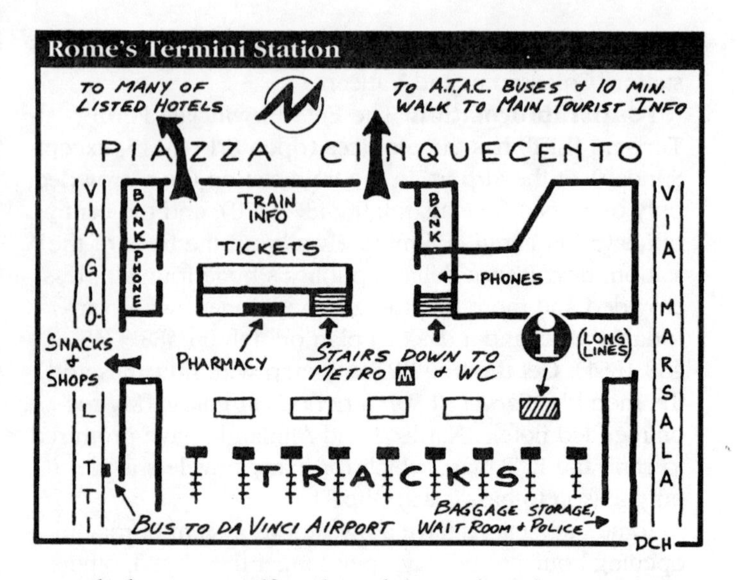

punch them yourself on board, buy a bunch so you can hop a bus without searching for an open tobacco shop or riding without a ticket—relatively safe but still stressful). Inspectors fine even innocent-looking tourists L50,000 if found on a bus without a ticket. If you do hop a bus without a ticket, most locals who use tickets rather than a monthly pass can sell you one from their wallet bundle. There are cheap all-day bus/metro passes (L2800 from regular ticket vendors). Learn which buses serve your neighborhood. Buses, especially the touristic #64, and the subway are havens for thieves and pickpockets. Assume any commotion is a thief-created distraction. Watch your pack and wear no wallet.

The Roman subway system (Metropolitana) has two simple, clean, cheap, and fast lines. While much of Rome is not served by its skimpy subway, these stops may be helpful to you: Termini (central train station, tourist office, National Museum), Barberini (Hotel Nardizzi, Capuchin Crypt, Trevi Fountain, Italy Italy cafeteria), Spagna (Spanish Steps, Villa Borghese, classiest shopping area), Flamino (Piazza del Popolo, start of the Via del Corso Dolce Vita stroll), Ottaviano (the Vatican, several recommended hotels), Colosseo (the Colosseum, Roman

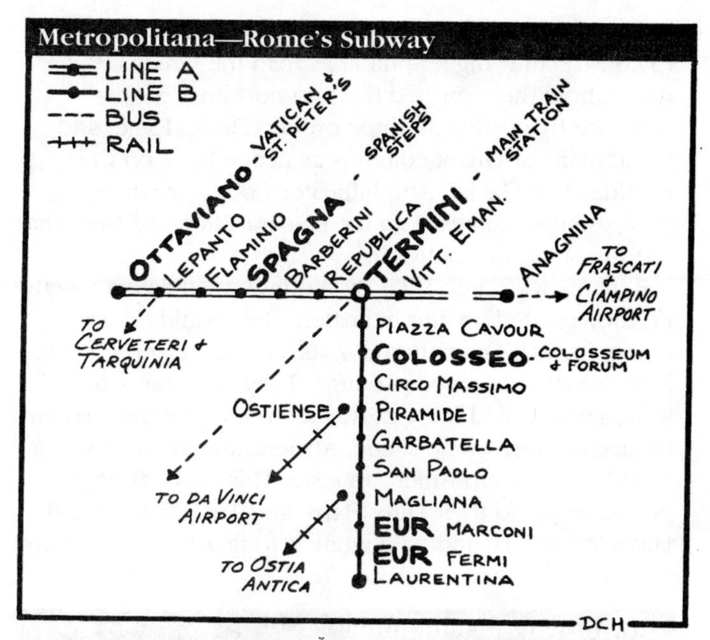

Forum, several recommended hotels), and E.U.R. (Mussolini's futuristic suburb). Buy your L800 subway tickets at tabacs, subway ticket counters, or from machines in some stations (if not Fuori Servizio—out of service—they take coins while neighboring machines change L1000 bills).

Metered taxis have a big drop charge (L6500), but it covers you for 3 kilometers. From the station to the Vatican costs about L12,000. Three or four traveling together with more money than time should taxi almost everywhere. Rather than wave and wave, ask in local shops for the nearest taxi stand ("Dové una fermata dei tassi?"). As long as they use the meter, they're fair.

Save time and legwork whenever possible by telephoning. When the feet are about to give out, sing determinedly, "Roman, Roman, Roman, keep those doggies movin' . . ."

Sightseeing Highlights—Rome

▲▲▲ **Colosseum**—This is the great example of Roman engineering 2,000 years ago. The Romans, using concrete, brick, and their trademark round arches, were able to construct far bigger buildings than the Greeks. But notice how they finished their no-nonsense mega-structure by pasting all three orders (Doric, Ionic, and Corinthian) of Greek columns as decorations on the outside. The Flavian Amphitheater's popular name, "Colosseum," comes from the colossal statue of Nero that used to stand in front of it.

Romans were into BIG. By putting two theaters together, they created an amphitheater. They could fill and empty its 50,000 numbered seats as quickly and efficiently as we do our super stadiums. They had teams of sailors who could hoist canvas awnings over the stadium to give the fans some shade. Ancient Roman taste was as bloody as modern American taste. This was where the people enjoyed their Dirty Harry and Terminator. Gladiators, criminals, and wild animals fought to the death in

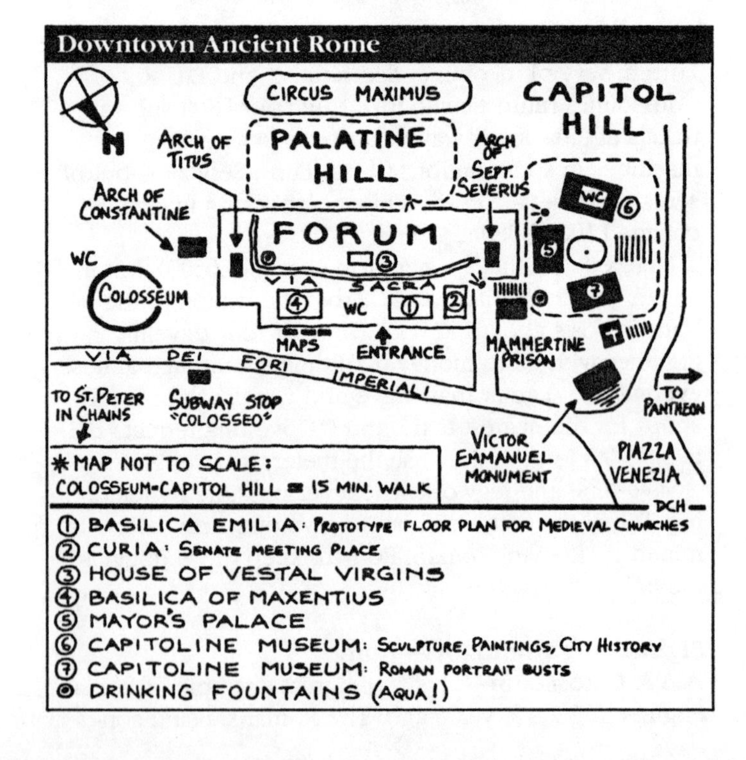

every conceivable scenario. They could even flood the place to wage mock naval battles.

After Rome fell, the Colosseum was cannibalized by centuries of medieval Romans who appreciated the place only as a quarry filled with precut stones. (Open daily 9:00 to 19:00 or an hour before sunset, Sunday and Wednesday 9:00-13:00, off-season 9:00-15:00, free, L6000 to go upstairs. tel. 7004261.)

▲▲▲ Roman Forum (Foro Romano)—Ancient Rome's birthplace and civic center, the Forum was the common ground between Rome's famous seven hills. To help resurrect this confusing pile of rubble, study the before-and-after pictures in the cheap city guidebooks sold on the streets. (Check out the small red *Rome, Past and Present* books with plastic overleafs, to un-ruin the ruins. They're priced at L25,000—pay no more than L10,000.)

Start at the Basilica Aemilia, on your right as you walk down the entry ramp. The floor plan of this ancient palace shows how medieval churches adopted this basilica design. Then walk the Via Sacra, the main street of ancient Rome running from the Arch of Septimus Severus on the right, past Basilica Aemilia, up to the Arch of Titus and the Colosseum on the left. The plain intact brick building near the Arch of Septimus Severus was the Curia where the Roman senate sat. Only the giant barrel vault remains of the huge Basilica Maxentius looming crumbly and weed-eaten to the left of Via Sacra as you walk to the Arch of Titus. As you stand in the shadow of the Bas Max try to reconstruct the place in your mind. The huge barrel vaults were just side niches. Extend the broken nub of an arch out over the vacant lot and finish your imaginary Roman basilica with rich marble and fountains. People it with toga-clad Romans. It must have been a sight.

At the Arch of Titus (carved with propaganda celebrating the defeat of the Jews, which began the Diaspora, which only ended with the creation of Israel in 1947), walk to the right up the Palatine Hill to the remains of the Imperial palaces. We get our word "palace" from this hill where the emperors chose to live. The pleasant garden overlooks the Forum; on the far side, look down on the dusty old Circus Maximus. (Open 9:00-18:00 or an hour before sunset, Sunday and Tuesday 9:00-13:00, off-season 9:00-15:00, L10,000, tel. 6990110.) Just past the entry there's a W.C. and a handy headless statue for you to pose behind.

▲ **Gypsy Thief Gangs**—If you know what to look out for, the omnipresent groups of children picking the pockets and handbags of naive tourists are no threat but an interesting, albeit sad, spectacle. Gangs of city-stained children, too young to really prosecute but old enough to be very effective at ripping you off, troll through the tourist crowds around the Forum and Colosseum. Watch them target tourists distracted with their video camera or overloaded with bags. They look like beggars and hold newspapers or cardboard signs to distract their victims. Every year they get bolder, but they'll still scram like stray cats if you're on to them. A fast-fingered mother with a baby is often nearby. With every visit to Rome, I meet tourists who've been ripped off. Be on guard.

▲ **St. Peter-in-Chains Church (San Pietro in Vincoli)**—On exhibit are the original chains and Michelangelo's *Moses* in an otherwise unexceptional church. Just a short walk from the Colosseum. (Open 6:30-12:30, 15:00-19:00, modest dress required.)

▲ **Mammertine Prison**—The 2,500-year-old converted cistern that once imprisoned Saints Peter and Paul is worth a look. On the walls are lists of prisoners (Christian and non-Christian) and how they were executed (Strangolati, Decapitato, Morto di Fame). At the top of the stairs leading to the Campidoglio, you'll find a refreshing water fountain. Block the spout with your fingers; it spurts up for drinking. The prison (donation requested) is open 9:00-12:30 and 14:30-18:00.

▲ **Capitoline Hill (Campidoglio)**—This hill was the religious and political center of ancient Rome. It's still the home of the city's government. Michelangelo's lovely Renaissance square is bounded by two fine museums and the mayoral palace.

The Capitoline Museum (Musei Capitolini) in the Palazzo Nuovo (the building closest to the river) is the world's oldest museum (500 years old) and more important than its sister (opposite). Outside the entrance, notice the marriage announcements. You may see a few blissfully attired newlyweds as well. Inside the courtyard have some photo fun with chunks of a giant statue of Emperor Constantine. (A rare public toilet hides near the museum ticket taker.) The museum is worthwhile, with lavish rooms housing several great statues including the original (500 B.C.) Etruscan Capitoline wolf and the enchanting Commodus as Hercules. Across the square is a museum full of ancient statues—great if you like portrait busts of forgotten emperors or want to see the newly restored equestrian statue of Marcus Aurelius that used to sit on the pedestal in the square. (Both open Tuesday to Saturday 9:00-13:30, Tuesday 17:00-20:00, Saturday 20:00-23:00, Sunday 9:00-13:00, closed Monday, L10,000, tel. 6782862.)

Don't miss the great view of the Forum from the terrace just past the mayor's palace on the right. To approach the square the way Michelangelo wanted you to, walk halfway down the grand stairway toward Piazza Venezia and walk back up from there. At the bottom of the stairs, look up the long stairway to your right for a good example of the earliest style of Christian church.

Way down the street on your left, you'll see a modern building actually built around surviving ancient pillars and arches. Farther ahead (toward Piazza Venezia), look into the ditch (on the right) and see how everywhere modern Rome is built on the countless bricks and forgotten mosaics of ancient Rome.

Piazza Venezia—This square is the focal point of modern Rome. The Via del Corso, starting here, is the city's axis, surrounded by the classiest shopping district. From the Palazzo di Venezia's balcony above the square (to your left with your back to Victor Emmanuel Monument), Mussolini whipped up the nationalistic fervor of Italy. Fascist masses filled the square screaming, "Four more years!" or something like that. (Fifteen years later, they hung him from a meat hook in Milan.)

Victor Emmanuel Monument—Most Romans call this oversized memorial to Victor Emmanuel "the wedding cake," "the typewriter," or "the dentures." It wouldn't be so bad if it weren't sitting on a priceless acre of ancient Rome. The soldiers there guard Italy's Tomb of the Unknown Soldier.

▲▲▲ **Pantheon**—For the greatest look at the splendor of Rome, this best-preserved interior of antiquity is a must (open 9:00-16:30 but often until only 14:00, Sunday 9:00-13:00, tel. 369831, free). Walk past its one-piece granite columns and through the original bronze door. Sit inside under the glorious skylight and study it. The dome, 140 feet high and wide, was Europe's biggest until Brunelleschi's dome was built in Florence 1,200 years later. You'll understand why this wonderfully harmonious architecture was so inspirational to the artists of the Renaissance, particularly Raphael who, along with Italy's first two kings, chose to be buried here. The Pantheon was a convenient place to contain (or hold hostage) the various gods of the people Rome conquered. The Pantheon went immediately from being a temple to all these gods to a church for the one Christian God. Since it has been continuously used since Roman times, it was never cannibalized. Stand in the center (notice the ancient rain drain) and look at the clouds rolling past the skylight. As you walk around the outside of the Pantheon, notice the "rise of Rome"—about 15 feet since it was built.

▲ **Curiosities near the Pantheon**—Santa Maria sopra Minerva is the only Gothic church you'll see in Rome. On a little square to the left behind the Pantheon, past the Bernini elephant and the Egyptian obelisk statue, it was built *sopra*, or over, a pre-Christian Temple of Minerva. Rome was at its low ebb, almost a ghost town through much of the Gothic period, and the little building done at that time was redone baroque later. This church is a refreshing exception. St. Catherine's body lies under the altar (her head is in Siena) and a little-known Michelangelo statue, *Christ Bearing the Cross*, stands to the left. Fra Angelico's tomb is in the left or north transept. Nearby (head out the church's rear door behind the Michelangelo statue and turn left) you'll find a church, **Chiesa di St. Ignazio**, a riot of baroque illusions. Study the ceiling in the back of the nave. Then stand on the yellow disk on the floor between the two stars. Look up at the central (black) dome. Keeping your eyes on the dome, walk under and past it. Church building project runs out of money? Hire a painter to paint a fake (and flat) dome. Turn around and look at the fresco over the entry. Walk left, then right . . . then look at the altar. What would you say if I told you it was a flat painting? (Both of these churches are open until 19:00, with a 12:00-16:00 siesta, are free and welcome modestly dressed visitors.)

A few blocks away, back across Corso Victor Emmanuel, is the very rich and baroque **Gesu church**, headquarters of the Jesuits in Rome. The Jesuits powered the church's Counter-Reformation. With Protestants teaching that all roads to heaven didn't pass through Rome, the baroque churches of the late 1500s were filled with propaganda church art. Check out the ceiling. The clouds are actually inside the building, casting shadows and interrupting the gilded ribs. Stop by the St. Ignatius Loyola Chapel in the left (or north) transept. Below a richly jeweled statue of the founder of the Jesuits, rests his body. Notice the marble statues on either side illustrating the valiant and apparently successful battle of the Roman church against its enemies. See on the left, the triumphant angel with the Roman Catholic eucharist and on the right, the wicked-looking Protestant heretics being thrown out and the really angry baby angel ripping out the "false teachings" of a Martin Luther book. Outside, on the square to the left, is the headquarters of the Christian Democrat party. The assassinated body of Italian prime minister Aldo Moro was found down the street behind this building (1978).

There are also three dramatic Caravaggio paintings (each showing a scene from the life of St. Matthew, in the fifth chapel on the left) in the nearby church of **San Luigi dei Francesi** (with your back to the Pantheon, take the first left, 7:30-12:30 and 15:30-19:00, closed Thursday afternoon).

▲ **Capuchin Crypt**—If you want bones, this is it: below Santa Maria della Concezione on Via Veneto, just off Piazza Barberini, are thousands of skeletons, all artistically arranged for the delight—or disgust—of the always wide-eyed visitor. Read the monastic message on the wall near the entry so you'll understand this as more than just a macabre exercise. Pick up a few of Rome's most interesting postcards. (Open 9:00-12:00, 15:00-18:30.) A bank with long hours and good exchange rates is next door, and the American Embassy is just up the street.

▲▲ **The Dolce Vita Stroll down Via del Corso**—The city's chic and hip cruise from the Piazza del Popolo down a wonderfully traffic-free section of the Via del Corso and up Via Condotti to the Spanish Steps each evening around 18:00. Shoppers, take a left on Via Condotti for the Spanish Steps and Gucci (shops open after siesta from 16:30 to 19:30). Historians, continue down the Via del Corso to the Victor Emmanuel Monument, climb Michelangelo's stairway to his glorious Campidoglio Square, and visit Rome's Capitoline Museum, open Tuesday and Saturday evenings. Catch the lovely view of the Forum (from past the mayor's palace on the right) as the horizon reddens and cats prowl the unclaimed rubble of ancient Rome.

▲ **Villa Borghese**—Rome's unkempt "Central Park" is great for people watching (plenty of modern-day Romeos and Juliets). Take a row on the lake, or visit its fine museums. The Borghese Gallery has some world-class baroque art, including the exciting Bernini statue of Apollo chasing Daphne and paintings by Caravaggio and Rubens (free, 9:00-19:00, Sunday 9:00-13:00, closed Monday, often open but with its best art "closed for restoration," call 854 8577 before going out). The nearby Museo di Villa Giulia is a fine Etruscan museum (same hours, also often closed, L8000, call 06/320 1951).

▲ **National Museum of Rome (Museo Nazionale Romano delle Terme)**—Directly in front of the station, it houses much of the greatest ancient Roman sculpture. (Open 9:00-14:00, Sunday until 13:00, closed Monday, L3000, tel. 488 0530.)

▲▲ **The Vatican City**—This tiny independent country of just over 100 acres is contained entirely within Rome. Politically powerful, the Vatican is the religious capital of 800 million Roman Catholics. If you're not Catholic, becoming one for your visit makes it a much better experience. Start your visit by dropping by the helpful tourist office just to the left of St. Peter's Basilica. (Open Monday-Saturday, 8:30-19:00, tel. 06/698 4466; L2000 map of the country and church.) Telephone them if you're interested in the pope's schedule (Sunday at noon for a quick blessing of the crowds in Piazza San Pietro from the window of his study above the square or Wednesday mornings when a reservation is necessary), their sporadic but very good tours of the Vatican grounds, or tours of the church interior. Very handy buses shuttle visitors between the church and the muse-

Vatican City and St. Peter's

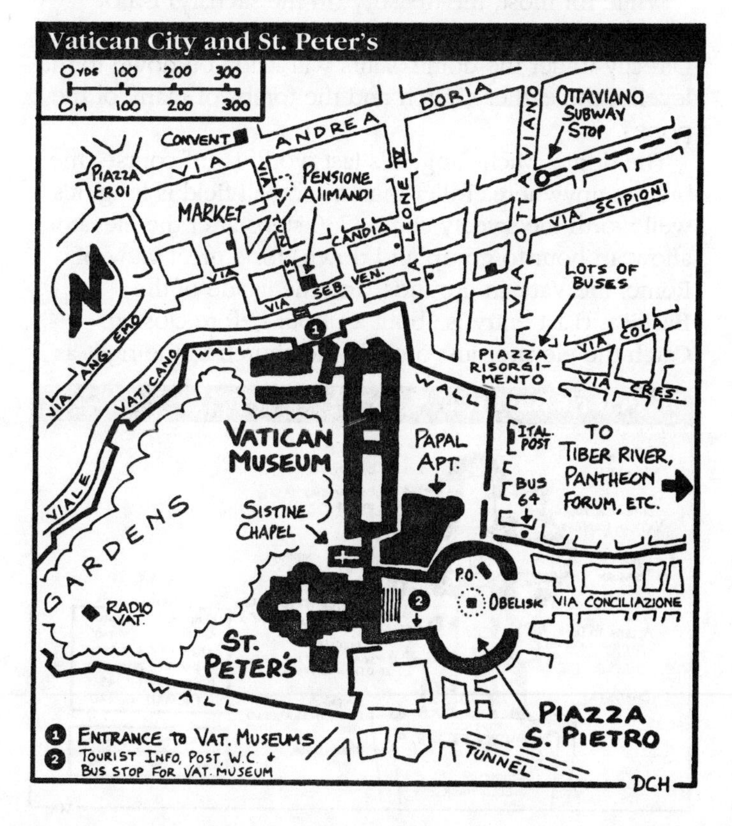

um twice an hour (8:45-13:45, L2000). This is far better than the exhaust-filled walk around the Vatican wall, and it gives you a pleasant peek at the garden-filled Vatican grounds.

▲▲▲ St. Peter's Basilica—There is no doubt: this is the richest and most impressive church on earth. To call it vast is like calling God smart. Marks on the floor show where the next largest churches would fit if they were put inside; the ornamental cherubs would dwarf a large man. Birds roost inside, and thousands of people wander about, heads craned heavenward, hardly noticing each other. Don't miss Michelangelo's Pietà (behind bullet-proof glass) to the right of the entrance. Bernini's altar work and huge bronze canopy (the *baldacchino*) are brilliant.

While for most, the treasury (in the sacristy) is not worth the admission, the crypt is free and worth a look. Directly under the dome, stairs will lead you down to the level of the earlier church and the tombs of many of the popes.

The dome, Michelangelo's last work, is (of course) the biggest anywhere. Taller than a football field is long, it's well worth the sweaty climb (330 steps after the elevator, allow an hour to go up and down) for a great view of Rome, the Vatican grounds, and the inside of the Basilica. (Last entry is about an hour before closing. Catch the elevator just outside the church to the right as

St. Peter's Basilica

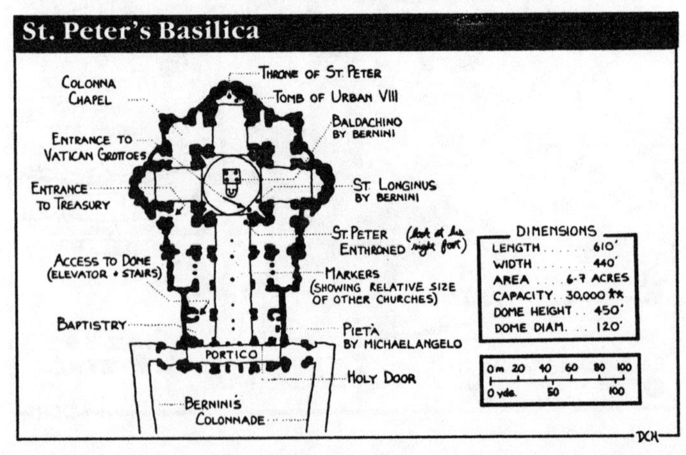

you face it. W.C. on the rooftop.) The church strictly enforces its dress code. Dress modestly—a dress or long pants, shoulders covered. St. Peter's is open daily from 7:00 to 19:00; crypt, treasury, and dome close an hour early. All are welcome to join in the mass (daily at 17:00). The church is particularly moving at 7:00 while tourism is still sleeping. Volunteers who want you to understand and appreciate St. Peter's give free 90-minute "Pilgrim Service" tours in English most days at 10:15 and 15:00. Check at the desk just after the dress code check as you're entering, for today's schedule. Seeing the Pietà is neat, understanding it is divine.

▲▲▲ The Vatican Museum—Too often, the immense Vatican Museum is treated as a cruel obstacle course, with four miles of displays separating the tourist from the Sistine Chapel. Even without the Sistine, this is one of Europe's top three or four houses of art. It can be exhausting, so plan your visit carefully, focusing on a few themes, and allow three hours. The museum uses a nearly-impossible-not-to-follow one-way system.

Required minimum stops, in this order: Etruscan Gallery (impressive for 500 B.C. and well explained in English), Egyptian mummies and statues; *Apollo Belvedere* and *Laocoön* in the Octagonal Courtyard and the *Belvedere Torso* (all three showing the classical mastery of the body and very influential to Renaissance artists); past the rooms of animals, the giant porphyry hot tub, between the porphyry sarcophagi of Constantine's mother and daughter, then down the hall of broken penises and past the tapestries and corridor of maps to huge rooms plastered with church propaganda (Constantine's divine vision and his victory at Milvian Bridge which led him to become Christian, the 19th-century Vatican declaration of the immaculate conception of the Virgin Mary), past a small chapel frescoed by Fra Angelico and into the Raphael rooms.

The masterpiece here is the School of Athens—which is remarkable for its blatant pre-Christian classical orientation—wallpapering the apartments of Pope Julius II. Raphael honors the great pre-Christian thinkers, Aristotle,

Plato, and company, who are portrayed as the leading artists of Raphael's day: Leonardo with the white beard in the center as Plato, Michelangelo brooding in the foreground, supposedly added late after Raphael snuck a peek at the Sistine Chapel and decided that his arch-competitor was so good he had to put their personal differences aside and include him in this tribute to the artists of his generation. Today's St. Peter's was under construction as Raphael was working. In this fresco he gives us a look at the unfinished new church.

Next (unless you detour through the modern Catholic art) is the newly restored Sistine Chapel. Michelangelo's pictorial culmination of the Renaissance shows the story of creation with a powerful God weaving in and out of each scene through that busy week. The centerpiece, God giving Adam the spark of life, shows the self-confidence of High Renaissance society as man is an impressive character from day one. The ceiling is newly restored and looking as bright and colorful as the day it was finished (experts think). The huge painting behind the altar is the *Last Judgment,* also by Michelangelo but from an entirely different age. This was years later when the church was split and embroiled in the Reformation wars and even the Catholic army of Spain had recently sacked Rome and the Vatican. Notice the vindictive Christ coming down with his angry fist raised on that day of reckoning. Some are going to heaven, some are going to hell, and some dangle literally by a rosary from the grip of eternal damnation. Michelangelo himself is in a kind of salvation limbo as St. Bartolomeo holds his flayed skin (showing the features of Michelangelo) and looks up at Jesus as if to ask, "Which way does this guy go?"

Now the museum is basically done. Occasionally, a door is open in the rear of the Sistine allowing visitors to pop out back on St. Peter's Square, but normally it's an eight-minute slalom through the tourists back to the entry/exit. Back near the entrance you'll find two more important galleries, the Pinacoteca painting collection with Raphael's *Transfiguration* and Caravaggio's

Deposition and the Christian art of ancient Rome, before exiting via the souvenir shop.

The museum clearly marks out four color-coded visits of different lengths. Rentable headphones (L6000) give a recorded tour of the Raphael rooms and Michelangelo's Sistine masterpiece. (Easter, July, August, September hours: 8:45-16:30, Saturday 8:45-14:00, closed Sunday, except last Sunday of month when museum is free; off-season 8:45-13:45. Last entry an hour before closing. Many minor rooms close from 13:45 to 14:45 or from 13:30 on. The Sistine Chapel is closed 30 minutes before the rest of the museum. L10,000.)

The museum's excellent book and card shop offers a priceless (L9000) black-and-white photo book of the Pietà—great for gifts. The Vatican post has an office in the museum and one on the Piazza San Pietro (comfortable writing rooms, open Monday-Friday 8:30-19:00, Saturday 8:30-18:00). The Vatican post is the most reliable mail service in Italy, and the stamps are a collectible bonus (Vatican stamps are good throughout Rome, Italian stamps are not good at the Vatican), but its bank has sinful rates.

▲ **E.U.R.**—Mussolini's planned suburb of the future (60 years ago) is a ten-minute subway ride from the Colosseum to Magliana. From the subway stop, walk through the park up to the Palace of the Civilization of Labor (Pal. d. Civilta d. Concordia), the essence of Fascist architecture with its giant, no-questions-asked, patriotic statues and its this-is-the-truth simplicity. (You heard it here: when similar art decorates your favorite mall, it's too late.) On the far side is its Museum of the Civilization of Rome (Piazza G. Agnelli, metro: EUR Magliana or Fermi, 9:00-13:30, Tuesday and Thursday 15:00-18:00, closed Monday, L5000, tel. 592 6041), including a large-scale model of ancient Rome.

▲▲ **Ostia Antica**—Rome's ancient seaport (80,000 people in the time of Christ, later a ghost town, now excavated) is the next best thing to Pompeii and, I think, Italy's most underrated sight. Start at the 2,000-year-old theater, buy a map, and explore the town, finishing with its fine little museum. Get there by taking the subway's B Line to the Magliana stop and catching the Lido train to Ostia Antica (twice an hour). Walk over the overpass, go straight to the end of that road, and follow the signs to Ostia Antica. (Open daily except Monday from 9:00 to one hour before sunset. The entry fee includes the museum, which closes at 14:00.) Just beyond is the filthy beach (Lido), an interesting anthill of Roman sun worshipers.

Overrated Sights—The Spanish Steps (with Italy's first, and one of the world's largest, McDonalds—McGrandeur at its greatest—just down the street); the unkempt, overpriced Villa d'Est garden of fountains at Tivoli; and the commercialized Catacombs, which contain no bones, are way out of the city, and are not worth the time or trouble.

▲▲▲ Floodlit Rome Hike: Trastevere to the Spanish Steps—Rome can be grueling. But a thoroughly enjoyable slice of this historian's fertility rite is an evening walk lacing together Rome's floodlit night spots. Fine urban spaces, real-life theater vignettes, sitting close enough to the Bernini fountain to hear no traffic, water flickering its mirror on the marble, jostling with local teenagers to see all the gelati flavors, enjoying lovers straddling more than the bench, jay-walking past flack-vested police, marveling at the ramshackle elegance that softens this brutal city for those who were born here and can imagine living no where else. These are the flavors of Rome best tasted after dark.

Taxi or ride the bus to **Trastevere** (#23 from the Vatican area), the colorful neighborhood across (*tras*) the Tiber (*tevere*). Start your hike at the city's oldest church, Santa Maria in Trastevere.

Trastevere offers the best look at medieval village Rome. Witness colorful street scenes: pasta rollers, streetwise cats, and crinkly old political posters caked like graffiti-laden baklava onto the walls. There are motionless men in sleeveless T-shirts framed by open windows, cobbles with centuries of life ground into their cleavages, kids kicking soccer balls into the cars that litter their alley-fields, and sultry cooks retailing pastries straight out of the bakery oven. Boys with prowling eyes whisper an approving and breathy *bella* as girls strut by pretending not to notice. (Boy-watching girls can say, "*Bello.*") The action all marches to the chime of the church bells. Go there and wander. Wonder. Be a poet. This is Rome's Left Bank.

Santa Maria in Trastevere from the third century (open 8:00-12:00 and 16:00-19:00) is one of Rome's oldest churches. Notice the ancient basilica floor plan and early Christian symbols in the walls near the entry.

From the square, Via del Moro (Mario's restaurant at #53 is good, see Eating in Rome below) leads to the river and Ponte Sisto, a pedestrian bridge with a good view of St. Peter's dome. Cross the bridge and continue straight ahead for one block. Take the first left, which leads through the scary and narrow darkness to Piazza Farnese with the imposing Palazzo Farnese. The palace's beautiful interior, designed, in part, by Michelangelo, is closed to the public. It's currently occupied by the French Embassy, which pays a rent of one lire every 99 years. If the ambassador walked straight out the door of his palace for one block, there's a fair chance he'd see me on my favorite square, Campo dei Fiori, eating dinner.

The **Campo dei Fiori** (Field of Flowers) offers a good look at village Rome, colorful produce and flower market in the morning and a romantic, affordable outdoor dining room after dark (Trattoria Virgilio is one of several decent restaurants). Drink to the dark moody statue of Bruno, who was burned with the steak for thinking scientific ahead of his time. (He one-upped Galileo, saying that not only was the earth not the center of the universe but that the universe had no center!)

If Bruno did a hop, step, and jump forward and turned right, he'd cross the busy Corso Vittorio Emanuele and find Piazza Navona.

Piazza Navona, Rome's most interesting night scene, features street music, artists, fire eaters, local Casanovas, ice cream, outdoor cafés (splurge-worthy if you've got time to sit and enjoy the human river of Italy), hippies, Polish entrepreneurs selling knickknacks, and three fountains by Bernini, the father of baroque art. The grand Fountain of the Four Rivers, built in 1651, symbolizes the four corners of the earth. Notice the Nile with its head covered (symbolizing either that its source was still unknown or Bernini's dislike of the church built by his artistic rival, Borromini, overlooking his fountain and the square). This oblong square is molded around the long-gone stadium of Domitian, an ancient chariot race track that was often flooded so the masses could enjoy mock naval battles.

Piazza Navona is famous for its chocolate ice cream specialty, Tartufo. Two places on the square offer homemade Tartufo for about the same steep price. Tre Scalini is most famous ("to go" is less expensive). Ai Tre Tartufi, next door, makes its special softer variation with less chocolate and more sugar and cream. Factory-made tartufos, just twenty yards down the lane from the square, are cheaper. I prefer Tre Scalini's, but it seems that as Tartufo's fame (and price) has increased, its quality has suffered. For those interested in just plain good gelato, face Tre Scalini and go to the left end of the square, take a right down Via D.G. Vecchio to #81, where Gelateria Pasquino offers great cups of homemade gelato for half the price of a Tartufo. At #114 on the same street is Pizzeria da Baffetto, a traditional old hole-in-the-wall place for real, and cheap, pizza (closed Sunday). For cheap picnic groceries or a quick slice of take-out pizza to eat on the square, walk two blocks down the street running from the square between the two tartufo places.

Leave Piazza Navona (walking down the lane directly across from the Tre Scalini café) past rose peddlers and palm readers, jog left around the guarded building, and follow the yellow sign to the Pantheon straight down Via del Salvatore (cheap pizza place on the left just before the Pantheon). From the obelisk (facing the Pantheon) head left to Casa del Caffe, then left down Via degli Orfani. At the square, pass the church on the left down Via Aquiro. At the obelisk (if its gelati time, head left behind Albergo Nazionale down Via degli Uffici del Vicario for a visit to the, at times, riotously popular

Gelateria Giolitti), turn right, walk between the Italian Parliament and the huge Il Tempo newspaper building to the busy Via del Corso. You'll pass the huge second-century column honoring Marcus Aurelius, cross the street noticing the Victor Emmanuel Monument way down to the right, and go into the lofty gallery. Take the right branch of this V-shaped gallery and exit continuing straight down Via de Crociferi to the roar of the water, light, and people of the Trevi fountain.

The newly restored **Trevi fountain** is an example of how Rome took full advantage of the abundance of water brought into the city by its great aqueducts. The watery baroque avalanche, built in 1762, features the figure of Ocean riding a chariot drawn by two sea horses and two tritons. Romantics toss two coins over their shoulder thinking it will give them a wish and assure their return to Rome. Every year I go through this touristic ritual. It seems to work very well.

Take some time to people-watch (whisper a few "bellos" or "bellas") before leaving. Facing the fountain, go past it on the right down Via delle Stamperia to Via del Triton. Cross the busy street and continue to the Spanish Steps (ask, Dové Piazza di Spagna?), a few short blocks and thousands of dollars of shopping opportunities away.

The Piazza di Spagna with the very popular Spanish Steps got its name 300 years ago when this was the site of the Spanish Embassy. It's been the hangout of many romantics over the years (Keats, Wagner, Openshaw, Goethe, and others). The Boat fountain at the foot of the steps was done by Bernini's father, Bernini.

Facing the steps, walk to your right about a block to tour one of the world's biggest and most lavish McDonald's. About a block on the other side of the steps is the subway, which will zip you home (unless it's after 23:30).

Entertainment

Nighttime fun in Rome is found in the piazzas, along the river, and at its outdoor concerts and street fairs. Pick up the local periodical entertainment guide, the English-language monthly *Carnet di Roma* for a rundown on special events.

A highlight for many is a grand and lavish opera performance on the world's biggest opera stage, the ruins of the ancient Baths of Caracalla (Terme di Caracalla). (Shows start at 21:00 and finish after midnight several nights a week in July; tickets L25,000-50,000; English scripts available; tel. 06/481 7003.) This spectacle is taking its toll on the ruins of the baths and will be stopped soon. "Soon" in Rome is kind of like the second coming.

Helpful Hints—Rome

There are absolutely no absolutes in Italy, and the hours I've listed will invariably vary. Museums are generally open 9:00 to 14:00. Most museums close on Mondays (except the Vatican) and at 13:00 on Sundays. Outdoor sights like the Colosseum, Forum, and Ostia Antica are open 9:00 to 19:00 (or one hour before sunset) and are often closed one day a week. The Capitoline Hill museums are Rome's only nocturnal museums, open Tuesdays 17:00 to 20:00 and Saturday 20:00 to 23:00. By the way, in museums, A.C. (*Avanti Cristo*, or Before Christ) after a year means the same as our B.C. D.C. (*Dopo Cristo*) is what we call A.D.

Churches open very early, close for lunch, and reopen for a few hours around 16:00. Dress modestly—no bare shoulders or shorts. Kamikaze tourists maximize their sightseeing hours by visiting churches before other sights open, seeing the major sights that don't close for siesta (St. Peter's and the Forum) when all good Romans are taking it cool and easy, and doing the nocturnal museums after dark.

Shops and offices are usually open 9:00-13:00 and 16:00-20:00. In the holiday month of August, many shops and restaurants close up; *Chiuso per feria* signs decorate locked doors all over town. Closed for Restoration is another sign you'll see all too often, especially in the winter.

One final theft alert: With seemingly likable, sweet-talking, well-dressed con artists, thieves on buses and at the station, and gypsy gangs at the ancient sights, Rome is a mine field of rip-offs. But, unless you are really looking for trouble, no one is going to mug you. If you keep on guard, remember that thieves strike when you're distracted, don't trust kind strangers, and keep nothing important in your pockets, you have nothing to fear in Rome.

The siesta is a key to survival in summertime Rome. Lie down and contemplate the extraordinary power of gravity in the eternal city. I drink lots of cold refreshing water from Rome's many drinking fountains (the Forum has three). If you get sick, the American hospital is at Via Emilio Longoni 69 (tel. 25671).

Sleeping in Rome (about L1300 = US$1)

The absolute cheapest sleepable doubles in Rome are L50,000, without shower or breakfast. A nicer hotel, providing an oasis/refuge, makes it easier to enjoy this intense and grinding city. If you're going door to door, prices are soft. Bargain. Easter, September, and October are the crowded times. July and August are too hot for crowds. I've focused on three areas. Most of the places are small with huge, murky entrances that make you feel like a Q-tip in a dustbin. Except for the convents, most of them speak a little English and will hold a room with a phone call.

Near the station: The cheapest hotels in town are on either side of the station (lining Via Palestro and Via Principe Amedeo). But, while many rooms are pleasant and the prices are soft enough to usually push down under L50,000 per double, the area just doesn't feel safe. The stairways leading to the top Frommer and *Let's Go* budget recommendations (Via P. Amedeo) are bouncing with prostitutes. With less than a dollar and five minutes on the metro zipping you into better zones, I'd avoid this area altogether. These recommendations are about a ten-minute walk toward the old town and river.

Hotel Nardizzi Americana (L100,000-120,000 doubles including breakfast, less 10% for 22 Days readers, Via Firenze 38, 00184 Roma, classic elevator to the fifth floor, tel. 06/488 0368) is my longtime favorite in the station area. Most of the beds are springy cots, and the traffic noise in the front rooms reminds you you're in a city of four million, but it's a tranquil haven, safe, handy, and central, a short walk from central station and Piazza Barberini on the corner of Via Firenze and Via XX Settembre. Sr. Nardizzi and his wife speak English, stock the TI's free ETP Rome maps, and provide a homey-and-you-belong atmosphere. Parking is actually workable here. Double-park below the hotel until a space without yellow lines becomes available, then grab it. The defense ministry is across the street, and you've got heavily armed guards all night. The nearby **Residence Adler** (L80,000-120,000 doubles, Via Modena 5, 00184 Roma, tel. 06/484 466) is also good—but not *as* good.

Hotel Pensione Italia (L90,000-110,000 doubles with shower and breakfast, promises a L20,000 discount for 22 Days readers, Via Venezia 18, just off Via Nazionale, tel. 06/482 8355, fax 06/474 5550) is in a busy, interesting, handy locale, placed safely next to the Ministry of the Interior. It's pleasant, clean, and friendly, and English is spoken.

Hotel Felicita (L100,000 doubles, all with showers, price guaranteed for my readers, Via Palermo 73, 00184 Roma, tel. 06/48 59 15 and 474 7363) is a friendly and happy place with quiet rooms.

Hotel Pensione Esedra (L60,000 doubles without shower, 47 Piazza della Repubblica, third floor, tel. 06/488 0334), on a formerly elegant piazza, a cigarette butt's toss from the station, is the best cheap deal I found close to the station. The place is spacious enough to make its dumpiness acceptable.

Near the Colosseum: An easy walk down Via Cavour or a couple of stops on the subway, most of these places are completely out of the station sleaze and buried in a very Roman world of exhaust-stained medieval ambience (listed roughly in order from the Colosseum to the station).

Pensione Beatrice (L28,000 singles, L46,000 doubles, L68,000 triples, baths down the hall, off Via Cavour at Via dei Serpenti 137, tel. 4824007) is a very homey gem in a decent village-Rome setting, family run, high ceilings, bright, clean, tasteful simplicity, offering Rome's best cheap beds and the closest thing to an elderly aunt's apartment to bed down in.

Hotel Flavio (five L77,000 doubles with showers down the hall, L98,000 doubles with shower, hiding almost torch-lit under vines on a tiny street a block toward the Colosseum from Via Cavour at Via Frangipane 34, 00184 Roma, tel. 06/6797203) is a real hotel with a classy TV lounge/lobby, an elevator, and elegant furnishings throughout in a quiet setting.

Albergo Perugia (two L50,000 doubles are a better value than their L80,000 doubles with showers, near the corner of Via Cavour and Via Fori Imperiali at Via del Colosseo 7, tel. 6797200) is yellow, peely, filled with furniture not fit for a garage sale but friendly, peaceful, and beautifully located.

Suore di Sant Anna (L25,000 per bed in singles and doubles, including breakfast, monkish lunch, or dinner for L15,000 more, just off the corner of Via dei Serpenti and Via Baccina at Piazza Madonna dei Monti 3, 00184 Roma, tel. 06/48 57 78) is a convent built for Ukrainian pilgrims (and rarely full except when groups hit in June, July, and September). The sisters, who speak Italian, Portuguese, and Ukrainian, are sweet, but the male staff doesn't seem to want your business. Although it's a clumsy and difficult place, once you're in, it becomes a comfortable home.

Hotel Cherie (L67,000 doubles, at the Cavour metro stop, Via Cavour 238, tel. 4741789), on a handy but noisy street, makes a clean, cheery, and safe place to call home if you don't mind the traffic.

Hotel Saturnia (L53,000 doubles without shower, L67,000 with shower, L80,000 with bath, halfway between the station and the Colosseum, just off Via Cavour at Via Ruinaglia 5, tel. 4828499) is a fine little hotel in a decent spot, but half the rooms suffer from street noise.

The **YWCA Casa Per Studentesse** (L24,000 per person in 3- and 4-bed rooms, L30,000 per person in spacious doubles, with breakfast, showers down the hall, locked up from midnight to 7:00, Via C. Balbo 4, 00184 Roma, five blocks toward the Colosseum from the station, tel. 06/488 0460 or 488 3917) accepts women, couples, and couples with children. It's a gray and institutional place, filled with maids in white and 75 single beds, with a raggedy fruit market out the front door.

Also in old Rome but nowhere near these others, the **Albergo del Sole** (L70,000-100,000 doubles, no breakfast, Via del Biscione 76, 00186 Roma, tel. 06/654 0873 or 06/687 9446, fax 689 3787) is just off the colorful Campo dei Fiori, right in the Roman thick of things. It's clean, impersonal, and very well run with 65 rooms, a roof garden, and lots of Germans.

Near the Vatican: These hotels are handy to the Ottaviano metro stop near the Vatican museum entry, surrounded by good places to eat and a shopping district favored by locals. To reach Pension Alimandi, follow the "M" signs from the train station into the subway system (see diagram), follow Linea A in the direction "Ottaviano" and ride to the last stop, Ottaviano. Exit that station smartest by walking straight to the far end underground and climbing the stairs to the left marked "v. le G. Cesare," continuing straight from the stairs for 4 or 5 blocks, past several handy and cheap eateries, up Via le G. Cesare (which becomes Via Candia), turning left at Via Tunisi.

Pension Alimandi (L75,000-95,000 doubles, optional but very good L12,000 breakfast, great roof garden; one block in front of the Vatican Museum, Via Tunisi 8, 00192 Roma, tel. 06/39726300, fax 06/397 23943, credit card accepted to secure telephone reservation) is a great value, run by friendly, English-speaking, and hardworking Paolo and Enrico and perfectly located (if you don't mind the Vatican out your bedroom window). They stock the TI's free EPT map.

Hotel Spring House (L125,000 doubles with breakfast, Via Mocenigo 7, one block from Alimandi, tel. 06/397 20948, fax 06/397 21047) offers clean, quiet rooms with balconies, TVs, and refrigerators, and a fine sixth-floor breakfast terrace but no personality. If you need a normal hotel, this is a good value.

Near Ponte Cavour (on the Vatican side): The **Pensione Anita** (L50,000 doubles, no breakfasts, showers extra, Via Marianna Dionigi 17, fifth floor with elevator, tel. 06/320 4677) has rooms big enough to dance in. Even with dirty walls and bare bulbs, it beats the Rome youth hostel.

Get Thee to a Nunnery: The convents of the city are your most interesting budget bet. The **Protezione delle Giovane** (in the train station near the day hotel, erratic hours, tel. 06/482 7594) is a helpful—to pilgrim-looking women only—convent and budget room-finding service. Convents operate tax-free and are therefore cheaper; these are peaceful, safe, and clean, but sometimes stern, and rarely does anyone speak English.

Suore Oblate dell Assunzione convent is a peaceful garden oasis for those lucky enough to get a place (L25,000 per bed, no meals, Via Andrea Doria 42, three blocks in front of the Vatican Museum entrance, buzz the big gray gate, tel. 06/372 9540, French and Italian spoken). Just across from the Vatican Museum and up the road is a **Convent** (L20,000 per person, in 1- to 4-bed rooms, Viale Vaticano 92, tel. 06/372 0209). They take men and women but no reservations and are normally full. It's worth a try if you have a good prayer life or know the people at Pension Alimandi, around the corner.

Pensione Suore Francescane (L30,000 doubles, five minutes walk from St. Peter's at Via Nicolo V 35, 00165 Roma, tel. 326 6531) is a simple, friendly, and clean convent with baths down the hall and the helpful English-speaking Sister Helen Agnes.

Similar places near the Vatican are: **Casa Valdese** (Via Alessandro Farnese, 18, tel. 06/321 1843), **Emaus** (Via di S. Maria alle Fornace 23, tel. 06/638 0370), and **Franciscan Sisters of the Atonement** (a 30-minute uphill walk from the Vatican at Via Monte del Gallo 105, tel. 06/63 07 82). Near Via Veneto is the convent **Nôtre Dame de Lourdes** (Via Sistina 113, tel. 06/474 5324).

Eating in Rome

The cheapest meals in town are picnics (from *alimentari* shops or open-air markets), self-serve **Rôtisseries**, and stand-up or take-out meals from a **Pizza Rustica** (pizza slices sold by the weight, 200 grams, or 2 *etti*, makes a light meal). Most alimentari will slice and stuff a sandwich *(panini)* if you buy the stuff there. Hotels can recommend the best nearby cafeteria or restaurant.

In Trastevere or on the Campo di Fiori: My best dinner tip is to go for Rome's Vespa street ambience and find your own place in Trastevere (bus 23 from the Vatican area) or on Campo di Fiori. Guidebooks list Trastevere's famous places, but I'd wander the fascinating maze of streets around the Piazza Santa Maria in Trastevere and find a place with barely a menu. For the basic meal, amazingly cheap, eat with the other tourists at **Mario's** (3 courses with wine and service for L15,000, near the Sisto bridge at Via del Moro 53, tel. 5803809, closed Sunday). For the ultimate romantic square setting, eat at whichever place looks best on Campo di Fiori (I like Virgilio, tel. 65 42 746, closed Wednesday).

Near the Pantheon: Il Delfino is a handy self-service cafeteria on the Largo Argentina square (7:00-21:00, closed Monday, not cheap but fast). For a classier meal (walk two blocks in front of the Pantheon, down Via Magdalena, left on Via della Coppelle), try **Hostaria La Nuova Capannina** (Piazza della Coppelle 8, tel. 06/654 3921, open for diner at 19:00, closed Monday), with good, moderately priced, sit-down, indoor or outdoor meals. The alimentari on the Pantheon square will make you a sandwich for a temple porch picnic. The **New Point** self-service is near Pizza Navona at 137 Vittorio Emmanuele.

Near the station, Nardizzi's, and Piazza Barberini: Italy Italy on Piazza Barberini is a good value for Italian fast food. The nearby **Ristorante de Giovanni** just off Via XX Settembre at Via Antonio Salandra 1, tel. 485950, closed Sunday) is a fine place for a sit-down real meal. Just down the street from Nardizzi's on Via Firenze is Chinese (**Lon Fon**, #44, elegant atmosphere with reasonable prices), **Snack Bar Gastronomia** (#34, really cheap hot meals dished up from under glass counter), and an alimentari (grocery store at #54).

Near the Vatican Museum and Pension Alimandi: Ristorante dei Musei (L15,000 menu, indoor/outdoor, corner of Via Sebastiano Veniero and Via Santamaura, closes at 17:00), or one of several good places along Via Sebastiano Veniero, such as **La Rustichella da Carlo** (more expensive but fine food, especially fish) at Via Angelo Emo 1 and the **Cipriani Self-Service Rosticceria** near the Ottaviano subway stop at the corner of Via Vespasiano and Viale Giulio Cesare (cheap, easy, with pleasant outdoor seating, several other cheap places on the busy street nearby). Don't miss the wonderful **Via Andrea Doria marketplace** two blocks in front of the Vatican Museum between Via Tunisi and Via Andrea Doria (closed by 13:30, Monday-Saturday). **Trattoria La Caravella** (corner of Vespasiano and Degli Scipioni) is a reasonable eatery three blocks from the recommended Pension Alimandi. And restaurant **Sport** has plenty of variety at reasonable prices (Via Andrea Doria 16, closed Monday).

DAY 14

ROME TO NAPLES TO SORRENTO

If you like Italy as far south as Rome, go farther south. It gets better. If Italy is getting on your nerves, think twice about going farther. Italy intensifies as you plunge deeper. Naples is a barrel full of cultural monkeys, Italy in the extreme—its best (birthplace of pizza and Sophia Loren) and its worst (home of Mafia-style organized crime). The puzzle of Italy is not complete without Naples.

After surviving the Vespa slalom called Naples and checking out Europe's top archaeological museum, escape via a sixty-minute commuter train to an entirely different world—the resort of Sorrento, gateway to the Amalfi coast and Italy's most stunning scenery.

Suggested Schedule

By Train:

7:00	Train to Naples.
9:30	Tour Archaeology Museum (closed at 14:00 and on Monday).
11:00	Do the "Slice-of-Neopolitan-Life" walk.
13:00	Pizza at Antica Pizzeria da Michele.
14:30	Train to Sorrento.
15:30	Set up in Sorrento, orientation walk.
17:30	Bus to Sant Agata for panorama and sunset.

By Car: Don't try it.

Speedy Option: To save a day and simplify your excursion south, make it a day trip from Rome, doing Naples (museum, walk, lunch) first, Pompeii in the afternoon, and returning that evening to Rome by train.

Transportation: Rome to Naples to Sorrento (150 miles)

It's a two- to three-hour trip from Rome's Termini station to Naples (hourly departures, more expensive express trains save nearly an hour). Catch the very early fast train and have breakfast in the cafeteria car (inexpensive, ask if Rome hotel will rebate your missed breakfast). Upon arrival in Naples, check all bags (Deposito Bagagli in front of track #24, L1500), visit the TI (pick up map and *Qui Napoli* booklet, if they say they're "finished" ask for an old one, 9:00-20:00, Sunday 9:00-13:00, tel. 081/268779, comes with a toupee-topped con man selling organized tours), and organize in the passenger waiting room (draw walking route on your map) before taking the Neapolitan plunge. Get an early start. In the afternoon, Naples's street life slows and museums close as the temperature soars. (Naples museums close on Monday.)

Rome trains arrive at one of several Naples stations. Naples Centrale is the main one (facing Piazza Garibaldi, baggage check, Circumvesuviana stop for commuter trains to Sorrento and Pompeii, TI). Since Centrale is a dead-end station, through trains often stop at Piazza Garibaldi (actually a subway station just downstairs from Centrale) or Napoli Mergellina (equipped with a TI, across town, a direct 10-minute subway ride to Centrale, train tickets to Napoli Centrale and train passes cover you for the connecting ride to Centrale, subway trains depart about every 10 minutes).

Naples' simple one-line subway, the Metropolitana, runs basically from the Mergellina station to the Centrale station through the center of town, stopping at Piazza Cavour (Archaeology Museum).

From Naples to Sorrento, Ferrovia Circumvesuviana trains (regional rail system separate from the main rail system, not covered on train passes but cheap) leave about hourly from the basement of the central station (well signposted). While there are several lines, the one sightseers use (marked Sorrento) goes from Piazza Garibaldi to Ercolano (Herculaneum, bus to Vesuvius, 15 minutes), Pompeii (40 minutes), and Sorrento (end of the line, 70 minutes, L4000 one way, cheaper round-trip).

Safety warning: Romans consider Neapolitans dishonest, disorganized, rude, and above all, poor drivers. Check all bags at the station, don't venture into neighborhoods that make you uncomfortable, walk with confidence as if you know where you're going and what you're doing, and assume able-bodied beggars are thieves. Keep your money belt completely hidden. Stick to busy streets, and beware of gangs of young street hoodlums. Remember, a third of the city is unemployed and the local government sets an example the Mafia would be proud of. Any jostle or commotion is probably a thief team's smoke screen. Lately Naples has been occupied by an army of police, which has made it feel safer. Still, err on the side of caution.

Naples

Italy's third largest city (2,200,000 people) has almost no open spaces or parks, which makes its position as Europe's most densely populated city plenty evident. Watching the police try to enforce traffic sanity is almost comical in Italy's poorest, worst-polluted, and most crime-ridden city. But Naples surprises the observant traveler with an impressive knack for living, eating, and raising children in the streets with good humor and decency. Overcome your fear of being run down or ripped off enough to talk with people and enjoy a few smiles and jokes with the man running the cobblestone tripe shop or the lady taking her day care class on a walk through the traffic.

Twenty-five hundred years ago, Neapolis (new city) was a thriving Greek commercial center. It remains southern Italy's leading city, offering a fascinating collection of museums, churches, eclectic architecture, and volunteers needing blood for dying babies. The pulse of Italy throbs in Naples. Like Cairo or Bombay, it's appalling and captivating at the same time, the closest thing to "reality travel" this tour offers. The U.S. military is still high profile here. You'll meet lots of American soldiers in Naples who, in their peculiar dialect and from their predictable perspective, will be sure to tell you what a hellhole this place is. But Naples is closer to global normalcy than any stop on our route . . . hotter and more crowded than ever . . . a tangled mess that still somehow manages to breath, laugh, and sing—with a captivating Italian accent.

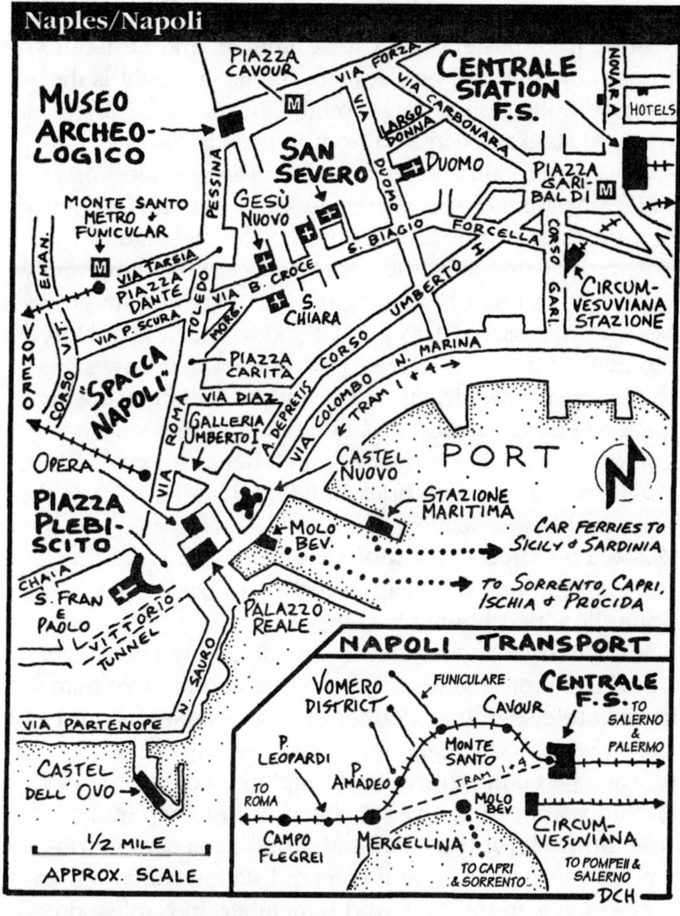

Sightseeing Highlights—Naples

▲▲▲ Museo Archeologico—For lovers of antiquity, this museum alone makes the side trip south from Rome worthwhile. This museum is the only peek possible into the artistic jewelry boxes of Pompeii and Herculaneum. The actual sights are vast and impressive but rather barren. Somehow, their best art ended up here.

Start on the top floor, a Pompeiian art gallery lined with paintings and bronze statues that make the relative darkness of medieval Europe obvious and that clearly show from where the Renaissance greats were inspired. The mezzanine, just off the central stairway, has a smaller but exquisite collection of Pompeiian mosaics. The ground floor has enough Greek, Roman, and Etruscan art to put any museum on the map, but its highlight is the Farnese Collection of huge, bright, and wonderfully restored statues excavated from Rome's Baths of Caracalla. You can almost hear the Toro Farnese snorting. This largest intact statue from antiquity was carved out of one piece of marble and restored by Michelangelo.

Amazingly for Italy, the entire collection is thoughtfully explained in English, making the L10,000 museum guidebook unnecessary (9:00-14:00, Sunday until 13:00, closed Monday, L8000). From the Centrale station, follow signs to Metropolitana (tickets from window on left, ask which track to Piazza Cavour, and ride the train one stop). As you exit turn right. At the end of cluttered Piazza Cavour, you'll see a huge pink brick building. Use the W.C. in the courtyard before leaving.

▲▲▲ The Slice-of-Neapolitan-Life Walk: From the museum through the heart of town and back to the station (allow two hours plus lunch).

Naples is a living medieval city and its own best sight. You'll see more fights and smiles per cobble here than anywhere else in Italy. Rather than see Naples as a list of sights, see the one great museum, then capture its essence by taking this walk through the core of the city. Should you become overwhelmed or lost, step into a store and ask for the nearest Metropolitana station (do-vay il Metropolitana?) or the central station (do-vay il sta-shee-o-nay cen-tral-ay?). And remember, in Naples, drivers consider red lights discretionary, and mopeds can mow you down from any place at any time.

As you leave the Archaeological Museum at the top of Piazza Cavour (Metro: Piazza Cavour), cross the street, veer right, and dip into the ornate galleria on your way to Via Pessina. Busy Via Pessina leads you downhill to Piazza Dante. Notice poor old Dante in the center looking out over the chaos with a hopeless gesture. Past the square, Via Pessina becomes Via Roma, Naples's principal shopping street. Follow it through Piazza Carita where it becomes Via Toledo. Wander down Via Toledo a few blocks past the Fascist architecture of two banks (both on your left). Try getting into the second one (Banco di Napoli, 178 Via Toledo). Up the hill to your right is the notorious Spaccannapoli ("split Naples") district. This is Naples at its rawest, poorest, and most historic. Thrill-seekers (or someone in need of a $20 prostitute) will take a stroll up one of these streets and loop back to Via Toledo. The only thing predictable about this Neapolitan tidepool is the ancient grid plan of the streets and the friendliness of its shopkeepers.

Continue down Via Toledo to the Piazza Plebiscito. From here you'll see the Church of San Francesco di Paola with its Pantheon-inspired dome and broad arcing colonnades. Opposite is the royal palace, which has housed Spanish, French, and even Italian royalty. The lavish interior is open for tours (daily 9:00-14:00, Sunday until 13:00, closed Monday, L6000). Next door, the neoclassical Teatro San Carlo is Italy's second most respected opera house (after Milan's La Scala). The huge castle on the harborfront just beyond the palace houses government bureaucrats and is closed to tourists.

From here, double back to the station. For a relaxing coffee break under the Victorian iron and glass of the 100-year-old Galleria Umberto I, go through the tall yellow arch at the end of Via Toledo or across from the opera house. Now, double back up Via Toledo to the Piazza Carita, then angle right down Via Morgantini, jog right and continue to a square with two bulky old churches, Piazza Gesu Nuovo. Check out the austere, fortresslike church of Gesu Nuovo with its peaceful but brilliant baroque interior. Across the street the simpler Gothic Church of Santa Chiara offers a stark contrast (church closes at noon, cloisters at 12:30).

Continue down Via B. Croce to the Piazza S. Domenico Maggiore. The castlelike church, San Domenico Maggiore, dominating the square has a surprisingly lavish baroque high altar. Walk behind San Domenico Maggiore (to the right as you face the church, taking the first right after that), following yellow signs to the Capella di Sansevero at Via de Sanctis 19. This small chapel is a baroque explosion mourning the body of Christ laying on a soft pillow under an incredibly realistic veil all carved out of marble. It's like no statue I've seen (by Giuseppe Sammartino, 1750). Lovely statues, carved from a single piece of marble, adorn the altar. Don't miss "Despair" struggling with a marble rope net (on the right, opposite "Chastity"). Then for the ghoul in all of us, walk down the stairway to the right for a creepy look at two 200-year-old studies in varicose veins (L4000, 10:00-13:30 and 17:00-19:00, Sundays 10:00-13:00).

Return to the Via B. Croce, turn left and run the gauntlet back to the train station. Keep going straight as Via B. Croce becomes Via S. Biagio dei Librai, cross the busy Via Duomo, and the street scenes intensify. Paint a picture with these thoughts: Naples has the most intact street plan of any ancient Roman city. Imagine life here as in a Roman city (retain these images for your visit to Pompeii) with street-side shop fronts that close up to form private homes after dark. Today is just one more page in a 2,000-year-old story of city activity: all kinds of meetings, beatings, and cheatings, kisses, near misses, and little boy pisses. You name it, it occurs right on the streets today, as it has since Roman times. For a peek behind the scenes in the shade of wet laundry, venture down a few side streets. A few streets after crossing Via Duomo veer right onto Via Forcella, which brings you to Corso Umberto.

For a tasty and typically Neapolitan finale, drop by the quintessential Naples pizzeria for lunch. From Via Forcella, you'll hit Corso Umberto near the **Antica Pizzeria da Michele** (cheap, filled with locals, 50 yards before you hit Corso Umberto on Via Cesare Sersale, look for the vertical red Antica Pizzeria sign, 8:00-22:00, closed Sunday). Here's your chance to taste pure pizza in its birthplace. Naples, baking just the right combination of fresh dough, mozzarella, and tomatoes in traditional wood-burning ovens, is famous for its pizzas. This place serves only two kinds of pizza: Margherita (tomato sauce and mozzarella) or Marinara (tomato sauce, oregano, and garlic with no cheese).

Turn left on Corso Umberto, which leads to the vast and ugly Piazza Garibaldi. On the far side is the Central Station. Good job!

Naples has many more museums, churches, and sights that some consider important. For a run-down on these, refer to the TI's free *Qui Napoli* publication.

Sleeping in Naples (about L1300 = US$1)
With Sorrento just an hour away, I can't imagine why you'd stay in Naples. But if needed, here are two safe, clean places near the station and one more out of the way. To find these hotels, turn right out of the station and walk up Corso Novara. In two minutes you're there, a thoroughly ugly but reasonably safe area. Be careful after dark.

Hotel Eden (L83,000, or L66,000 with this book, Corso Novara 9, tel. 081/285 344, fax 202 070) is a fine establishment run with panache by Nicola (Danny Devito), the helpful owner. Very clean, good beds, brown and gray tones and all the comforts in sterile surroundings, which is exactly what you're after here. Ask to see the hall lighting ambience.

Hotel Ginerva (L50,000-60,000, across the street from the Eden and down Via Genoa to #116, tel. 081/283 210) is bright and cheery. You'll find this a pleasant respite from the streets below. No English spoken, but they try hard. New beds, floral wallpaper, and the owner will let you use his washing machine for a bargain L3000 per load.

Ostello Mergellina (L18,000 beds including sheets and breakfast, membership required or you'll pay extra, small rooms with two to six beds, Metro to Mergellina, take two right turns, and walk 15 minutes to Salita della Grotta a Piedigrotta 23, tel. 081/761-2346, closed 9:00-16:30 and at 23:30, cheap meals) is well run, cheap, and pleasant but a headache to get to.

Sorrento
Wedged on a ledge under the mountains and over the Mediterranean, surrounded by lemon and olive groves,

Sorrento is an attractive resort of 20,000 residents and easily as many tourists. It's as well located for regional sightseeing as it is a pleasant place to stay and stroll, without a hint of Naples. The Sorrentines have gone out of their way to create a pleasant, completely safe, and relaxed place for tourists to come and spend money. Everyone seems to speak fluent English and work for the chamber of commerce. Sorrento has a pleasant and unspoiled old quarter, a lively main shopping street, and a spectacular cliffside setting. Skip the port and its poor excuse for a beach unless you're taking a ferry. Sorrento exists for tourism. For our purposes, it's a good place to lick your wounds after Naples and a handy home base for exploring Capri and the Amalfi coast.

Orientation

Sorrento is long and narrow. The main drag, Corso Italia (50 feet in front of the station), runs parallel to the sea from the station through the town center and out to the cape, where it's renamed Via del Capo. The commercial center, TI, and most services are five minutes walk from the station. To reach the TI (Soggiorno e Turismo), turn left on Corso Italia, walk the five minutes to Piazza Tasso, Sorrento's main square, then turn right at the end of this square down Via L. de Maio through the Piazza Sant Antonino and to the mansion at #35 (8:30-14:00 and 17:00-20:00, or 8:30-14:00 and 16:00-19:00 in off-season, tel. 081/878 2229, ask for the free Sorrentum magazine, boat, bus and events schedules). You'll pass many fake "tourist offices" on the way (travel agencies selling bus and boat tours) which, with longer hours and town maps, can be helpful. Telephone code: 081. Postal code: 80067.

Sleeping in Sorrento (about L1100 = US$1)

Unlike many resorts, Sorrento offers the whole range of rooms. If you splurge, make sure you get a balcony and view. Hotels listed here are either near the station and city center or out toward the Punta del Capo, a good 30-minute walk from the station (taxi or bus from the station). The TI can book you into a private home for

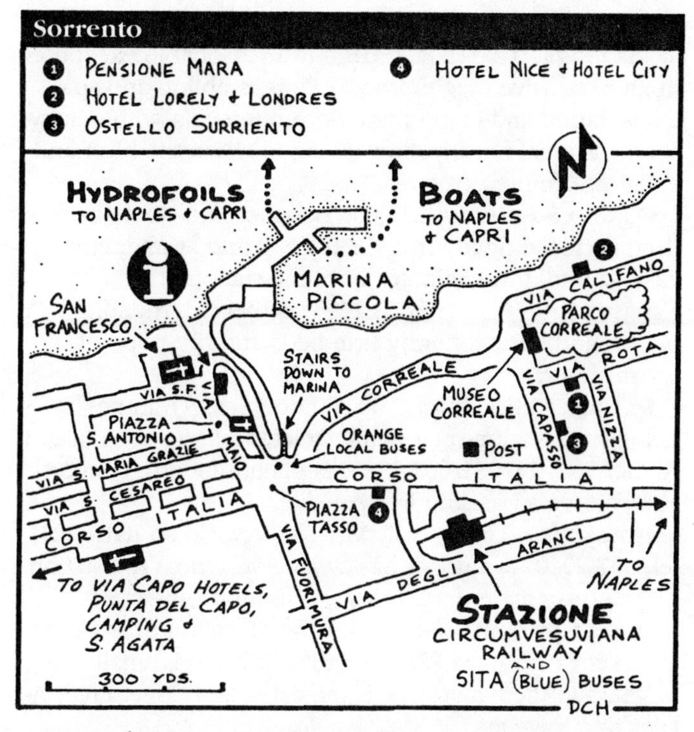

around L60,000 per double. Many hotels close in the winter until April, though you'll have no trouble finding a room off-season. Note: the more exotic Amalfi coast town of Positano (explained below) is also a good place to spend the night.

Near the station and in the town center: From the station, turn right onto the Corso Italia, then left down Via Capasso for the first three listings. For the others, turn left on Corso Italia.

Pension Mara (L60,000 doubles, ask for a balcony, from Via Capasso, turn right onto the unmarked Via Rota just past the youth hostel, Via Rota 5, tel. 081/878 3665). Very friendly, non-English-speaking owners provide simple, relatively clean rooms in a dull building with a great location.

Hotel Lorely and Londres (L80,000 doubles with breakfast, in July, August, and September half-pension, L70,000 per person, is required, follow Via Capasso to the water and turn right to see the big rose-colored hotel at Via Califano 2, tel. 807 3187) is a reasonable exception in an expensive neighborhood. This rambling and spacious, faded and colorful old Sorrentine villa with rickety rooms is ideal for anyone wishing to sit on the bluff and contemplate their navy.

Ostello Surriento (L14,000 per spot in 6- to 10-bed dorms, closed tightly from 9:30-17:00 and at midnight, easy to find, three minutes from the station at Via Capasso 5, tel. and fax 878 1783) is relaxed, friendly, bright, and basic, offering firm beds and the hope of warm water.

La Caffetteria Hotel (L60,000 doubles, 3 minutes behind the station on a dull characterless street, Via degli Aranci 160, tel. 081/807 2925) is plain, modern, comfortable, above a bar, and inexpensive.

Hotel Nice (L65,000, all with shower, Corso Italia 221, tel. 877 2210) is a good, basic value very near the station on the busy main drag. Ask for a room off the street.

Hotel City (L50,000-60,000, handy location near Piazza Tasso at Corso Italia 221, tel. 081/877 2210) is small and bright, and the manager, Gianni, caters to budget English-speaking travelers.

Hotel Del Corso (L70,000, all with facilities, half-pension at L70,000 per person is required in the summer, in the town center at Corso Italia 134, tel. 878 1299), a well-worn Old World hotel is central, clean, comfortable, and quiet enough. I'm not sure if the manager is wry or unfriendly.

View hotels out the Via Capo: These hotels are outside of town near the cape (straight out the Corso Italia which turns into Via Capo, thirty minutes on foot, five by taxi, or a bus ride away). It's an easy walk to the Punta del Capo from here.

Pension La Tonnarella (L65,000 doubles, obligatory L80,000 per person half-pension with a fine dinner in the summer, many rooms with view balconies, Via Capo 31, tel. 878 1153) a splurge worth every lire if you've got it. A classic Sorrentine villa, beautifully maintained inside and out with several terraces, stylish tiles, killer views, and an elevator down to its private beach. Ideally, reserve long in advance.

Hotel Minerva (L140,000 doubles with no summer half-pension requirement, Via Capo 30, tel. 878 1011). Very friendly, fluent English-speaking owners have lovingly restored this dream place. Great Mediterranean views, a spectacular terrace, and cliff-hanging swimming pool complement large tiled rooms with balconies. Peasants sneak in a picnic dinner and just enjoy hanging out here.

Pension Elios (L60,000-70,000 depending on plumbing, Via Capo 33, tel. 878 1812) is the Via Capo bargain. Luigi and Maria, an adorable couple who speak no English, offer simple but spacious rooms, many with balconies and views. A fine roof terrace and a warm welcome hide behind its ugly exterior.

Eating in Sorrento

Dining out is reasonable here. If you fancy a picnic dinner on your balcony or the hotel terrace or in the public garden, you'll find many markets and take-out pizzerias in the old town.

Splurges: **La Tonnarella** (see accommodations for directions, a 20-minute walk from the Piazza Tasso) offers fine views, terraces, and exquisite Sorrentine cooking. En route you'll pass another well-reputed view restaurant, **La Minervetta**. Arrive at either of these restaurants before sunset. In the city center, try the **Parruchana** (Corso Italia 71) for fine regional cooking.

For a less expensive meal in the center, **Sant Antoninos** offers friendly service, red checkered tablecloths, an outdoor patio, and good pasta (just off the P. Sant Antonino on Santa Marie delle Grazie 6). The nearby and smaller **Pizzeria Da Gigino** (first road to the right of Sant Antonino) is also good. **Pizzeria Giardiniello** (Via Accademia 7) is a family show offering great food and great prices.

Sorrento Area Sightseeing Highlights

See tomorrow.

DAY 15

SORRENTO SIDE TRIPS: POMPEII, AMALFI, CAPRI

Depending on your energy, you can spend today enjoying Sorrento with a quick trip to Pompeii. Or you can be more aggressive and plug in some more travel either to the Amalfi coast or over to the touristic but scenic island of Capri.

Suggested Schedule	
9:00	Train to Pompeii, tour sight.
12:00	Return to Sorrento, lunch and siesta.
15:00	Either bus to Amalfi coast town or boat to Capri.

Transportation around Sorrento and Amalfi Trains to Pompeii: Circumvesuviana trains leave at least hourly—30 minutes to Pompeii, 45 minutes to Herculaneum, 70 minutes to Naples, all on the same line.

Boats to Capri, Iscia, Naples, and Positano on the Amalfi coast: Several lines compete with regular boats and hydrofoils all leaving from Sorrento's port. Capri boats go about hourly for L9000 round-trip (the 15-minute hydrofoil ride is more expensive). Boats to Positano cost L7000 or L12,000 return. Shop around the town center for tickets. Walk down from Piazza Tasso or catch the bus to the port.

Buses to Amalfi coast towns and Salerno: Blue SITA buses depart from the train station about every two hours, stop at all Amalfi coast towns (Positano in 45 minutes, Amalfi in 90 minutes), and end up in Salerno at the far end of the coast in just under three hours. Buy tickets at the station before boarding. You may have to change in Amalfi to get to Salerno.

Within and around Sorrento: The orange city buses skirt the town center, running along Via degli Aranci from the station to the Punta del Capo, in the other direction to the beach at Meta, and down to the port (L1000 tickets, good for 90 minutes, sold at tabacchi shops).

Getting your own wheels: You could spend L35,000 to rent a moped or L50,000 for a vespa (and L650,000 if it's stolen, Corso Italia 210, tel. 878 1386). Forget renting a car unless you enjoy traffic jams in the Italian sun.

Sightseeing Highlights—South of Naples

▲ **Sorrento**—Take time to stroll and explore the surprisingly pleasant old city. Don't miss the evening passegiata along the Corso Italia, peaking at Piazza Tasso. If you need immediate tanning, you could rent a chair on the pier by the port, though the best nearby sandy beach is at Meta, 20 minutes toward Naples via orange city bus from the station. The Foreigners Club (backyard of the TI, public W.C.) was established to provide reasonably priced snacks and drinks, relaxation and views, and a handy place for visitors to meet locals. It has live music on summer evenings.

▲ **Bus trip to Sant Agata, Il Deserto**— Like the Amalfi coast road, this is another beautiful cliff-hanger punctuated by lemon groves, olive orchards, and wild flowers. Finish your day here for the single best view over both sides of the peninsula. From the end of the line, Sant Agata, walk toward Sant Agata's church. The village of Sant Agata is nothing special, but you'll find it refreshingly unspoiled and a decent place for dinner (20 minutes one way, departures via blue SITA bus about every 30 minutes from the station, buy 2 one-way L1600 tickets in the station café).

▲ **Bus ride, bike ride, or walk to Punta del Capo**—
From Sorrento walk 40 minutes or take the 10-minute bus ride (orange city bus from station, two departures per hour, L1000) to the end of the road for a rocky but accessible traffic-free swimming area and a stunning view of Sorrento and Naples. The very ruined Roman Villa di Pollio marks this discovered but beautiful cape. If you're walking, cross from the Hotel Solara, down the street with the small grocery store on the corner. No matter how you arrive, walk to the end of the dead-end street with the modern church to the left, then veer left down a narrow, very cobbled lane to the beach where the street ends.

▲▲▲ **Pompeii**—Pompeii, stopped in its tracks by the eruption of Mount Vesuvius in A.D.79, offers the best look anywhere at what life in Rome must have been like 2,000 years ago. An entire city of well-preserved ruins is yours to explore. Once a thriving commercial port of 20,000, Pompeii grew from Greek and Etruscan roots before becoming an important Roman city. When Vesuvius blew, it buried Pompeii under 30 feet of hot mud and volcanic ash. For archaeologists this was a windfall, teaching them much about ancient Roman culture. It was rediscovered in the 1600s, and the first excavations began in 1748 (open from 9:00 to an hour before sunset, L10,000).

Orientation and Tips on Touring Pompeii
While the modern town of Pompei is spelled with one "i," the ancient site has two. Pompeii is halfway between Naples and Sorrento, a half hour from either by the Circumvesuviana train. Get off at the Villa dei Misteri, Pompei Scavi stop. (You can check your bag here for L1000 or as you enter the site for free.) From the station, veer right and cross the street to the entrance. You'll be signed down a path about 150 meters to buy your ticket (L10,000), then returned to the same entry (Porta Marina) to enter. Don't pay more than L5000 for the guidebook to Pompeii. The L10,000 *Pompeii, Past and Present* book allows you to re-create the ruins with overlays. The TI has a Pompeii layout (just beyond the ticket office on the side of the large restaurant to the right, look for the blue "i"). Allow two to three hours to see Pompeii. To understand what you're seeing, a guidebook is a good investment.

Entering through the Porta Marina, you'll walk straight past the Antiquarium (first building on your right, see its various artifacts and several eerie casts of well-preserved victims) to the Forum.

The Forum was Pompeii's commercial, religious, and political center. Probably the most ruined part of Pompeii, this area is, nonetheless, impressive with a market

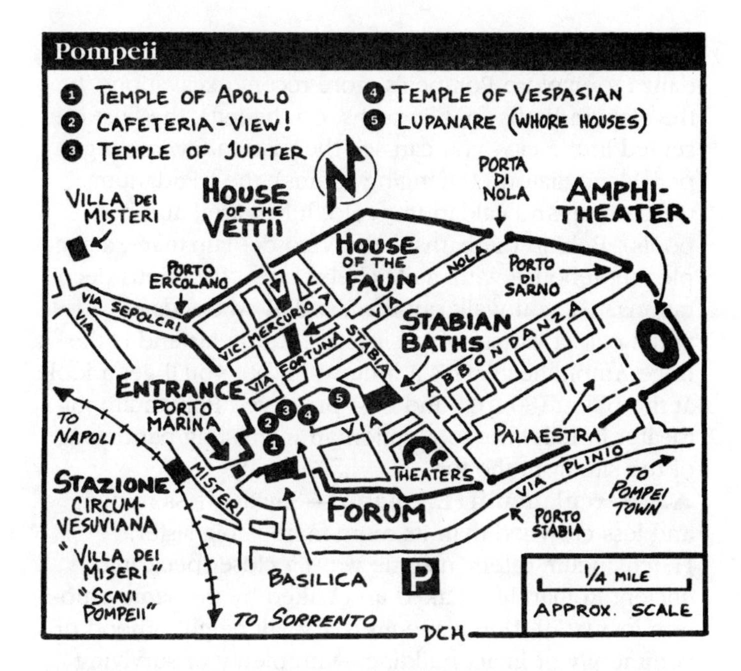

building (Macelleum), several temples, the "basilica" (Pompeii's largest building), which was used for legal and commercial business, and some interesting casts of volcano victims displayed on the side (nearest the Porta Marina entrance). From the Forum, walk past the twentieth-century cafeteria (which offers a rooftop view of the site) down Via del Foro, which becomes Via di Mercurio, into Pompeii's oldest quarter where you'll find the most interesting houses. Don't miss the House of Vettii, home of two wealthy brothers, both merchants, who enjoyed erotic wallpaper (for a tip, the guard will give you a peep). As you wander through the site, ask guards to let you into various houses and buildings, many of which are locked, or tag along with a tour if you can. Inside homes, you'll find frescoes, paintings, and mosaics that give you a feel for—at least the rich man's—workaday Roman life. The flat stones that cross the streets like crosswalks allowed pedestrians to cross during rain-storms.

Return to the Forum and walk left out Via dell' Abbondanza to explore Pompeii's more recent excavations. In the Stabian Baths (public baths, on the left), the best preserved in the city, you can see the piscina (swimming pool), spogliatorio (changing rooms), the frigidarium, tepidarium, and caldarium (cold, lukewarm, and hot pools). Behind the baths is the Vico del Lupanare, a simple whorehouse with, as Michelin says, "licentious decorations." As you walk out the Via dell' Abbondanza, you'll pass a variety of businesses. At the far end is the huge Amphitheater. It's a long walk, but you'll get a look at the oldest (80 B.C.) and best-preserved Roman amphitheater in Italy, not to mention an interesting panorama of the site from the top.

▲▲ Herculaneum (Ercolano)—Smaller, less ruined, and less crowded than its more famous big sister, Herculaneum offers in some ways a closer peek into ancient Roman life. Caked and baked by the same eruption in A.D. 79, Herculaneum is a small neighborhood or community of intact buildings with plenty of surviving detail (15 minutes from Naples on the same train that goes to Pompei and Sorrento, turn right and follow the yellow signs, 5 minutes downhill from the Ercolano station, open 9:00 until one hour before sunset, L10,000).

A Volcanic Bus Ride? For an easy trip up to the 4,000-foot summit of Vesuvius, mainland Europe's only active volcano (sleeping restlessly since 1944), catch the blue Vesuvio bus from the Ercolano (Herculaneum) station (45-minute ride, six a day), which drops you a 30-minute hike from the top for a commanding view, desolate lunarlike surroundings, and hot rocks. You'll have to be escorted by a "guide" (bus and guide costs around L10,000 total).

▲▲▲ Bus ride along Amalfi coast—One of the world's great bus rides, this trip will leave your mouth wide open and your film exposed. You'll gain a respect for the Italian engineers who built the road—and even more respect for the bus drivers who drive it. The hyperventilation caused by winding around so many breathtaking cliffs makes the Mediterranean, 500 feet below, really

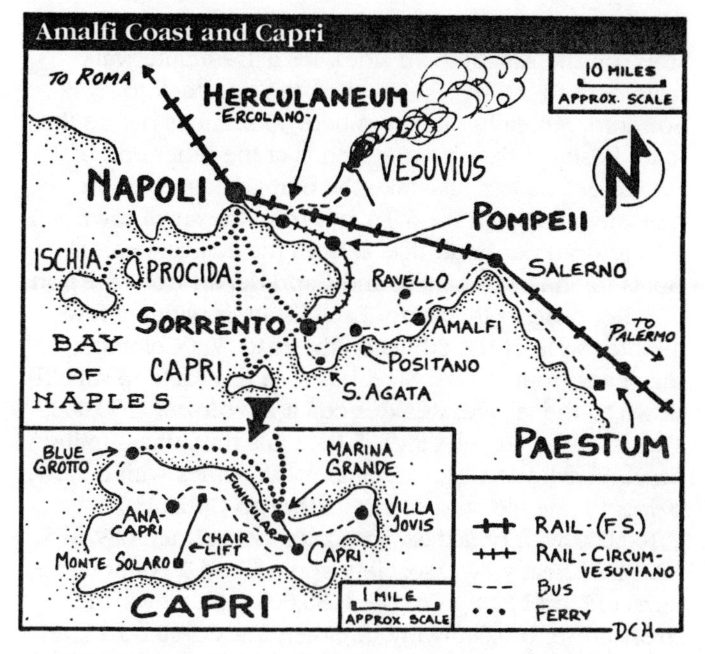

twinkle. Cantilevered garages, hotels, and villas cling to the vertical terrain, and beautiful sandy coves tease from far below and out of reach. Gasp from the right side of the bus as you go and the left on the way back (if you return by bus). Traffic is so heavy that in the summer, local cars are allowed to go in one direction only (buses and tourists foolish enough to drive are excluded). The Amalfi coast towns are pretty to look at but generally touristic, congested, overpriced, and a long hike above tiny beaches. The real thrill here is the scenic drive, which I'd do tomorrow on the way to Paestum.

▲ **Positano**—Specializing in scenery and sand, Positano sits halfway between Sorrento and Amalfi at the most spectacular stretch of the coast. The village, a three-star sight from a distance, is a pleasant, if expensive, gathering of women's clothing stores and cafés with a superb beach. There's little to do here but enjoy the beach and views and window shop. Consider a day trip from Sorrento; take the bus out and afternoon ferry back. After dark, walk out of town to see the village glitter.

To minimize your climb, use the last Positano bus stop (on the Amalfi town side). It's a 15-minute walk from here to the beach. To catch the bus back to Sorrento, remember it leaves here 15 minutes before the main Positano departure, which is at the other end of Positano. You can also take the orange bus up to the highway and catch the SITA bus from the small town square (two per hour, tickets from the adjacent café). Boats to Sorrento, Amalfi, and Capri depart from the port.

Sleeping in Positano: Each listing is within a few minutes walk of the others on the road, Via Colombo, that leads from the last SITA bus stop (en route to Amalfi) down to the village. **Residence La Tavolozza** (L90,000, Via Colombo 10, tel. 089/875 040) is a tiny, unassuming hotel. Flawlessly restored, each room comes with a view, balcony, fine tile, and silence. **Albergo California** (L100,000 with breakfast, Via Colombo 141, tel. 089/875 382) has great views, spacious rooms, and a comfortable terrace. **Hotel Bougainville** (L80,000 with views and street noise, L60,000 without either, Via Colombo 25, tel. 089/875 047), Positano's bargain, is a fine, spotless place with eager-to-please owners and comfortable rooms. The pizzerias on the beach are a bit overpriced but pleasant. Consider a balcony, terrace, or beach picnic dinner.

Amalfi—I'd skip this most overrated of the Amalfi coast villages. The waterfront is dominated by a bus station, a parking lot, and two gas stations. The main street through the village, hard for pedestrians to avoid, is packed with cars and bully mopeds. If marooned here, stay at the **Hotel Amalfi** (Via dei Pastai 3, tel. 089/87 24 40) or hike 15 minutes to the tiny town of Atrani, right on the beach, and stay in the A Scalinatella, an informal hostel with cheap beds and a user-friendly management (near the main square, tel. 871492).

▲▲ Capri—Made famous as the vacation hideaway of Roman emperors Augustus and Tiberius, these days Capri is a world-class tourist trap packed with gawky tourists in search of the rich and famous and finding only their prices. The four-mile by two-mile "Island of Dreams" is a zoo in July and August. Other times of year it provides a relaxing and scenic break from the cultural gauntlet of Italy. While Capri has some Roman ruins and an interesting monastery, its chief attraction is its famous Blue Grotto, and its best activity is a scenic hike.

To most, a visit to the Blue Grotto is a must. While most go by ferry from Marina Grande, you can save money by catching the bus from Anacapri or hiking. Admission, by rowboat with a guide, is L12,000. Touristy and commercial as this ail is, the grotto, with its eerily beautiful blue sunlight reflecting through the water, is an impressive sight (open daily 9:00 until an hour before sunset except in stormy weather).

From Anacapri, ride the chair lift to the 1,900-foot summit of Monte Solaro for a commanding view of the Bay of Naples and a pleasant downhill hike through lush vegetation and ever-changing views, past the fourteenth-century Chapel of Santa Maria Cetrella and back into Anacapri.

Emperor Tiberius's now-ruined Villa Jovis is a very scenic one-hour hike from Capri town. Supposedly, Tiberius ruled Rome from here for a decade (in about A.D. 30).

While you can take the boat from Naples, the ride from Sorrento is much quicker and cheaper. From the ferry dock at Marina Grande, a funicular will lift you 500 feet to the cute but most touristy town, Capri. From there buses go regularly to the still cute but more bearable town of Anacapri. The tourist information office (tel. 081/837 0634, room-finding service) and a baggage check service are next to the dock in Marina Grande.

DAY 16

AMALFI COAST, PAESTUM, NIGHT TRAIN TO VENICE

After Italy's probably most hair-raising coastal joy ride, take a one-hour train ride back 2,500 years into the days when this part of Italy was called Magna Graecia (Greater Greece) to see the best bit of ancient Greece this side of Athens, the temples of Paestum. Then for a major change in scenery, sleep northbound on the train, past everything you've already seen, and wake up in Venice.

Suggested Schedule	
8:00	Catch the first bus along the Amalfi coast from Sorrento to Salerno.
12:00	Picnic on train (or bus) to Paestum.
14:00	Tour Greek ruins at Paestum.
17:00	Catch train back to Naples, Rome, and overnight to Venice.

Transportation by Bus or Train: Sorrento–Salerno–Paestum–Venice

From Sorrento, allow four hours to reach Paestum by scenic, hair-raising bus or three hours by smooth, no scenery train. Both options take you via Salerno, from which Paestum is an hour away by frequent bus or infrequent rail service. The Salerno–Paestum bus is usually more efficient than the train, but check at the Salerno station.

The Sorrento–Salerno blue SITA bus drops you 75 yards from the Paestum bus stop and 150 yards from the train station. Ask the driver to direct you to the station and/or Paestum bus stop. Check your bags at the train station (unless you think you'll find a direct Paestum–Naples train) and see if there's a convenient train to Paestum. If not, head back to the bus stop. Buses leave for Paestum about every half hour, and several companies offer the service from the same stop. Buy the L4000 ticket on board. (Schedules for rides to Paestum are potentially very frustrating on Sunday.)

To connect Sorrento to Paestum by train requires a

change back in Naples. Sorrento–Naples and Naples–Salerno are both about one-hour trips with hourly departures. (Note: the last Circumvesuviana stop is a 5-minute walk from Centrale station. Turn right from the exit and you'll hit Piazza Garibaldi. You may want to check your bag at Naples's, Centrale station.) To get from Salerno to Paestum, see above. From the Paestum train station, walk straight down the road for half a mile to the ruins.

Returning from Paestum to Salerno to Naples to Rome to Venice: Northbound buses leave from the far side of the street that borders the ruins. Flag down any bus, ask "Salerno?" and buy the ticket on board. Trains go regularly from Salerno to Naples to Rome. Some are direct. From Rome's Termini station you'll catch the night train to Venice. (There may be a night train from Naples. For safety and comfort, reserve a couchette in advance.)

Salerno Connections

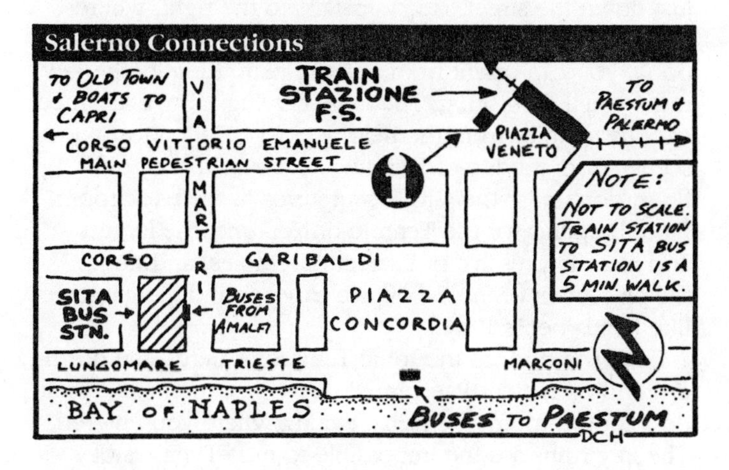

▲▲▲ Paestum

Paestum is one of the best Greek temples anywhere—and certainly one of the most enjoyable to tour. Serenely situated, it is surrounded by fields and wild flowers and has only a modest commercial strip. Founded as Poseidonia in the sixth century B.C., a key stop on an important trade route, its name would be changed to Paestum by occupying Romans in the third century B.C.

The final conquerors of Paestum, malaria-carrying mosquitoes, kept the sight wonderfully desolate for nearly a thousand years. Rediscovered in the eighteenth century, Paestum today offers the only well-preserved Greek ruins north of Sicily. (Open daily from 9:00 until one hour before sunset, museum closed Mondays, ticket sales end two hours before sunset, L8000 tickets include the museum across the street. Allow about two hours to tour the museum and site. Tel. 0828/811023.)

Orientation—Paestum

Salerno buses stop at the "secondary entrance" that leads to the lonely Temple of Ceres, across from a good bar/café with sandwiches and cappuccino. Get a feel for the very manageable scale of these ruins by looking through the fence, then visit the museum, opposite the entrance, just down the street. Head upstairs to the right, where you'll find a plan of the site. If you don't buy a guidebook, you can orient from this site plan. Identify the key ruins you'll be visiting. The large carvings above adorned various temples from the nearby city of Hera. Most are scenes from the life of Hercules. Back on the ground floor, don't miss the Greek sculptures in the back room. Find the plans for the Temple of Neptune, the largest and most impressive of Paestum's temples, and notice the placement of the decorative carvings and the gargoyle-like heads behind you.

Enter the ruins at the Ionic Temple of Ceres, the northern end of ancient Paestum. Survey the entire site. You'll do a loop through the ruins, exiting where you entered. The key ruins are the impossible-to-miss Temples of Ceres and Neptune and the Basilica. But the scattered village ruins are also interesting. Faint remains of swimming pools, baths, houses, a small amphitheater, and lone columns will stretch your imagination's ability to re-create this ancient city.

The misnamed Temple of Neptune, constructed in 450 B.C., a textbook example of the Doric style, dedicated to Hera, is simply overwhelming. Better preserved than the Parthenon in Athens, this huge structure is a tribute to

Greek engineering and aesthetics. Walk right in, sit right down, and contemplate the word "renaissance"—rebirth of this grand, Greek style of architecture. Notice how the columns seem to angle out (in fact they do). This was a trick ancient architects used to create the illusion from a distance of a perfectly straight building. All important Greek buildings were built using this technique. Now, imagine it richly and colorfully decorated with marble and statues.

Adjacent is the almost delicate Basilica (also dedicated to the Goddess Hera, 550 B.C.). Beyond these temples, you'll find traces of the old wall that protected Paestum. If you have time, walk out toward the train station to see the wall's eastern limit.

Should you get stuck in Paestum, the Albergo della Rosse (L55,000 doubles, tel. 0828/811070), which has a respectable restaurant, is just across from the main entry.

DAYS 17 and 18

VENICE

Soak—all day—in this puddle of elegant decay. Venice is Europe's best-preserved big city, a car-free urban wonderland of 100 islands, laced together by 400 bridges and 2,000 alleys.

Born in a lagoon 1,500 years ago as a refuge from barbarians, Venice is overloaded with tourists and slowly sinking (unrelated facts). In the Middle Ages, after the Venetians created a great trading empire, they smuggled in the bones of St. Mark (San Marco), and Venice gained religious importance as well.

Today, Venice is home to about 75,000 people in its old city, down from a peak population of around

Suggested Schedule

Day 17	
8:00	Arrive by train, find room.
9:30	Tour the Grand Canal by vaporetto, orient on Piazza San Marco.
11:00	Tour Doge's Palace, the Basilica San Marco, ride to top of Campanile, glass-blowing demonstration.
13:00	Lunch. How about a picnic in the breeze while you circle the city on Vaporetto 5?
15:00	Siesta in your hotel.
17:00	Shopping and strolling.
19:30	Dinner, or commence pub crawl.
Day 18	**Art lovers' plan**
9:00	Basilica dei Frari, Scuola di San Rocco.
10:00	Accademia Gallery.
12:00	Peggy Guggenheim modern art gallery.
14:00	Cruise the lagoon, leave early to see Verona or get more time in the Dolomites for hiking, or siesta and shop. Big decision: a second night in Venice or more time in the mountains.

200,000. While there are about 500,000 in greater Venice counting the mainland, not counting tourists, the old town has a small-town feel. Try to see small-town Venice through the touristic flack. Venice is worth at least a day on even the speediest tour.

Orientation and Arrival

The island city of Venice is shaped like a fish. Its major thoroughfares are canals. The Grand Canal snakes through the middle of the fish, starting at the mouth where all the people and food enter, passing under the Rialto Bridge, and ending at St. Mark's Square (San Marco). Leave your car and twentieth-century perspective at the mouth and let Venice swallow you whole.

The city has no real streets, and addresses are hopelessly confusing. There are six districts, each with about 6,000 address numbers. Navigate by landmarks, not streets. Actually, it's easy to find your way, since nearly every street corner has a sign pointing you to the nearest major landmark, such as San Marco, Rialto, and Ferrovia (for the train station), and most hotels and restaurants have neighborhood maps on their cards. (If you get lost, they love to hand them out to prospective customers.)

The tourist office's free "Pianta de Venezia" map, which shows the boat lines and landmarks, is adequate for most visits. A better 1:7,000 scale Venice map is sold at most souvenir stands. Consider buying the little sold-with-the-postcards guidebook with a city map, various walking tours, Grand Canal tour, and explanations of the major sights. Most people who have anything to sell to tourists (beds, meals, souvenirs) speak some English. Bank rates vary.

Only three bridges cross the Grand Canal, but several *traghetti* (little L500 ferry gondolas) shuttle locals and smart tourists across the canal, where necessary.

The public transit system is a fleet of bus-boats called *vaporetti*. They work like city buses except that they never get a flat, the stops are docks, and if you get off between stops you may drown. Most tickets cost L2200 and are bought at the dock before you board. Some

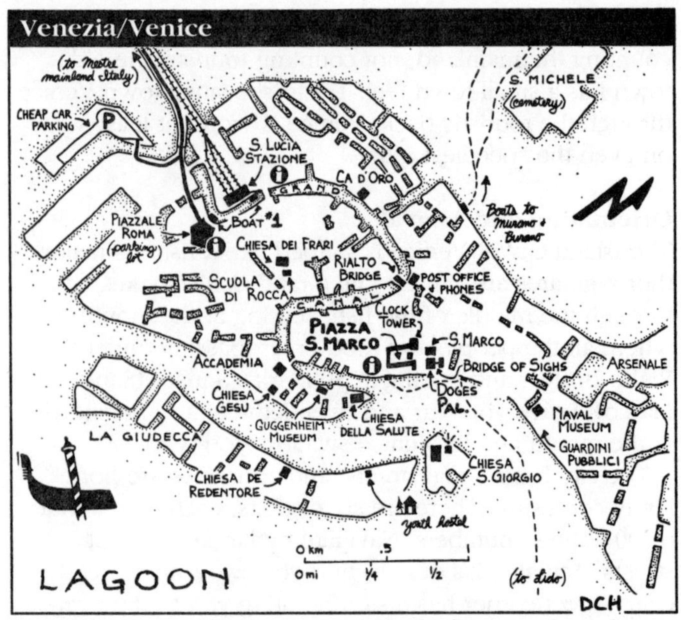

boats cost more. Stamp your ticket before you board or you may be fined. The 24-hour and 3-day passes are generally not worthwhile. Any city map shows the boat stops and routes. The TI or the boat information office at Piazzale Roma can give you the free ACTV Venice public transportation map.

Boat #1 is the slow boat down the Grand Canal (boats every 10 minutes, making every stop from Piazzale Roma to San Marco in about 45 minutes). Boat #34 does the Grand Canal trip (Piazzale Roma-train station-Rialto-San Marco) faster, with only a few stops. Boat #5 gives you an interesting circular tour of this island city (ride clockwise from San Marco, and get off at Fondamenta Nuove to avoid the long lagoon trip).

The best tourist information office is on St. Mark's Square (tel. 041/522 6356, hours vary, about 8:30-19:00 daily). Confirm your sightseeing plans, and get a map, a list of events, and the latest museum hours. Anyone under 30 with a photo can get a free *Carta Giovani* (youth pass) giving you discounts all over town (about 30% off at museums). You can grab the free periodical entertainment guide, *Un Ospite de Venezia,* at the reception desk of any expensive hotel. Telephone code: 041.

Accept the fact that Venice was a tourist town 400 years ago. It was, is, and always will be crowded. The crowds and tacky souvenir stalls vanish when you hit the back streets.

Parking in Venice: At Venice, the freeway ends like Medusa's head. Follow the green lights directing you to a parking lot with space. The standard place is Tronchetto (across the causeway and on the right) with a huge new multistoried garage. From there you'll find travel agencies masquerading as TIs and vaporetto docks for the boat connection to the town center.

Sightseeing Highlights—Venice

▲▲▲ Piazza San Marco—Surrounded by splashy and historic buildings and filled with music, lovers, pigeons, and tourists from around the world by day, and your pri-

Piazza San Marco

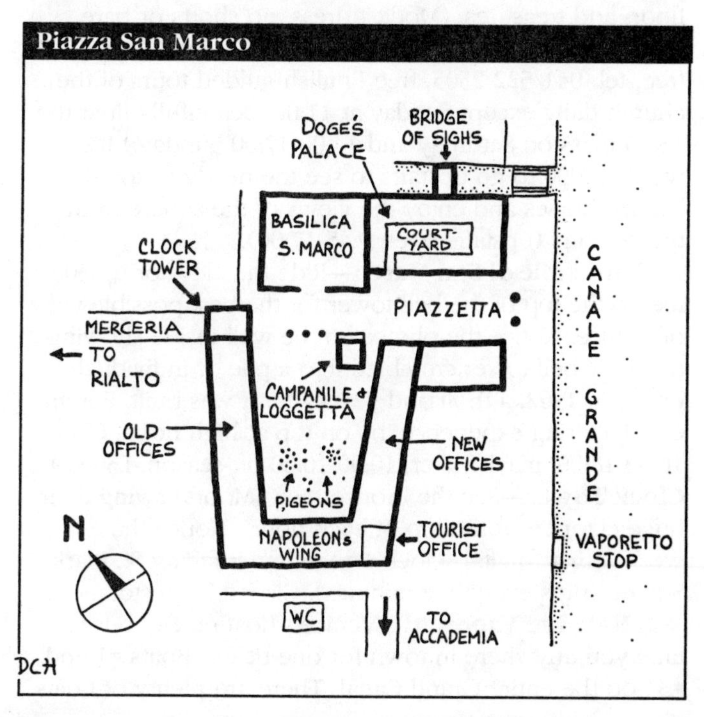

vate rendezvous with the Middle Ages late at night, Europe's greatest dance floor is the romantic place to be. This has the best tourist information office in town (in the rear corner), fine public rest rooms (behind the TI, see Helpful Hints below), and elegant cafés (L7500 for beer, but great people-watching and live music, explore their fine interiors, mooch a W.C.). Piazza San Marco is the first place to flood when the city gets a wind and a high tide.

▲▲ Doge's Palace (Palazzo Ducale)—The former ruling palace has the second largest wooden room in Europe, virtually wallpapered by Tintoretto, Veronese, and other great painters. The attached Bridge of Sighs leads to the prison; wave to the tourists gawking at you from the bridge (open 9:00-19:00, L8000). No tours: buy a guidebook on the street, or use *Mona Winks*.

▲▲ St. Mark's Basilica—For a thousand years, it has housed the saint's bones. Study the ceiling mosaics, the floor, and treasures. (Modest dress, no shorts or bare shoulders admitted, open 9:00-17:00, Sunday 14:00-17:00, free, tel. 041/522 2505, free English guided tours of the church daily except Sunday at 11:00, beautifully lit at the 18:45 mass on Saturday and 14:00-17:00 Sunday.) It's worth L2000 to go upstairs to see the newly restored bronze horses and enjoy the views of the square from the balcony (upstairs open 9:45-17:00).

▲ Campanile di San Marco—Ride the elevator up 300 feet to the top of the bell tower for the best possible view of Venice. Notice the photos on the wall inside showing how this bell tower crumbled into a pile of individual bricks in 1902, a thousand years after it was built. For an ear-shattering experience, be on top at high noon. (Open 10:00-18:00, maybe later, 10:00-16:00 off-season, L3000.)

Clock Tower—See the bronze men (Moors) swing their huge clappers at the top of each hour. Notice the world's first "digital" clock on the tower facing St. Mark's Square (flips every five minutes). Closed for restoration.

▲▲ Ride the Vaporetti—Venice's floating city buses take you anywhere in town for one ticket. Boats #1 and #34 do the entire Grand Canal. There are plenty of boats leaving from San Marco to the beach (Lido), as well as speedboat tours of Burano (a quiet, picturesque fishing and lace town), Murano (the glassblowing island), and Torcello (with the oldest churches and mosaics on an otherwise dull and desolate island).

▲▲ Grand Canal Tour—Grab a front seat on boat #34 (fast, 20 minutes) or #1 (slow, 45 minutes) to cruise the entire Canale Grande from the car park or train station to San Marco. While Venice is a barrage on the senses that hardly needs a narration, these notes will give the cruise a little meaning and help orient you to this great city. The small L2500 city map (on sale at most postcard racks) has a handy Grand Canal map on its back side.

Venice is built in a lagoon and sits on pilings—pine trees driven 15 feet into the mud. Over 100 canals, about 25 miles in length, drain the city. If they are streams, the Grand Canal is the river.

Venice is a city of palaces and the most impressive were built fronting this canal. This ride is the best way to really appreciate this unique and historic chorus line of lavish homes from the days when Venice was the world's richest city. Those days are long gone, and today many of these buildings are inhabited only by the green slime that lines lower steps of their now quiet canalside front doors. Europe's best-preserved medieval city is protected by strict laws that prohibit any changes in these buildings.

You'll start at Tronchetto or Piazzale Roma (the bus and car park) or the train station. Each night the steps of the modern concrete train station (first stop) are lined with backpackers in sleeping bags boycotting the city's expensive rooms. The gray building on the corner just before the station is the Mensa DLF, the public transportation workers' cafeteria, very cheap and open to you. The bridge across from the station is one of only three that cross the Canale Grande.

Vaporetto stop #4 (San Marcuola-Ghetto) is near the old Jewish quarter. This district was the world's original ghetto.

As you cruise, notice the traffic signs. This is the main thoroughfare of the city, and it's busy with traffic. You'll see all kinds of boats: taxis, police boats, garbage boats, even brown-and-white UPS boats.

Venice has about 500 sleek, black, and graceful gondolas. They are a symbol of the city, cost about $35,000, and are built with a slight curve so they can be propelled in a straight line by one oar. At several places along the Grand Canal you'll see traghetti gondolas ferrying pedestrians across where there are no bridges.

At the Ca d'Oro stop, notice the palace of the same name. For years it's been under a wooden case of scaffolding for reconstruction. Named the "House of Gold," it's considered the most elegant Venetian Gothic palace on the canal.

Just before the Rialto Bridge (on the right) you'll see the outdoor produce market. It bustles in the morning but is quiet and sleepy, with only a few grazing pigeons, the rest of the day.

The huge post office, usually with a postal boat moored at its blue posts, is on the left.

A symbol of Venice, the Rialto Bridge is lined with shops and tourists. Built in 1592, with a span of 42 meters, it was an impressive engineering feat in its day. Locals call the summit of this bridge the "ice box of Venice" for its cool breeze.

The Rialto was a separate town in the early days of Venice. It has always been the commercial district, while San Marco was the religious and governmental center. Today a street called the Merceria connects the two, providing travelers with a gauntlet of shopping temptations.

Take a deep whiff of Venice. What's all this nonsense about stinky canals? By the way, how's your captain? Smooth landings?

Notice how the rich marble facades are just a veneer covering no-nonsense brick buildings. Notice also the characteristic chimneys.

After passing the British consulate you'll see the old wooden Accademia Bridge, leading to the Accademia Gallery, which is filled with the best Venetian paintings.

Cruising under the bridge you'll get a classic view of the Salute church. They claim to have used over a million trees for the foundation of this church alone. Venice deforested much of the surrounding countryside. Trees were needed both to fuel the furnaces of its booming glass industry and to prop up this city in the mud.

The low white building on the right is the Peggy Guggenheim Gallery. She willed the city a fine collection of modern art.

As you prepare to deboat at stop 15—San Marco—look from left to right out over the lagoon. The green area in the distance is the public gardens, the only sizable park in town. Farther out is the Lido, with its beaches, casinos, and cars. The dreamy church that seems to float is the architect Palladio's San Giorgio (an interesting visit, great view from the top of its bell tower, L2000, 9:00-13:00, 14:00-18:00). And farther to the right is an island called the Guidecca.

▲▲ **Galleria dell' Accademia**—Venice's top art museum is packed with the painted highlights of the Venetian Renaissance (Bellini, Giorgione, Veronese, Tiepolo, and Canaletto). It is just over the wooden Accademia Bridge (Tuesday-Friday 9:00-19:30, Saturday and Monday 9:00-14:00, Sunday 9:00-13:00, expect delays as they allow in only 180 at a time, L8000, tel. 041/522 2247).

▲ **Museo Civico Correr**—The city history museum offers interesting snippets of Venetian life in the old days as well as great views of Piazza San Marco from its windows. Entry is on Piazza San Marco opposite the church (9:00-19:00 daily, 9:00-16:00 off-season, L5000).

▲ **Chiesa dei Frari**—This Gothic Franciscan church, an artistic highlight of Venice featuring three great masters, offers more art per lira than any other Venetian sight. Freeload on English-language tours to get the most out of the Titian *Assumption* above the high altar. Then move one chapel to the right to see Donatello's wood carving of St. John the Baptist almost live. And for the climax, continue right into the sacristy to see Bellini's *Madonna and the Saints.* Perhaps the greatest Venetian painter, Bellini's genius is obvious in the pristine clarity, believable depth, and reassuring calm of this three-paneled altarpiece. Notice the rich colors of Mary's clothing and

Venice "Downtown"

how good it is to see a painting in its intended setting. For many, these three pieces of art make the Accademia Gallery unnecessary. Before leaving, pay a visit to the neoclassical pyramid-shaped tomb of Canova and (opposite) the grandiose tomb of Titian, the Venetian. Compare the carved marble Assumption behind his tombstone portrait with the painted original above the high altar. (L1000, 9:00-12:00, 14:30-18:00.)

▲ **Scuola di San Rocco**—Next to the Frari church, another lavish building offers the richest collection anywhere of Tintoretto paintings (about 50 canvases painted over 22 years). The best paintings are upstairs, especially the *Crucifixion* in the smaller room. View the neck-breakingly splendid ceiling paintings with the mirrors (*specchio*) available at the entrance. (9:00-17:30 daily in summer, 10:00-13:00 off-season, last entrance a half hour before closing, L6000.)

▲ **Peggy Guggenheim Collection**—A popular collection of far-out art that so many try so hard to understand, including works by Picasso, Chagall, and Dali (11:00-18:00, closed Tuesdays, L7000; Saturday 18:00-21:00 and free).

Also, for modern art fans: in even-numbered years, Venice hosts a "World's Fair" of art, the Biennale, at the fairgrounds on Venice's "tail" (vaporetto: Biennale).

▲ **Gondola Rides**—This tradition is a must for many but a rip-off for most. Gondoliers charge about L70,000 for a 40-minute ride. You can divide the cost—and the romance—by up to six people (some take seven if you beg and they're hungry). For cheap gondola thrills, stick to the L500 one-minute ferry ride on the Grand Canal traghetti, or hang out on a bridge along the gondola route and wave at the romantics (such as along the Rio del San Lorenzo and Rio della Tetta).

▲ **Glassblowing**—It's unnecessary to go all the way to Murano Island to see glassblowing demonstrations. For the best show, wait near one of several glassworks near St. Mark's Square and follow any tour group into the furnace room for a fun and free ten-minute show. You'll usually see a vase and a horse made from molten glass. (I like the Murano Glass Factory across the hall from recommended Hotel San Gallo. See accommodations for directions). The commercial that always follows in the showroom is actually pretty entertaining. Be careful. Prices around San Marco's have a sizable tour guide commission built in. Serious glass shoppers will save plenty by finding a small shop on Murano Island.

▲▲ **Evening: The Stand-up Progressive Venetian Pub Crawl Dinner**—Venice's residential back streets hide plenty of characteristic bars with countless trays of interesting toothpick munchie food (*cicheti*). This is a great way to mingle and have fun with the Venetians. Real cicheti pubs are getting rare in these fast-food days, but locals can point you in the right direction, or you can follow the plan below.

Italian cicheti (hors d'oeuvres) wait under glass in bars; try fried mozzarella cheese, blue cheese, calamari, artichoke hearts, beans (*fagioli*), and anything ugly on a toothpick. Ask for a *piatto misto* (mixed plate). Drink the house wines. A small beer (*birrino*) or house wine costs less than L1000, meat and fish munchies are expensive, veggies are around L4000 for a meal-sized plate. When you're good and ready, ask for a glass of *grappa*. A good precaution might be to give each place L20,000 (or whatever) for your group and explain you want to eat and drink until it's dead (money morto-basta). Bars don't stay open very late, so start your evening by 19:00. Ask your hotel manager for advice—or to join you.

First course: Start on Campo San Bartolomeo near the Rialto Bridge. If the statue stepped back 20 yards, turned left, went under a passageway, over one bridge, to Campo San Lio, took a left past Hotel Canada, and over another bridge, he'd hit **Alberto's Osteria**, called simply Osteria on Calle Malvasia. This fine local-style bar has plenty of snacks and cicheti, available cheap from the bar. Say hi to Alberto, order with your best Italian (and by pointing), then sit or stand for same price (open until 20:30, closed Sunday, tel. 041/522 9038).

Second course: Leaving Alberto's, turn left and go basically straight with a jog to the left through a couple of squares to Campo Santa Maria di Formosa. Split a pizza with wine on the square (**Piero's Bar all' Orologio**, opposite the canal, has the worst pizza with the best setting.) When in doubt, I order the capricioso, the house specialty.

Third course: Fresh fruit and vegetables. After 50 years, **Giuseppe** still actually enjoys selling fresh fruit and vegetables on the square next to the water fountain (open until about 20:30).

Fourth course: Cicheti and wine. From Bar all' Orologio (on Campo S.M. Formosa), with your back to the church, head down the street to **Osteria Mascaron** (Gigi's bar, closes at 23:00 and on Sunday).

Fifth course: More cicheti and wine. Go down the alley across from Gigi's bar (Calle Trevisana o Cicogua), over the great gondola voyeurism bridge, down Calle Brasano to Campo S. Giovanni e Paolo. Pass the church-looking hospital (notice the illusions painted on its facade, maybe with a drink under the statue at Sergio's Caffe Bar Cavallo). Go over the bridge to the left of the hospital to Calle Larga Gallina, and take the first right to **Antiche Cantine Ardenghi de Luigi** (another Gigi) **Ardenghi** at #6369 under the red telephone (no sign for tax reasons, tel. 041/523 7691). This is a *cicheteria* (munchie bar supreme), and this Gigi, his sister, Barbara, and his mom, Germania, have made this bar very popular with locals. Open nightly, except Sunday, until 23:00.

Sixth course: Gelati. The unfriendly but delicious gelateria on Campo di Formosa closes at about 20:00 and on Thursdays. Those on San Marco stay open very late (the best is opposite the Doge's Palace on the bay).

You're not a tourist, you're a living part of a soft Venetian night. Street lamp halos, floodlit history, and a ceiling of stars make St. Mark's magic at midnight. The live music is an invitation to dance (no cover charge on Europe's finest open-air dance floor). Shine with the old lanterns on the gondola piers where the sloppy Grand Canal splashes at the Doge's Palace. Comfort the four frightened tetrarchs (ancient Byzantine emperors holding their swords and each other) under the moon near the Doge's Palace entrance. Smoke a breadstick. Cuddle history.

Side Trips from Venice

Several interesting places hide out in the Venice Lagoon. **Burano**, famous for its lace making, is a sleepy island with a sleepy community, giving you a look at village Venice without the glitz. Lace fans enjoy Burano's Scuola di Merletti (L5000, 9:00-18:00, Sunday until 16:00, closed Monday, tel. 730034).

Torcello is another lagoon island. This one's dead except for its church, which claims to be the oldest in Venice (L2000, 10:00-12:30, 14:00-17:00, tel. 730084). It's impressive for its mosaics but not worth a look on a short visit unless you really had your heart set on Ravenna and weren't able to make it there.

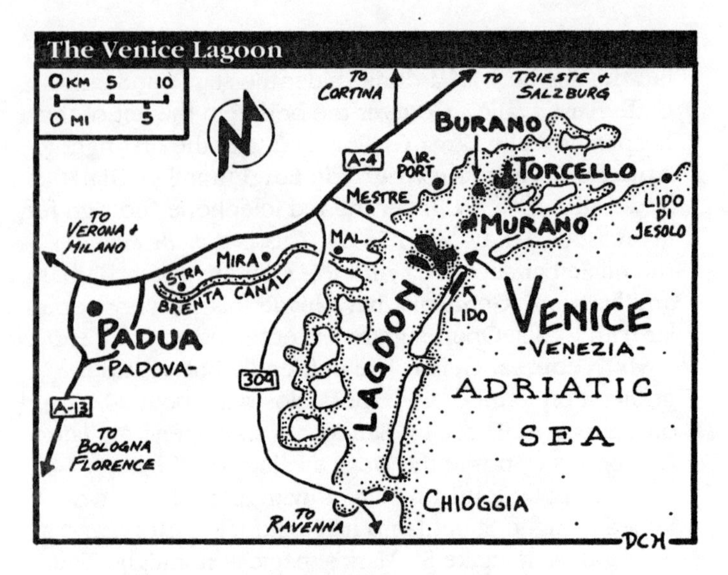

The island of **Murano**, famous for its glass factories, has the Museo Vetrario, which displays the very best of 700 years of Venetian glassmaking (L5000, 9:00-19:00, closed Wednesday, shorter hours off-season, tel. 739586). While the islands are reached easily but slowly by vaporetto, four-hour speedboat tours of these three lagoon destinations leave twice a day from the dock near the Doge's Palace.

The **Lido**, a quick boat ride from San Marco, is the Venice beach strip with fancy hotels, casinos, nightlife, a fun, if congested, beach scene . . . and cars.

Farther away, interesting but forgotten in the shadow of Venice, are Chioggia (Italy's top fishing port, a Venice with cars), Grado (a resort calling itself the "Mother of Venice," with lots of history and the fine Roman ruins of Aquileia), and Palmanova (a Renaissance planned town, the 1593 town of the future, with a unique snowflake street plan within a ten-sided wall).

Helpful Hints

Venetian churches and museums keep erratic hours. Double-check opening times, especially off-season (by telephone or with the TI's hours sheet). Churches are usually open at least from 10:00 to 12:00 and 16:00 to 18:00. Venice is the ideal town to explore on foot. Walk and walk to the far reaches of the town. Don't worry about getting lost. Get as lost as possible. Keep reminding yourself, "I'm on an island and I can't get off." When it comes time to find your way, just follow the directional arrows on building corners, or simply ask a local, "Dovè (DOH-vay) San Marco?" ("Where is St. Mark's?")

Try a siesta in the Giardini Publici (public gardens, in the tail area), on the Isle of Burano, or in your hotel. The area in the tail of the fish is completely untouristy, just canals, laundry, sleepy dogs, and Venetians.

Venetians pride themselves in having pure, safe, and tasty tap water, which is piped in from the foothills of the Alps.

While Venice is expensive, the window-shopping is fascinating. The best shopping area is around the Rialto Bridge and along the Merceria, the road connecting St. Mark's and the Rialto. Things are cheaper on the non-San Marco side of the Rialto Bridge. *Saldi* means "on sale."

Laundry time? There's a handy family-run *lavanderia* (laundromat) near St. Mark's and most of my hotel listings. The full-service Laundry Gabriella (open Monday-Friday 8:00-19:00, Rio Terra Colonne, one bridge off the Merceria near San Zulian church, tel. 5221758) does 9 pounds of laundry, wash and dry with a smile, for L15,000. Drop it by in the morning, pick it up that afternoon.

If bombed by a pigeon, resist the initial response to wipe it off immediately—it'll just smear into your hair. Wait until it dries and flake it off cleanly.

Sleeping in Venice (about L1300 = US$1)

Finding a room in Venice is actually easy if you go with one of my recommendations, call a few days in advance, reconfirm by telephone the morning of the day you plan to arrive, and arrive no later than midafternoon. While many choose to stay in a nearby less crowded place and side-trip to Venice, I can't imagine not sleeping with this beautiful city.

If you come in on the overnight train, chances are your room won't be ready, but any hotel will store your bag and move it in when the room is vacant and ready. So leave your bag and get out to enjoy the town.

There are clear hotel rules. The maximum price is posted in the lobby, including all extras; breakfast price is uncontrolled and, technically, must be optional. For any complaints, call 041/520 0911. Unless otherwise stated, all of the prices listed here include breakfast.

L60,000 is about rock bottom for a sleepable Venetian double. I've let location and character be my priorities. It's worth budgeting the money to stay in the old center and not in a dorm.

Near the Rialto Bridge or between it and San Marco: Albergo Guerrato (L65,000 doubles, L72,000 with shower, L95,000 with bath, walk over the bridge away from San Marco, go straight about two blocks, continue on Ruga dei Spezieri about 30 yards past long pink arcaded building; at the drugstore turn right on Calle drio la Scimia and you'll see the red sign, Calle drio la Scimia 240a, Rialto, tel. and fax 041/5227131 or 5285927), in a handy and colorful produce market, one minute from the Rialto action, is warmly run by English-speaking Biba, her husband, Roberto, and dog, Lord. Their old building is simple, airy, and wonderfully characteristic.

Locanda Sturion (L110,000-150,000 doubles, 5-bed room for L200,000, S. Polo, Rialto, Calle Sturion 679, 30125 Venezia, tel. 041/523 6243, fax 522 5702) is newly renovated with all the modern comforts overlooking the Grand Canal. Sergio, Sandro, and Nicole speak English and will hold a room until 16:00 with no deposit. Their 700-year-old hotel is located 100 yards and as many stairs from the Rialto Bridge (it's opposite the vaporetto dock, go over the bridge, left along the canal past four lamp posts, and you'll see the simple sign down an alley). The Rialto/canal view from the breakfast room makes the climb more bearable. You'll see this hotel's sign of the sturgeon (*sturion*) in a 400-year-old painting in the Accademia. Read the history on the lobby wall.

Hotel Canada (L125,000 doubles, Castello San Lio 5659, 30122 Venezia, tel. 041/522 9912, fax 041/523 5852) has 25 rooms, all with private showers, W.C., phones, and air-conditioning. In a "typical noble Venetian home," it's ideally located on a quiet square, just behind Campo San Bartolomeo between the Rialto and San Marco. (See directions to Alberto's under Evening highlight.)

Hotel Riva (two L70,000 shower-across-the-hall doubles on the fourth floor, campanile view but no elevator, L92,000 doubles with very modern showers, Ponte dell'Angelo 5310, Venezia, tel. 041/522 7034) is entirely redone, with gleaming marble hallways and bright modern rooms and is romantically situated on a canal along the gondola serenade route. You could actually dunk your breakfast rolls in the canal (but don't). Sandro will hold a corner (*angolo*) room if you ask. It's a couple blocks behind San Marco where the canals Rio di San Zulian and Rio del Mondo Nouvo hit Rio Canonica o Palazzo.

Hotel San Gallo (L90,000-125,000 doubles, San Marco 1093/A, 30124 Venice, tel. 041/522 7311 or 528 9877, fax 522 5702) is about 100 yards off Piazza San Marco (with back to the church, take the second to last archway right off St. Mark's Square) is on a very quiet little square, clean, and serves breakfast on the chirpy breezy roof garden. English is spoken by Antoinella, Luca, and Sandro, the same people who bring you Locanda Sturion.

Albergo Doni (twelve L80,000 doubles, showers down the hall cost extra, Riva Schiavoni, San Zaccaria N. 4656—Calle del Vin, tel. 041/5224267) is a dark, woody, clean, and quiet little place run by a likable smart-aleck named Gina. One minute from San Marco, it's two bridges behind the church, or walk east along the San Marco waterfront (Riva Degli Schiavoni), over two bridges, take the first left, and follow the signs.

Locanda Casa Petrarca (L60,000-80,000 doubles without breakfast, Calle Schiavone 4386, with your back to St. Mark's, take the last right off the square, it's two blocks before Campo San Luco, just down Calle dei Fuseri, second turn on left, tel. 520 0430), wicker-cozy, and my listing closest to a private home, hangs like an ivy-framed painting over a dead-end alley. Nelli, a friend as well as a host, speaks English. With only six rooms and listed in seven guidebooks, she doesn't need to serve breakfast and holds rooms only until 13:00 with a phone call.

Alloggi Ai Do Mori (L55,000 doubles without breakfast, or L25,000 in shared four-bed rooms, Calle Larga San Marco, 658 San Marco, tel. 041/520 4817) is incredibly central, one block off St. Mark's and the bell tower with the two Moors, which it's named after (next to Wendy's). The place has lots of long, narrow stairways and peeling green wallpaper, and the finishing touches are pretty flimsy, but the rooms and facilities are clean and functional, the management is friendly, and it's much handier than the hostel.

In other parts of Venice: Hotel Marin (L54,000 doubles, L80,000 with bath, breakfast an optional L7000, from the train station, cross the bridge and go behind the big green domed church—right, left, right, and right to San Croce 670b, tel. and fax 041/718022) is directly across the canal and over a church from the station but out of the touristic bustle of the Lista di Spagna. Cozy, plain, and cheery, it will seem like home the moment you cross the threshold.

Albergo alla Salute 'Da Cici (L80,000-120,000, 222 Salute, a few blocks to the right of the Salute church, a long walk but just one vaporetto stop from San Marco, tel. 041/523 5404, fax 522 2271) is a close but off-the-beaten-path alternative, with a peaceful garden.

Locanda Sant' Anna (L70,000-80,000, Castello 269, tel. 041/528 6466) is a garden of peace tucked away from all the hustle and bustle of Venice out in the "tail of the fish." Go to the far end of Venice, walk down Via Garibaldi almost to Isolo di San Piero, turn left over a bridge onto Ponte Sant' Anna street, then first right into a small square. The sign is a very small plaque on a door. Son, Walter, speaks English.

Foresteria della Chiesa Valdese (L22,000 dorm beds or L60,000 doubles with sheets and breakfast included, more expensive for one-night stays, with some larger "apartments" for small groups, from Campo Santa Maria Formosa walk past the Orologio bar to the end of Calle Lungo and cross the bridge, Castello 5170, tel. 041/5286797, closed 13:30-18:00) is run by a Protestant church offering cheap dorm beds at nearly youth hostel prices in a handier location (halfway between San Marco and Rialto) and more intimate setting. It's located in a run-down but charming old palace with elegant paintings on the ceilings and has a friendly management.

The **Venice youth hostel** (L18,000 per person with sheets and breakfast in 4- to 6-bed rooms, on Giudecca Island, tel. 041/523 8211, Zittele stop on boat #5) is crowded, clean, cheap, efficient, and newly remodeled. Reception accepts no telephone reservations but can tell you what's available (desk open 7:00-9:00, 18:00-21:00, lock-up at 23:00). Their budget cafeteria welcomes non-hostelers.

Each summer, the city uses a few elementary schools to house budget travelers with sleeping bags. The tourist office has a list of these options, but they're not much cheaper than simple pensions.

Eating in Venice, near Campo San Bartolomeo

While none of these places are worth a journey, they are each handy, decent values. All are just off the very central Campo San Bartolomeo (a block toward San Marco from the Rialto Bridge). Directions are based on the statue in this square's center.

The very local, hustling **Rosticceria San Bartolomeo/Gislon** (Calle della Bissa 5424, 20 yards behind the statue to its left, under a passageway, tel. 041/522 3569, open 10:00-14:30, 17:00-21:00, closed Monday) is a cheap and confusing self-service restaurant on the ground floor (L5000 pasta, prices listed at door, stools along the window) with good but pricier meals in its full-service restaurant upstairs.

If the statue on the square were to jump off his pedestal, walk ahead 50 yards, and look down a narrow alley to the left, he'd see a fat hula girl. That's the **Pizzeria Bora Bora**, with a fun menu and good prices (less a 10% discount if you show them this book, closed Wednesday). Across the alley from Bora Bora is the **Devil's Forest Pub**, English decor and self-service Italian food (L6000 pasta, no cover, open late, closed Monday).

Ristorante Pizzeria da Nane Mora (behind the statue, past PTT, over the bridge, and right at the red Santuario Madonna della Grazie church, on a tiny triangular square) has good pizza and indoor/outdoor seating.

For low-stress budget meals, you'll find plenty of self-service restaurants (*Self-service* in Italian). One is right at the Rialto Bridge. Pizzerias are cheap and easy. The **Wendy's** just off San Marco on Calle Larga San Marco serves a L7000 all-you-can-eat salad bar. Another budget saver is bar snacks. You'll find plenty of stand-up mini-meals in out-of-the-way bars. Order by pointing.

My favorite Venetian dinner is the **pub crawl** described above under Sightseeing Highlights. Any of the listed bars would make a fine stop for a sit-down dinner.

The produce market that sprawls for a few blocks just past the Rialto Bridge is a great place to assemble a picnic. The nearby street, Ruga Vecchia, has good bakeries and cheese shops.

Warning: Any place serving food on the Grand Canal, on St. Mark's, or along the main road connecting the two, may have a pleasant setting but is not a good value.

Itinerary Options for Day 18: Distractions West of Venice

Five important towns and possible side trips in addition to the lakes and the Dolomites make zipping directly from Venice to Milan (3-hour trip, hourly departures) a route strewn with temptation.

The towns of Padua, Vicenza, Verona, Bergamo, and Ravenna are all, for various reasons, reasonable stops. But none are essential parts of the best 22 days Italy has to offer. The side trips to the lakes and the Dolomites are unique and distinct from anything we've seen so far and are worked in as part of the core suggested itinerary below (covered in Days 19 through 22). Of the towns

Temptations: Venice to Milan

discussed below, only Ravenna (2.5 hours from Padua or Florence) is not on the main train line.

Padua

Just 30 minutes by train from Venice, Padua is seen by some as an easy home base from which to explore Venice. I'd rather flip-flop it, sleeping in Venice and side-tripping to Padua. Living under Venetian rule for four centuries seemed only to sharpen Padua's independent spirit. Nicknamed "the brain of Veneto," Padua has a prestigious university (founded 1222) and was called home by smart guys like Galileo, Dante, and Petrarch.

The old town is a colonnaded time-tunnel experience, and Padua's museums and churches hold their own in Italy's artistic big league, with masterpieces by Giotto (a well-preserved cycle of over thirty frescoes in the Chapel of the Scrovegni, Mantegna, important, but devasted by WW II bombs, frescoes in the Church of the Eremitani) and Donatello (his Crucifixion with statues of Mary and Padua's six patron saints on the high altar of the Basilica di Sant'Antonio and his great equestrian statue—the first since ancient Roman times—of the Venetian mercenary general Gattamelata, on Piazza del Santo outside the Basilica).

The tourist information office is in the station (tel. 049/8750655). **Hotel Piccolo Vienna** (L40,000-50,000, Via Beato Pellegrino 133, tel. 049/8716441) is small and near the station. **Hotel Verdi** (L40,000, bus #6 from the station to Teatro Verdi, Via Dondi dell'Orologio 7, tel. 049/663450) is in the old center. The well-run **Ostello Citta di Padova** (bus #8 or #12 from the station, Via Aleardi 30, tel. 8752219) packs over a hundred L15,000 beds into 13 rooms as comfortably as a hostel can. Many budget travelers enjoy making this hostel a low-stress, low-price home base from which to tour Venice.

Vicenza

To many architects, Vicenza (less than an hour by train from Venice) is a pilgrimage site. Entire streets look like the back of a nickel. This is the city of Palladio, the sixteenth-century Renaissance architect who gave us the "Palladian" style, so influential in Britain (countless country homes) and the U.S.A. (It was the style of choice for American slave owners, like Thomas Jefferson, whose Monticello was inspired by Palladio's Rotonda, a private but sometimes tourable Palladian residence on the edge of Vicenza.)

For the casual visitor, a quick stop offers plenty of Palladio. From the train station, catch any bus (L1000) to Piazza Matteotti where you can visit the tourist office (Piazza Matteotti 12, tel. 0444/320854, pick up a map). From there see the Olympic Theater, Palladio's last and one of his greatest works. This oldest indoor theater in Europe is still used and is considered one of the world's best.

From the Olympic Theater begin your stroll down Vicenza's main drag, a steady string of Renaissance palaces and Palladian architecture peopled by Vicenzans who keep their noses above the tourist trade and are considered by their neighbors as uppity as most of their colonnades.

After a few blocks, you'll see the huge Basilica standing over the Piazza dei Signori, which has been the town center since Roman times. It was young Palladio's proposal to redo the dilapidated Gothic palace of justice in his neo-Greek style that established him as Vicenza's favorite architect. The rest of his career was a one-man construction boom. Notice the thirteenth-century 280-foot-tall tower and the Loggia del Capitanio (opposite the basilica), one of Palladio's last works.

Finish your Corso Palladio stroll by walking to Piazzale Gasperi (where the PAM supermarket is a handy place to grab a picnic for the train ride) and walk five minutes down Viale Roma back to the station. Trains leave about every half hour toward Venice and Milan/Verona. **Hotel Vicenza** (L50,000-70,000, Piazza Signori at Stradella dei Nodari, tel. 0444/321512) is a rare, reasonable place in the Palladian center of things.

Verona

Verona is a household word because it's the hometown of Romeo and Juliet. But, alas, a visit here has nothing to do with those two star-crossed lovers. While you can pay to visit the house falsely claiming to be Juliet's, with an almost believable but slathered-with-tour-groups balcony, and you can even make a pilgrimage to what isn't La Tomba di Giulietta, the town has been an important crossroads for 2,000 years and is therefore packed with history. (R and J fans will take some solace in the fact that two real feuding families, the Montecchi and the Capellos, were the models for Shakespeare's Montagues and Capulets. And, if R and J existed and were alive today, they would recognize much of their "hometown.")

Verona's main attraction is its wealth of Roman ruins, the remnants of its thirteenth- and fourteenth-century political and cultural boom, and its twentieth-century, quiet, pedestrian's-only ambience. After Venice's festival of tourism, Veneto's second city (in population and in artistic importance) is a cool and welcome sip of just plain Italy.

Orientation

From the train station catch one of many buses to Piazza Brå (or walk about 15 minutes up boring Corso Porta Nuova) where you'll see the well-preserved Roman Arena (amphitheater). The Tourist Information office is behind the Arena to the right (Via Leoncino 61, tel. 045/592828). The most enjoyable core of Verona is along Via Mazzini between Piazza Brå and Piazza Erbe, Verona's medieval market square.

Sightseeing Highlights—Verona

Verona's Arena, on Piazza Brå, dates from the first century A.D. This elliptical, 140 by 120 meter amphitheater, the third largest in the Roman world, is well preserved and looks great in its pink marble. Over the centuries as many as 25,000 spectators at a time have cheered through Roman gladiator battles, medieval executions, and modern plays, including a popular opera festival every summer. Climb to the top for a fine city view (8:00-18:30, closed Monday, L6000).

Piazza Brå, down Via Mazzini, to Piazza Erbe—The highlight of Verona for me is the evening passagiata from the elegant cafés of Piazza Brå, through the old town on Europe's first major pedestrian-only street, to the bustling and colorful medieval market square, Piazza Erbe. (To see the House of Juliet, detour right from Piazza Erbe to Via Cappello #23.) Piazza Erbe is a photographer's delight with pastel buildings corralling the stalls, fountains, pigeons, and people that have come together here for centuries. Walking under the "arch of the whales rib" (look up) you'll continue into the Piazza dei Signori with its statue of a very pensive Dante. Poke around here. At the far end (through an arch on the right) you'll find the strange and very Gothic tombs of the Scaligeri family, who were to Verona what the Medici family was to Florence.

Walking further toward Ponte Pietra (a Roman bridge that survived until WW II), you'll come to two impressive churches (the Duomo and Sant' Anastasia) and just across the river, built into the hill above the Ponte Pietra, is

Verona's Roman Theater, which stages Shakespeare plays every summer (only a little more difficult to understand in Italian than in old English). From the Duomo, if you hike upstream you'll pass the well-preserved first-century Roman gateway, the Porta Borsari. Then, just before the castle, is the Roman triumphal arch, the Arco dei Gavi. The huge medieval castle, the Castlevecchio, is now an art museum (fine sixteenth- to eighteenth-century paintings, 8:00-18:30, closed Monday). Finally, a few blocks farther up the river, you'll find the twelfth-century Church of San Zeno Maggiore. This offers not only a great example of Italian Romanesque but a set of 48 paneled eleventh-century bronze doors nicknamed "the poor man's Bible" (pretend you're an illiterate medieval peasant and do some reading), and Mantegna's San Zeno Triptych (normally 7:00-12:30, 15:30-18:00).

Sleeping in Verona (about L1300 = US$1)
Cheap hotels in Verona are drab. **Albergo Volto Cittadella** (L36,000, just off Corso Porta Nuova, two blocks toward the station from Piazza Brå, Vicolo Volto Cittadella 8, tel. 045/8000077) is very simple but quiet, with an elevator, and handy to the center and station. **Hotel Catullo** (L35,000-55,000, off Via Mazzini between 1D and 3A at Via Valerio Catullo 1, tel. 8002786) is also sleepable and right in the middle of the old town. Tiny **Albergo Ristorante Ciopeta** (5 doubles, showers down the hall, L40,000-75,000, Vicolo Teatro Filarmonico 2, tel. 045/8033722, Sr. Cristofoli speaks un poco English) is more ristorante than albergo, but it's a cute little place right off Piazza Brå.

Two classier places just off Piazza Brå toward the river are **Hotel Cavour** (L77,000, two doubles with no shower for L48,000, no singles, Vicolo Chiodo 4, tel. 045/590508) and the noisier but newly remodeled **Albergo Al Castello** (L60,000, one L48,000 double, Corso Cavour 43, tel. 045/8004403).

The **Verona youth hostel** (L15,000 beds, bus #2 from the station, over the river beyond Ponte Nuovo at Salita Fontana del Ferro 15, tel. 045/590360) is one of Italy's best hostels.

Ravenna

Ravenna is on the tourist map for one reason—its 1,500-year-old churches decorated with best-in-the-West Byzantine mosaics. Briefly a capital of Eastern Rome during its fall, Ravenna was taken by the barbarians. Then in 539, the Byzantine emperor Justinian made the city Byzantium's lieutenant in the west. Ravenna was a light in the Dark Ages. Two hundred years later the Lombards booted Byzantine out and Ravenna melted into the backwaters of medieval Italy. Apart from being Dante's last home, Ravenna didn't made a history book for a thousand years. Today the city booms with a big chemical industry, the discovery of offshore gas deposits, and the construction of a new ship canal. It goes busily on its way while busloads of tourists slip quietly in and out of town for the best look at the glories of Byzantium this side of Istanbul.

Central Ravenna is quiet, with more bikes than cars and a pedestrian-friendly core. While not worth an overnight, it's only a 90-minute detour from the main Venice–Florence train line, and worth the effort for those interested in old mosaics. While all agree that Ravenna has the finest mosaics in the West, many will find their time better spent taking a careful look at the good but not as sublime Byzantine-style mosaics in Venice.

A visit to Ravenna can be as short as a two-hour loop from the train station. From the station, walk straight down Viale Farini to Piazza del Popolo. A right on Via IV Novembre takes you a block to the colorful covered market (Marcato Coperto, open for picnic fixings from 7:00-13:30). The tourist office is a block away (Via Salara 8, tel. 0544/35404, get a map). The two most important sights, Basilica di San Vitale and the Mausoleum of Galla Placidia, are two blocks away down Via San Vitale. On the other side of Piazza del Popolo is the Church of Sant'Apollinare Nuovo, also worth a look. From there you're about a five-minute walk back to the station. (Sights are open from 9:00-19:00, 9:00-16:30 October to March.)

Jot down on a scrap of paper when the next few trains depart for Ferrara (Venice) or Bologna (Florence). Three cheap hotels near the station are **Al Giaciglio** (Via R. Brancaleone 42, tel. 0544/39403), **Hotel Minerva** (Via Maroncelli 1, tel. 34549), and **Hotel Ravenna** (Via Varoncelli 12, tel. 22204). The **youth hostel** is a ten-minute walk from the station (follow the signs for Ostello Dante, Via Nicolodi 12, tel. 420405).

Ravenna's Sightseeing Highlights

▲▲ Basilica di San Vitale—It's impressive enough to see a 1,400-year-old church. But to see one decorated in brilliant mosaics that still convey the intended feelings of "this peace and stability was brought to you by your emperor and God" is rare indeed. Study each of the scenes: the arch of apostles with a bearded Christ at their head, the lamb on the twinkly ceiling, the beardless Christ astride a blue earth behind the altar and the side panels featuring Emperor Justinian, his wife Theodora (an aggressive Constantinople showgirl who used all her charms to gain power with—and even over—her emperor husband), and their rigid and lavish courts. San Vitale can be seen as the last of the ancient Roman art and the first of the Christian era. This church was the prototype for Constantinople's Hagia Sophia built 10 years later, and it inspired Charlemagne to build the first great church in northern Europe in his capital of Aix-la-Chapelle (present-day Aachen).

▲▲ Mausoleum of Galla Placidia—Just across the courtyard is the humble-looking little mausoleum with the oldest and, to many, the most impressive mosaics in Ravenna. The little light that sneaks through the thin alabaster panels brings a glow and a twinkle to the very early Christian symbolism (Jesus the good shepherd, Mark's lion, Luke's ox, John's eagle, the golden cross above everything) that fills the little room. Cover the light of the door with your hand to see the beardless Christ as the good shepherd. This was a popular scene with the early church.

▲ **Basilica of St. Apollinare Nuovo**—This austere sixth-century church, in the typical early Christian basilica form, has two huge and wonderfully preserved side panels. One is a procession of haloed virgins each bringing gifts to the Madonna and the Christ Child. Opposite, Christ is on his throne with four angels awaiting a solemn procession of 26 martyrs.

There are several other sights in town that can be explained at the TI. The **Church of Sant'Apollinare in Classe** with more great Byzantine art (three miles out of town, easy bus and train connections, tel. 47 30 04) is generally considered a must among mosaic pilgrims. For a quick stop, I'd see the three downtown sights, enjoy the covered market and the Piazza del Popolo, and catch the train. The nearby beach town of Rimini is an over-crowded and polluted mess.

DAYS 19 and 20

THE DOLOMITES, ITALY'S ALPS

Italy's dramatic limestone rooftop, the Dolomites, offers some of the best and certainly most unique mountain thrills in Europe. A special bonus is a feeling that the good weather is here to stay. You have a high-altitude world of Dolomite options.

Suggested Schedule

Day 19

8:00	Depart Venice.
12:00	Bolzano, get hike info, buy picnic at Erb Market.
14:00	Catch bus to Kastleruth.
16:00	Set up in Kastleruth.

Day 20

9:00	Long all-day Alpi di Suise hike.
18:00	Evening in Kastleruth.

For rugged hikers:

Day 18

12:00	Depart Venice, visit Bolzano, set up in Kastleruth.

Day 19

9:00	Catch bus to Alpi di Suise.
10.00	Hike to mountain hut.
Day 20	Continue hike from hut over mountain and back into Alpi di Suise. Sleep in Kastleruth.

Orientation

The Dolomites are well developed, and the region's famous valleys and towns suffer from an après ski fever. But the bold limestone pillars flecked with snow over green meadows under a blue sky offer a unique and worthwhile mountain experience. The cost for the comfort of reliably good weather is a drained-reservoir feeling. Lovers of the Alps may miss the lushness that comes with the unpredictable weather farther north.

A hard fought history has left the region bicultural with an emphasis on the German. Locals speak German first, and some wish they were still part of Austria. In the Middle Ages, the region faced north, part of the Holy Roman Empire. Later they were firmly in the Austrian Hapsburg realm. By losing World War I, Austria's South Tirol became Italy's Alto Adige. Mussolini did what he could to Italianize the region, including giving each town an Italian name. Even in the last decade, secessionist groups have agitated violently for more autonomy. The government has wooed locals with economic breaks that make it one of Italy's richest areas (as local prices attest) and today all signs and literature in the autonomous province of Süd Tirol/Alto Adige are in both languages. Many include a third language, Ladin, the ancient Latin-type language still spoken in a few traditional areas. (I have listed both the German and Italian so the confusion caused by this guidebook will match that caused by your travels.) The Dolomites are pronounced "doe-loe-mee-tin" in German and "doe-loe-MEE-tee" in Italiano.

In spite of all the glamorous ski resorts and busy construction cranes, the local color survives in a warm, blue-aproned, ruddy-faced, long-white-bearded way. There's yogurt and yodeling for breakfast. Culturally as much as geographically, the area reminds me of Austria. (Tirol is named for a village that is now actually in Italy.)

Lifts, trails, outdoor activity-oriented tourist offices, and a decent bus system make the region especially accessible. But things are expensive. Most towns have no alternative to hotels, which charge at least L30,000 per person, or private homes, which offer beds for as low as L20,000 but are often a fair walk from the town centers. Beds nearly always come with a hearty breakfast. Those traveling in peak season or staying for only one night are often penalized. Local TIs can always find budget travelers a bed in a private home (*Zimmer*).

The seasons are brutal. Everything is open, booming, full price, and normally crowded from July 20 through September 20. June 20 to July 20 and September 20 until the end of October are shoulder season. After about a month off, the snow hits and it's busy again until April. May and early June are dead. No lifts are running. The most exciting trails are still under snow. And most huts and budget accommodations are closed as locals are more concerned with preparing for another boom season than catering to the stray off-season tourist.

This is one region that understands the importance of tourist information. Each town has an excellent tourist office that can find you rooms in private homes and give you all the details you'll need to choose the right hike. They have excellent free maps and even entire books on local hikes available for free in English.

Before choosing a hike, get advice at the TI. Ideally, pick a hike with an overnight in a hut. Most huts, called *refugios*, offer reasonable doubles, cheaper dorm (*Lager*) beds, and good inexpensive meals. Telephone any hut to secure a spot before hiking there. A few Dolomite budget tips: Jausenstation is a place that serves cheap, hearty, and traditional mountain-style food to hikers. In local restaurants, there is no cover charge and tipping is not expected. If you're low on both money and scruples, Süd Tirolian breakfasts are the only ones in Italy big enough to steal lunch from.

Transportation: Venice to Bolzano and into the Dolomites

While you can tackle the Dolomites from the east as a side trip from Venice, those relying on public transportation and with limited time will maximize mountain thrills and minimize connection headaches by side-tripping in from Bolzano (about an hour north of Verona, 3.5 hours from Milan) in the west. Frequent buses connect Bolzano to most western Dolomite valleys. Unfortunately, there is no direct public route covering the Great Dolomite Road. (There are, of course, L100,000 day-long bus tours from Bolzano.)

By car, it's ideal to circle north from Venice and drive the famed Great Dolomite Road (Belluno–Cortina–Pordoi Pass–Sella Pass–Val di Fassa–Bolzano). The drive from Cortina to Bolzano is 130 breathtaking miles.

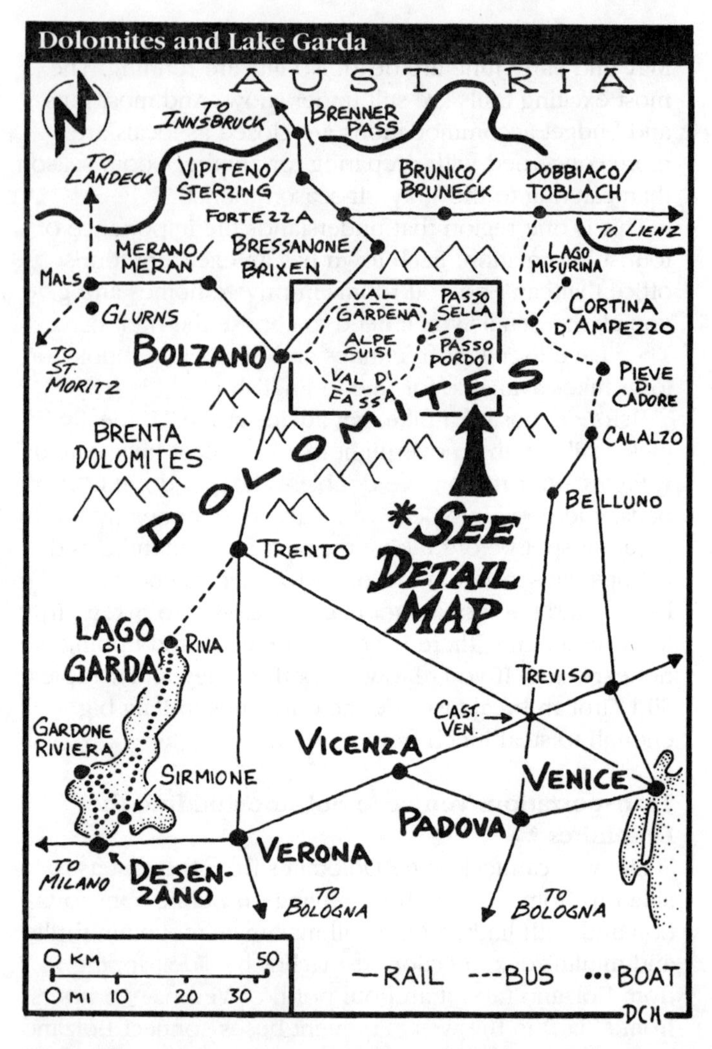

Remember, in the spring and early summer, passes labeled "closed" are often bare, dry, and, as far as local drivers are concerned, wide open.

Into the Dolomites from Bolzano: While there are no trains, the local buses are inexpensive and go to most destinations (usually twice a day off-season, 4 to 8 times a day in the summer). For example: Bolzano to Val di Fassa (easier from Trent, from Bolzano to Vigo di Fassa and Canazei twice a day, four times daily in summer, 2 hours); Bolzano to Val di Gardena (to St. Ulrich/Ortisei, St. Christina, Selva, and Plan, four times daily, 1 hour); Bolzano to Kastelruth (eight times a day, 1 hour); and on to Saltria in Seiser Alpe/Alpe di Siusi (twice daily, five times in summer). Shuttle buses go nearly hourly from Kastelruth into the Seiser Alpe. In the summertime, this park is closed to cars, so the bus goes even more often.

Bozen/Bolzano

Willkommen to the Italian Tirol! If it weren't so sunny, you could be in Innsbruck. This enjoyable old town (of 100,000) is worth a stop to gather Dolomite information and for a Tirolian stroll. From the station, walk to Piazza Walther. Follow arcaded Via dei Portici to the Piazza Erbe with its ancient and still healthy open-air produce market.

All your orientation help is at your toes. City tourist information is on Piazza Walther (tel. 0471/975656). The excellent Dolomites information office is just down the street (open Monday-Friday 8:30-12:30, 14:00-17:30, Parrocchia 11, tel. 0471/993809). The bus station with an information office is between the train station and Piazza Walther.

Sleeping in Bolzano: While the cool, scenic, and nearby Dolomites make sleeping in Bolzano relatively hot, humid, and questionable, it has substantial charm. **Gasthof Weisses Kreuz** (L45,000-60,000, a block off Piazza Walther in the old town at Kornplatz 3, tel. 0471/977552) is your best bet. It couldn't be better located or more German. The modern, clean, institutional **Kolpinghaus Bozen** (L76,000 with breakfast, in the center also at Spitalgasse 3, tel. 0471/971170) has more rooms and less character. Each room has all the comforts and twin beds. Its cheap cafeteria (L10,000 dinners, 18:30-19:30 Monday-Friday) is open to all.

Many are tempted to wimp out on the Dolomites and see them from a distance by making the popular quick trip into the hills above Bolzano (cable car from near the Bolzano station to the cute but very touristy village of

Oberbozan where you'll have a long pastoral walk to the Pemmern chair lift, ride to Schwarzseespitze and walk 45 more minutes to the Rittner Horn). You'll be atop a 7,000-foot peak with distant but often hazy Dolomite views.

Seiser Alpe/Alpe di Siusi from Kastelruth/Castelrotto
Less than an hour by bus from Bolzano lies Europe's largest high alpine meadow, the Alpe di Siusi. The area is a natural preserve, and in the summer it's car-free. Only the park bus service shuttles hikers closer to the base of the postcard dramatic Sasso peaks (Sassolungo, 3,180 meters). Trails are well marked, and the brightly painted numbers are keyed into local maps. Pick up the appropriate 1:25,000 "Tobacco" map at the TI.

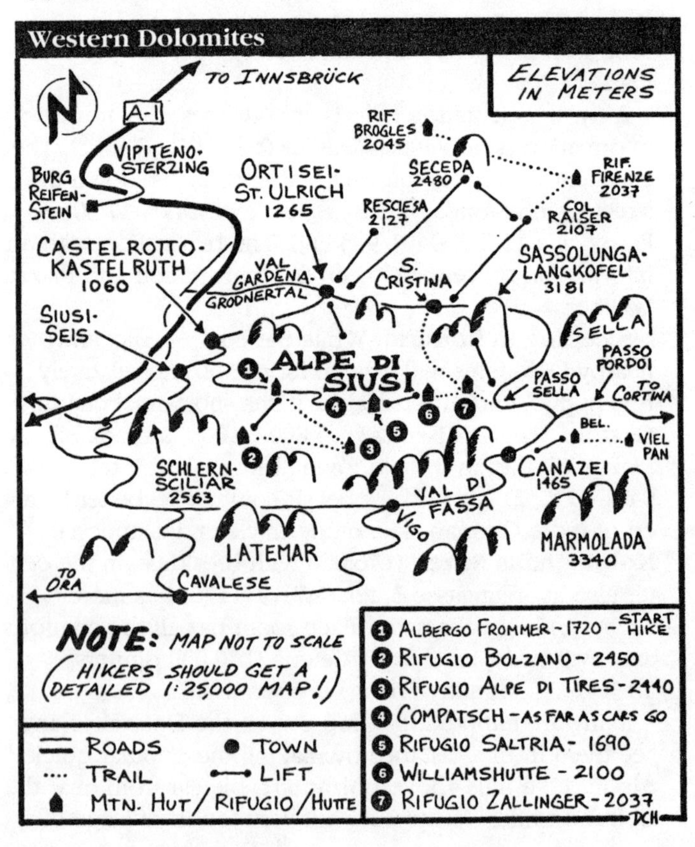

Western Dolomites

Easy meadow walks abound, giving tender feet classic Dolomite views from baby carriage trails. Experienced hikers should consider two tough and exciting treks from the Alpe di Siusi. For an 8-hour (18-km) day hike or an ideal two-day hike with an overnight in a traditional mountain refuge, consider the summit of Schlern/Sciliar and spending a night in Refugio Bolzano. From the bus stop at Albergo Frommer catch the chair lift, hike across the meadow, and climb steeply to the plateau of the tabletop Schlern/Sciliar. From the Schlernhaus/Refugio Bolzano (2,450 meters, with doubles and a dorm, tel. 0471/612024, call for a reservation), hike (12 km) past Refugio Alpe di Tires (smaller than Bolzano, also with doubles and dorm beds, tel. 727958), drop 1,000 meters back down to the Alpe di Siusi and a long easygoing meadow walk back.

More difficult is the long day's hike around Sassolungo. Ride the bus to Saltria, the end of the line, ride the chair lift to Williamshutte, walk to Refugio Zallinger (overnight possible), and circle the Sasso group. Before attempting either of these more difficult hikes, confirm your understanding of the time and skills required through the local tourist office.

Sleeping in Kastelruth/Castelrotto

Kastelruth/Castelrotto has more village character than any town I saw in the region. It's full of real people (be in town as the moms bring home the grade schoolers). And it isn't a resort (TI, 8:30-18:00, 0471/706333). Good reasonable beds are at **Gasthof Zum Turm** (L70,000 with breakfast, behind the TI at Kofelgasse 8, tel. 0471/706349) and **Gasthof Zum Wolf** (L70,000 with breakfast, in front of the TI at Wolkenstein strasse 5, tel. 0471/706332). Ask the TI for the latest on L20,000 beds with breakfast in private homes (**Pfarrhaus Kastelruth** at Krausenweg 1, tel. 706380; **Pramstrahler Martha** at Grondlbodenweg 23, tel. 706775; and **Haus Oswald** at Wolkenstein strasse 25, tel. 706607 are each inexpensive, open all year and central) or for a dormitory in a mountain hut (around L15,000). There are several lagers with dorm beds near Saltria in the Alpe di Siusi.

Val di Fassa

This is Alberto Tomba country. Free postcards featuring Italy's most famous Olympian are all over the valley. In the summer, the whole place reminds me of a ski resort without the snow. But there are plenty of lifts and accommodations and some spectacular high country hikes.

The town of Canazei, at the head of the valley and the end of the bus line, has the most ambience and altitude (4,600 feet). From there a lift takes you to Col dei Rossi Belvedere where you can hike past the Refugio Belvedere along an easy but breathtaking ridge to the Refugio Viel del Pan. This is a 3-hour round-trip hike with views of the highest mountain in the Dolomites, the Marmolada, and the quintessentially Dolo-mighty Sella group along the way.

Grodner Tal/Val Gardena

Famous for its woodcarvers (ANRI is from a Val di Gardena town called St. Christina), its traditional Ladin culture, and now its skiing and hiking resorts, Val Gardena is a bit overrated. Even if its culture has been suffocated by the big bucks of hedonistic European fun seekers, it remains a good jumping-off point for trips into the mountains.

St. Ulrich/Ortisei is the main town and best base. From here, you can ride the lifts into the high country for some fine hikes. Consider hikes from the top of either the Rasciesa or the Seceda lifts, hiking to Refugio Brogles and/or Refugio Firenze, and riding the Col Raiser lift into St. Cristina for some of the most dramatic views within easy striking distance. (TI tel. 0471/796328, open 8:30-18:30, Sunday 10:00-12:00, best reasonable sleeps at the Aurelia Guesthouse, Streda Rezia 236, tel. 0471/796258, open all year, L60,000-70,000 doubles with breakfast and pass to swimming pool.)

Itinerary Options

▲▲ Reifenstein Castle—For one of Europe's most intimate looks at medieval castle life, let the lady of Reifenstein (Frau Blanc) show you around her wonderfully preserved castle. She leads tours on the hour, in Italian and German. She's friendly and will squeeze in what English she can.

Just before the Austrian border, leave the autostrada at Vipiteno/Sterzing (the town, like many in this area, has both a German and an Italian name), follow signs toward Bolzano, then over the freeway to the base of the castle's rock. It's the castle on the west. Telephone 0472/76 58 79 in advance to confirm your tour. The pleasant mini-park beside the drawbridge is a good spot for a picnic. (Pack out your litter.) Tours normally Easter through November at 9:30, 10:30, 14:00, and 15:00, closed Friday, L3000.

▲ Glurns—If you decide to connect the Dolomites and Lake Como by the high road via Meran and Bormio or the southwest of Switzerland, spend the night in the amazing little fortified town of Glurns (45 minutes west of touristy Meran between Schluderns and Taufers). Glurns still lives within its square wall on the Adige River, with a church bell tower that has a thing about ringing and real farms rather than boutiques filling the town courtyards. This is a refreshing break after so many cute and wealthy tourist towns. There are several small hotels in the town, but I'd stay in a private home 100 yards from the town square, near the church, just outside the wall on the river (Family Hofer, tel. 0473/81597, well marked).

DAYS 21 and 22

LAKE COMO, BEST OF THE ITALIAN LAKES

To round out our tour of Italy, finish with a visit to the best of Northern Italy's "Lakes District." Lake Como, on the Swiss border, is our target. Once you're set up there, it's hard to imagine you're just an hour or two from hustling Milan and the end of our 22-day itinerary.

Suggested Schedule

9:00	Leave Dolomites.
11:00	Sightsee, lunch in Verona (see Day 18).
14:00	Continue to Milan, train to Lake Como.
18:00	Set up in Varenna on the lake.

Day 22

Depending on your schedule, relax on the lake, return to Milan, or head north for more of Europe.

Lake Como (Lago di Como)

The million-lire question is, Which lake in the Italian Lakes district? For the best mix of handiness, scenery, and off-beatness that gives you a complete dose of Italian lakes wonder and aristocratic old days romance, Lake Como is my choice.

Lined with elegant nineteenth-century villas, crowned by snowcapped mountains, and buzzing with ferries, hydrofoils, and little passenger ships, this is a good place to take a break from the intensity and obligatory turnstile culture of central Italy. It seems half the travelers you'll meet on Lake Como have tossed their itinerary into the lake and are actually relaxing.

Today, the lake's only serious industry is tourism. Thousands of lakeside residents travel daily to nearby Lugano, in Switzerland, to find work. The area's isolation and flat economy have left it pretty much the way the nineteenth-century romantic poets described it.

Transportation: Into and around Lake Como
By car, it's a short drive north of Milan. While you can easily drive around the lake, the road is narrow, congested, and lined by privacy-seeking walls, hedges, and tall fences. It costs L12,000 to take your car onto a ferry. And parking is rarely easy where you need it, especially in Bellagio. I'd park in Varenna and cruise. If you're driving to Como, it's a straight cheap shot on the autostrada (exit just before the Swiss border). Find a garage and walk into the old town.

By train it's easy. Milan Centrale to Varenna (60 minutes, ten departures daily, note: some Milan trains depart to Varenna from the Garibaldi station, an easy Metro connection from the Central station), Milan to Como (40 minutes, hourly departures). The quickest Milan connection to any point at midlake (Bellagio, Menaggio, or Varenna) is via the train to Varenna.

Lago di Como is well served by pricey little boats. When you consider the scenery that comes with the transportation, the L4000 per one-stop hop doesn't seem quite so expensive. Passengers pay the same for car or passenger ferries but 50 percent more for the enclosed, stuffy, less scenic, but very quick hydrofoil. The free schedule (Navigazione sul Lago di Como, available at any tourist office or boat dock) lists all times and prices. Stopovers aren't allowed, and there's no break for round-trips, so you buy a ticket for each ride. The L25,000 all-day lake pass and a L15,000 midlake day pass don't make much sense.

Consider side-tripping from Varenna, or leaving Varenna and visiting Bellagio and maybe Villa Carlotta by boat and taking the scenic ride down to Como (90 minutes and L10,000 on slow boat) where you're an easy train trip from Milano.

▲▲ Varenna is the best of all lake worlds. Easy train access, on the less driven side of the lake, with a romantic promenade, a tiny harbor, narrow lanes, and its own villa. Most important, it is the right place to savor a cappuccino and ponder the place where Italy is welded to the Alps.

A steep trail leads to Varenna's ruined castle capping the hill above. It's as intriguing as a locked-up castle can be. While you can't get in, there's a fine view and a peaceful traffic-free, one-chapel, and no-coffee town behind it.

Varenna is very quiet at night. The *passerella* (lakeside walk) is adorned with caryatid lovers pressing silently against each other in the shadows. For a reasonable meal, try the pizzeria (#1, Piazza San Giorgio) across from the church. For a splurge, the Vecchio Varenna restaurant, right on the old harborfront, is good.

In Bellano, just to the north, is the Orrido, an impressive gorge cutting into the mountainside (9:00-12:30, 14:00-18:00). The next town south, Fiumelatte, is named for its milky river, which is only 800 feet long. (It runs only during the tourist season.)

▲ **Bellagio** is "the Pearl of the Lake," a classy combination of tidiness and Old World elegance. If you don't mind that "tramp in a palace" feeling, it's a fine place to surround yourself by the more adventurous of the soft travelers and shop for umbrellas and ties. The heavy curtains between the arcades keep the visitors from sweating. Steep stepped lanes rise from the harborfront, and the shady promenade leads to the Lido (beach). The town has a tourist office (on Piazza Chiesa next to the church, tel. 031/950204, loosely open 9:00-18:00, closed for lunch and Sundays), a worth-a-look church, and some surprisingly affordable funky old hotels.

Bellagio, the administrative capital of the midlake region, is located where the two southern legs split off. For an easy break in a park with a great view, wander right on out to the crotch. Walk past the rich and famous Hotel Villa Servelloni, past the little Ortofrutta market (cheap fruit and juice for the view point), and walk a few minutes to the Punta Spartivento, literally "the point that divides the wind." You'll find a bar, a tiny harbor, and a fine chance to sit on a bench and stare north past Menaggio and Varenna into the Swiss Alps and the end of the lake.

▲ **Lake Como's West Side Story:** Menaggio, just eight miles from Lugano in Switzerland, has more substance as a real town than its neighbors. Since the lake is getting a bit dirty for swimming, consider its fine public pool. This is the starting point for a few hikes. Only 25 years ago, these trails were used by cigarette smugglers. As many as 180 people a night would sneak through the darkness from Switzerland back into Italy with tax-free cigarettes. The hostel has information about catching the bus to trailheads on nearby Mount Grona or to the top of the pass on the Lugano road.

Villa Carlotta is the best of Lake Como's famed villas. I see this part of our trip as a break from Italy's art, but if you are in need of a place that charges admission (L6000), Villa Carlotta offers an elegant neoclassical interior, a famous Canova statue, and a garden (its highlight, best in spring). If you're touring one villa on the lake, this is probably the best. Nearby Tremezzo and Cadenabbia are pleasant lakeside resorts an easy walk away. Boats serve all three places. Open 9:00-18:00 daily.

Just to the south, Isola Comacina is Como's only island. It's filled with ruins and connected by ferry from scenic little Ospedaletto. As you cruise around the peninsula just north of the island, check out the lovely Villa Balbianello. As WW II was winding up, Mussolini was fleeing to Switzerland. He was caught at Dongo, a town on the north end of the lake, and shot in Azzano with his mistress on April 28, 1945.

Como, on the southwest tip of the lake, has a good traffic-free old town, an interesting Gothic/Renaissance cathedral, and a pleasant lakefront with a promenade. It's an easy walk from the boat dock to the train station where hourly trains get you to Milan in 40 minutes.

Sleeping in mid-Lake Como (about L1300 = US$1)

The area is tight in August, snug in July, and wide open most of the rest of the year. All places listed are family-run, speak some English, and have lake-view rooms. Usually the price is the same all year, and view rooms cost no extra. They are given to those who telephone reservations and request a view. If ever I was to kill, it would be here . . . for the view. Off-season prices in the cheaper places seem soft. Spend some time on the phone confirming the view and price. Breakfasts are normally an optional L7000. Most places have singles for about 70 percent of the double price.

Varenna: Albergo Olivedo (L50,000-85,000, sit-down tub showers and toilets across the hall, 22050 Varenna/ Lago di Como, tel. 0341/830115), right at the ferry dock, is a neat old hotel. Each room has lumpy old beds and a glorious little lake-view balcony. It's a fine place to hang out and watch the children play, the boats come and go, and the sun set. **Albergo Milano** (L100,000, discounted for two nights, off-season, or with a side view, Via XX Settembre 29, 22050 Varenna [Como], tel. 0341/830298), located right in the old town with a magnificent breakfast terrace and very friendly but non-English-speaking management, is your best splurge. Each of its nine rooms is small, modern, comfortable, with a shower and a view. Rooms 1 and 2 have the royal balconies. **Albergo Beretta** (L45,000-70,000, room 9 without a shower has a view balcony for only L45,000, tel. 0341/830132) is off the water and on the main road with no character or atmosphere but good beds.

Bellagio: Hotel du Lac (L120,000-140,000 with breakfast, Leono family, 22021 Bellagio/Como, tel. 031/950320, fax 951624) is your best splurge. Right on the harbor with a roof garden, it's completely remodeled (air-conditioning, TVs, mini-bars) and gives you the old flavor with absolutely no loss of comfort. **Hotel Suisse** (L66,000 doubles with breakfast, Piazza Mazzini 8, 22021 Bellagio, tel. 031/950335, fax 951755) somehow landed right on the harbor next to the stuffy places. It's frumpy with simple rooms and hardwood floors. The similar one-star **Hotel Roma** (L45,000-65,000, breakfast extra, elevator, tel. 031/950424) cranes its neck above Hotel Suisse. Until they remodel, the fifth floor has the cheapest rooms (shower down the hall) with great view balconies. **Hotel Giardinetto** (L40,000-55,000, Via Roncati 12, tel. 950168), near the tourist office, about 100 steps above the waterfront, offers squeaky, clean, cool, quiet, and spartan rooms, above a breezy and peaceful garden.

Menaggio: La Primula Youth Hostel is a rare hostel. Family run for ten years by Ty and Paola, it caters to a quiet, savor-the-lakes crowd and offers the only cheap beds in the area. Located just south of the Menaggio dock (you'll see the sign from the boat), it has a view terrace, lots of games, a members' kitchen, a washing machine, bike rentals (L15,000 a day), discount tickets to Villa Carlotta, easy parking, and a creative and hardworking staff. (Closed 10:00-17:00 daily and from mid-November through mid-March, L13,000 per night in a 4- to 6-bed room with sheets and breakfast, hearty dinners with a local flair and wine are only L12,000.) Ty and Paola print a newsletter to advertise their activities programs (inexpensive 14-day Italian language, 3- to 7-day hikes, bike trips, cooking classes). Ostello La Primula, Via 4 Novembre 86, 22017 Menaggio, tel. and fax 0344/32356.

Lake District Options

Bergamo—If you need another medieval hill town, this place is a northern Siena. Skip the lower town and head right for Bergamo Alta (bus 1 from the station to the funicular, free with bus ticket, drivers follow the signs to citta alta). Hang out on Piazza Veccia and stroll Via Colleoni. To sleep in the center of this medieval atmosphere, try **Albergo Agnello D'Oro** (L75,000, Via Gombito 22, tel. 035/249883).

Lake Garda (Lago di Garda)—The largest, most visited and most Italian of the lakes is also the last developed and therefore more contemporary and dedicated to wind surfing, suntanning, and paddle-boating rather than strolling and high teas. Tour groups, German wind surfers, and Italian fun-in-the-sun seekers pack the entire lake in the summer. A quick stop is easy, but for the summer traveler, I think the lake's overrated.

The towns at either end of the lake, Riva in the north and Desenzano in the south, have enough substance to keep their crenellated heads above the flood of tourists. Riva is a pleasant little castle port town with good bus connections to Trento farther north. Boats cruise the entire lake regularly (Riva to Desenzano, 2 hours and L20,000 by hydrofoil, 4 hours and L15,000 by slow boat).

Desenzano—While English-language guidebooks mention Desenzano only as a gateway, on the Venice–Milan train line and just off the autostrada, it was my favorite town on the lake. Walk straight from the station ten blocks to the lakefront and a helpful tourist information office. The waterfront area has several gelati-licking piazzas, tiny harbors, a promenade, and the ferry dock. (Free parking is safest on the waterfront on Piazza XXV Aprile.)

Sleeping in Desenzano: There are no great values in town, but it is the handy base for a quick visit to Garda. **Hotel Alessi** (L45,000-70,000, one block off the harbor, perfectly central on a pedestrian street, Via Castello 3, tel.

030/9141980, fax 9141756) is clean, simple, and shipshape, with an elevator. The **Splendid Hotel Mayer** ("splendid" is part of their name, not my description, L70,000 doubles, Piazza Ulisse Papa, tel. 030/9142253) is a huge old place, central as can be and right on the water, popular with groups, with handy parking and a faint smell of sewer. **Albergo Du Lac** (L50,000, Via Anelli 8, tel. 030/9141612) is right on the lake but pretty dreary.

Sirmione—This is the lake's cover-girl town. A skinny two-mile pin of land is capped by this mini-Dubrovnik. It's a fairy-tale island town as untouristy and barely more real than Disneyland. The pin is lined with hotels and people looking for a parking spot. The fortified old town has a Venetian flavor with a clichetic castle complete with swan tail crenellations. The town's Grotte di Catullo is the ruins of a Roman spa with fine mosaics. Sirmione is a quick bus ride or 20 minutes and L4000 by boat from Desenzano.

Posttrip Transportation Tips

Getting out of Italy by train: There are regular overnight trains from Milan to Paris, the French Riviera, Munich, Vienna, and Amsterdam. After lots of Italy, Switzerland is particularily pristine and storybookish. From Milan, trains go north tunneling you under the Continental Divide and back into the German-speaking Alpine world in an hour or two.

Getting to Milan's airports: To get from Milan to either of its airports is a matter of catching a quick shuttle bus (inexpensive and regular departures from the Central Station, see Day 1 for more specifics).

That's my idea of the best 22 days Italy has to offer. I hope you had a great trip, and best wishes for many more. Ciao!

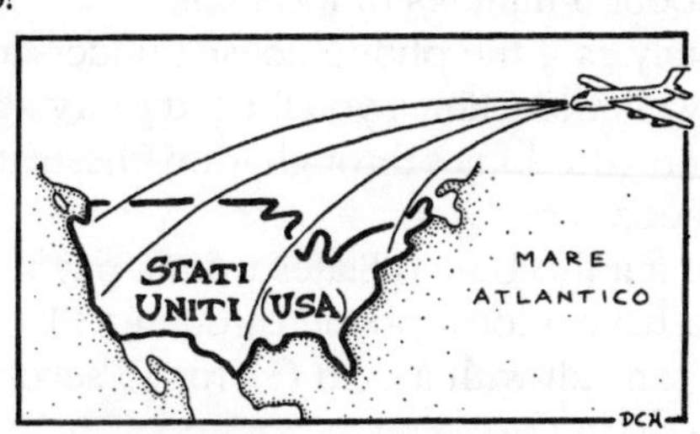

APPENDIX

TELEPHONE INFORMATION

Smart travelers use the telephone every day. Hotel reservations by phone the morning of the day you plan to arrive are a snap. If there's a language problem, ask someone at your hotel to talk to your next hotel for you.

The key to dialing long distance is understanding area codes and having a local phone card. Hotel room phones are reasonable for local calls, but a terrible rip-off for long distance calls. Never call home from your hotel room (unless you are putting the call on your credit card).

For calls to other European countries, dial the international access code (00 in Italy), followed by the country code, followed by the area code without its zero, and finally the local number (four to seven digits). When dialing long distance within Italy, start with the area code (including its zero), then the local number. Post offices have fair, metered long-distance booths.

Use Italy's new phone cards. The L5000 or L10,000 phone cards (worth from $4 to $8, buy at post offices, tobacco shops, and machines near phone booths; many phone booths indicate where the nearest phone card sales outlet is located) are much easier than coins for long distance calls. Buy one on your first day to force you to find smart reasons to use the local phones. The old vandal-plagued coin- and token-operated phones, which are getting more and more difficult to find, work if you have the necessary pile of coins or *gettoni* (slotted tokens which also function as L200 coins). One token gets you about 5 minutes of local talk.

Dial in Italy as if the phone doesn't understand numbers very well. Sometimes you'll need to try again and again. When you do get through, don't hestitate to nearly scream if necessary.

Telephoning the United States from a pay phone is easy if you have a local phone card, an ATT or MCI credit card, or can call with a coin ($1 for 15 seconds) to have the other person call you back at a specified time at your hotel. From the United States, they would dial 011-39-your area code without the zero-and the local number. Italy-to-United States calls are twice as expensive as direct calls from the United States. Midnight California is breakfast time Rome.

If you plan to call home much, get an ATT or MCI card. Each card company has a toll-free number in each European country which puts you in touch with an American operator who takes your card number and the number you want to call, puts you through and bills your home telephone number for the call (at the cheap USA rate of about a dollar a minute plus a $2.50 service charge). If you talk for 3 minutes, you save more than enough in the rates to cover the $2.50 service charge. SPRINT, MCI, and ATT numbers are listed below.

Telephone Directory

Italy's International Access Code - 00
Italian country code - 39
MCI operator - 172-1022
ATT operator - 172-1011
SPRINT operator - 172-1877
Emergency (English-speaking help) - 113
Emergency (police) - 112
Road Service - 116
Directory Assistance - 12
English language telephone help - 170
To call Italy from the USA - 011-39-area code without the zero-local number
To call USA from Italy - 00-1-area code-local number

Italy: Public Transportation
Paris
Chamonix
Pre S. Didier
Domo.
Luzern
Loc.
St. Moritz
Innsbruck
Salzburg
Men.
Tirano
Brenner
Lugano
Varenna
San Candido
Wien
Aosta
Como
Lecco
Fort.
Chivasso
Stresa
Bolzano
Cortina
Vill.
Torino
Berg.
Riva
Trent
Verona
Udine
Milan
Vicenza
Cal.
Nice
Vent.
Finale
Genova
Desenzano
Trieste
S. Marg.
Parma
Padua
Venice
Vernazza
Florence
Bologna
La Spezia
Lucca
Pisa
Ravenna
Emp.
Terentola
Rimini
Siena
Perugia
Pesaro
Elba
Falconara
Assisi
Chiusi
Fossato
Orvieto
Civitá di Bagnoregio
Foligno
Ancona
Spoleto
Porto Torres
Orte
Olbia
Roma
Pescara
Anzio
Chilivani
Naples
Capri
Foggia
Pompeii
Meta-ponto
Sorrento
Barletta
Calagri
Salerno
Paestum
Bari
Tunis
Palermo
Lam.
Brindisi
Messina
Taranto
Crot.
Trapani
Calt.
Mil.
Villa S.G.
Lecce
Cast.
Taormina
Marsala
Catania
Reggio Calabria
To Corfu & Patra (Greece)
Agrigento
Siracusa
KEY: — Rail --- Bus .... Ship
Not to scale
Overnight stops (on 22 days route)
DCH

TRAIN CONNECTIONS:

from . . . to	duration of trip	frequency	cost 2nd cl
Milan-La Spezia	3-4 hours	6/day	L20,000-25,000
La Spezia-Pisa	1 hour	hourly	L6,000
Pisa-Florence	60-90 minutes	hourly	L7,000-9,000
Florence-Siena	80-120 minutes	hourly	L7,200
Siena-Orvieto	2-3 hours, 1 change	7/day	L10,000
Siena-Assisi	3.5 hours, 2 changes	4/day	L16,000
Assisi-Rome	2-3 hours, 1 change	8/day	L14,000-20,000
Siena-Rome	3 hours, 1 change	6/day	L20,000-25,000
Orvieto-Rome	75-90 minutes	10/day	L11,000
Orte-Rome	40-80 minutes	20/day	L7,000
Rome-Naples	2-3 hours	hourly	L16,000
Salerno-Naples	40 minutes	2/hour	L4,500
Rome-Venice	5-7 hours	22:15-6:10, 23:10-6:28	L50,000
Venice-Bolzano	3.5-4 hours, 1 change	8/day	L20,000-28,000
Bolzano-Milan	3.5 hours, 1 change	8/day	L20,000

Europe
Through the Back Door
ITALIAN PHRASE BOOK

"Only my son could assemble such a practical little phrase book. I won't travel without it."

— June Steves

The *Europe Through the Back Door Phrase Book: Italian* contains all the words and phrases that Rick Steves has found necessary to enjoy over 20 years of foot-loose and fancy-free travel throughout Italy.

You'll find key Italian words and phrases covering:

- communication
- transportation
- shopping, money
- finding a room
- tongue-twisters and gestures
- budget skills
- eating
- help, health
- conversations, politics, profanity, romance
- the Rolling Rosetta Stone Italian word guide

Rick Steves is the author of *Europe Through the Back Door*, *2 to 22 Days in Europe*, *2 to 22 Days in Italy*, and seven other travel books. Rick also co-writes and hosts the Public Television Series *Travels in Europe*.

INDEX

Alpi di Suise 175, 180
Amalfi 136, 140-143
Assisi 90-92
Bagnoregio 85-88
Bellagio 187
Bergamo 190
Bolzano 175-179
breakfast 5
Burano 159
Capri 136, 142
car rental 11-13
Cinque Terre train schedule 43
Cinque Terre 42-54
- Cinque Terre train schedule 43
- Corniglia 45
- La Spezia 42
- Mama Rosa's hostel 50
- Manarola 45
- Monterosso al Mare 47
- Riomaggiore 44
- Vernazza 45-49

Civita di Bagnoregio 85-88
Corniglia 45
culture shock 10
Desenzano 190
Dolomites, Italy's Alps 175-182
- Alpi di Suise 175, 180
- Bolzano 175-179
- Glurns 183
- Kastleruth 175, 181-182
- Reifenstein Castle 183
- Seiser Alpe 175, 180
- Val di Fassa 182
- Val Gardena 182
- Vipiteno/Sterzing 183

driving 11-13
eating Italian 7-9
Etruscan museum 84
Etruscan tomb 88
Florence 53-70
Fra Angelico 59
Glassblowing 157
Glurns 183
Gondola rides 157
guidebooks, recommended 15-17
Gypsie Thief gangs 102
Herculaneum 140
Hilltowns of Tuscany and Umbria 85-92
- Assisi 90-92
- Bagnoregio 85-88
- Civita di Bagnoregio 85-88
- Orvieto 82-85
- San Gimignano 70-71
- Siena 70-82

hotels 5, 7
Iscia 136
Italian phrasebook 195
Italian wine exhibition 77
Italy cultural overview 25-27
itinerary overview 21-24
jet-lag 28
Kastleruth 175, 181-182
La Spezia 42
Lake Como/Lago di Como 184-190
Lake Garda/Lago di Garda 190
Lake Bolsena 88
Lakes District 184-191
- Bellagio 187
- Bergamo 190
- Desenzano 190
- Lake Como/Lago di Como 184-190
- Lake Garda/Lago di Garda 190
- Menaggio 187
- Sirmione 191
- Varenna 185

Leaning Tower 55
Leonardo di Vinci 37, 38
Lido, Venice's beach 160
mail 14
Malpensa airport, Milan 30
Mama Rosa's hostel 50
Manarola 45

Maps, in 22 Day route order:
Italy in 22 Days Tour Route 1
Italy 22
Milan Subway 33
Milan 35
Cinque Terre, Italian Riviera 44
Vernazza 46
Siena 73
Orvieto area 83
Civita di Bagnoregio 85
Hilltowns of Central Italy 89
Rome area 95
Rome 96
Rome's Termini Station 98
Rome's subway 99
Downtown Ancient Rome 100
Vatican City and St Peter's 107
St Peter's Basilica 108
Naples 127
Sorrento 132
Pompeii 139
Amalfi Coast and Capri 141
Salerno 145
Venice 150
Piazza San Marco, Venice 151
Venice "Downtown" 156
Venice Lagoon 160
Temptations: Venice to Milan 167
Dolomites and Lake Garda 178
Western Dolomites 180
Lago di Como/Lake Como 186
Italy: Public Transportation 194

maps 17
Menaggio 187
Michelangelo 58
Milan 29-42
Monterosso al Mare 47
Murano 160
Mussolini 111
Naples 124-131
Naples Area:
  Amalfi 136, 140-143
  Capri 136, 142
  Herculaneum 140
  Iscia 136
  Pasteum 144-147
  Pompeii 136, 138-140
  Positano 141
  Salerno 136
  Sorrento 124, 131-137
  Vesuvius 140
Orvieto 82-85
Orvieto Classico wine 89
Ostia Antica 111
Padua 167
Palio, Siena 75
Palladio 168
Panforte 81
Pasteum 144-147
philosophy, back door 20
picnics 9
Pisa 53-55
Pompeii 136, 138-140
Positano 141
Positano 136
Pub Crawl dinner, Venice 157
Ravenna 172-174
Reifenstein Castle 183
Renaissance, Florentine 57-62
restaurants 8
Riomaggiore 44
Riviera 42-54
Rome 93-124
  Gypsie Thief gangs 102
  Mussolini 111
  Ostia Antica 111

St Peter's Basilica 108
Vatican City 107-111
Vatican Museum 109
Romeo and Juliet 169
Saint Francis 90-92
Salerno 136
San Gimignano 70-71
Seiser Alpe 175, 180
Siena 70-82
Sirmione 191
Sorrento 124, 131-137
St Peter's Basilica 108
St Catherine 77
Steves, Rick guidebooks 15-17
Telephone Info/Directory 192, 193
terrorism 14
Torcello 159
tourist information 17-18
train travel 10
train 2, 10, 11
Train connections 195
transportation 10-13
Uffizi Gallery 62
Val Gardena 182
Val di Fassa 182
Varenna 185
Vatican City 107-111
Vatican Museum 109
Venice 148-167
Vernazza 45-49
Verona 169-171
Vesuvius 140
Vicenza 168
Vipiteno/Sterzing 183
when to go 3

Rick Steves' BACK DOOR CATALOG

All items field tested, highly recommended, completely guaranteed, discounted below retail and ideal for independent, mobile travelers. Prices include tax (if applicable), handling, and postage.

The Back Door Suitcase / Rucksack $70.00

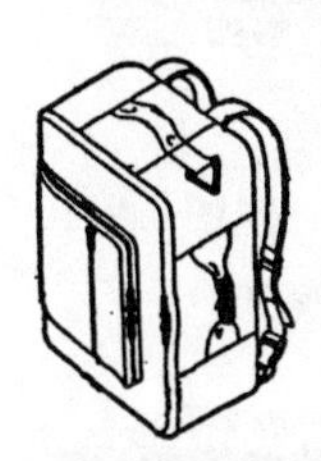

At 9"x22"x14" this specially designed, sturdy functional bag is maximum carry-on-the-plane size (fits under the seat) and your key to foot-loose and fancy-free travel. Made of rugged water resistant Cordura nylon, it converts easily from a smart-looking suitcase to a handy rucksack. It has hide-away padded shoulder straps, top and side handles and a detachable shoulder strap (for toting as a suitcase). Lockable perimeter zippers allow easy access to the roomy (2,700 cubic inches) central compartment. Two large outside pockets are perfect for frequently used items. Also included is one nylon stuff bag. Over 40,000 Back Door travelers have used these bags around the world. Rick Steves helped design and lives out of this bag for 3 months at a time. Comparable bags cost much more. Available in navy blue, black, or grey.

Moneybelt $8.00

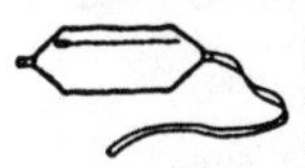

This required, ultra-light, sturdy, under-the-pants, nylon pouch is just big enough to carry the essentials (passport, airline ticket, travelers checks, and so on) comfortably. I'll never travel without one and I hope you won't either. Beige, nylon zipper, one size fits nearly all, with "manual."

Catalog FREE

For a complete listing of all the books, travel videos, products and services Rick Steves and Europe Through the Back Door offer you, ask us for our 64-page catalog.

Eurailpasses . . .

...cost the same everywhere. We carefully examine each order and include for no extra charge a 90-minute Rick Steves VHS video Train User's Guide, helpful itinerary advice, Eurail train schedule booklet and map, plus a free 22 Days book of your choice! Send us a check for the cost of the pass(es) you want along with your legal name (as it appears on your passport), a proposed itinerary (including dates and places of entry and exit if known), choice of 22 Days book (Europe, Brit, Spain/Port, Scand, France, or Germ/Switz/Aust) and a list of questions. Within 2 weeks of receiving your order we'll send you your pass(es) and any other information pertinent to your trip. Due to this unique service Rick Steves sells more passes than anyone on the West Coast and you'll have an efficient and expertly-organized Eurail trip.

Back Door Tours

We encourage independent travel, but for those who want a tour in the Back Door style, we do offer a 22-day "Best of Europe" tour. For complete details, send for our free 64 page tour booklet/catalog.

All orders will be processed within 2 weeks and include tax (where applicable), shipping and a one year's subscription to our Back Door Travel newsletter. Prices good through 1993. Rush orders add $5. Sorry, no credit cards. Send checks to:

Europe Through The Back Door • 120 Fourth Ave. N. Box 2009 • Edmonds, WA 98020 • (206) 771-8303

Other Books from John Muir Publications

Adventure Vacations: From Trekking in New Guinea to Swimming in Siberia, Bangs 256 pp. $17.95
Asia Through the Back Door, 3rd ed., Steves and Gottberg 326 pp. $15.95
Belize: A Natural Destination, Mahler, Wotkyns, Schafer 304 pp. $16.95
Bus Touring: Charter Vacations, U.S.A., Warren with Bloch 168 pp. $9.95
California Public Gardens: A Visitor's Guide, Sigg 304 pp. $16.95
Costa Rica: A Natural Destination, 2nd ed., Sheck 288 pp. $16.95
Elderhostels: The Students' Choice, 2nd ed., Hyman 312 pp. $15.95
Environmental Vacations: Volunteer Projects to Save the Planet, 2nd ed., Ocko 248 pp. $16.95
Europe 101: History & Art for the Traveler, 4th ed., Steves and Openshaw 372 pp. $15.95
Europe Through the Back Door, 11th ed., Steves 448 pp. $17.95
Europe Through the Back Door Phrase Book: French, Steves 112 pp. $4.95
Europe Through the Back Door Phrase Book: German, Steves 112 pp. $4.95
Europe Through the Back Door Phrase Book: Italian, Steves 112 pp. $4.95
Floating Vacations: River, Lake, and Ocean Adventures, White 256 pp. $17.95
A Foreign Visitor's Survival Guide to America, Baldwin and Levine 224 pp. $12.95
Great Cities of Eastern Europe, Rapoport 256 pp. $16.95
Guatemala: A Natural Destination, Mahler 288 pp. $16.95
Gypsying After 40: A Guide to Adventure and Self-Discovery, Harris 264 pp. $14.95
The Heart of Jerusalem, Nellhaus 336 pp. $12.95
Indian America: A Traveler's Companion, 2nd ed., Eagle/Walking Turtle 448 pp. $17.95
Interior Furnishings Southwest: The Sourcebook of the Best Production Craftspeople, Deats and Villani 256 pp. $19.95
Mona Winks: Self-Guided Tours of Europe's Top Museums, 2nd ed., Steves and Openshaw 456 pp. $16.95
Opera! The Guide to Western Europe's Great Houses, Zietz 296 pp. $18.95
Paintbrushes and Pistols: How the Taos Artists Sold the West, Taggett and Schwarz 280 pp. $17.95
The People's Guide to Mexico, 9th ed., Franz 608 pp. $18.95
The People's Guide to RV Camping in Mexico, Franz with Rogers 320 pp. $13.95
Ranch Vacations: The Complete Guide to Guest and Resort, Fly-Fishing, and Cross-Country Skiing Ranches, 2nd ed., Kilgore 396 pp. $18.95
The Shopper's Guide to Art and Crafts in the Hawaiian Islands, Schuchter 272 pp. $13.95
The Shopper's Guide to Mexico, Rogers and Rosa 224 pp. $9.95
Ski Tech's Guide to Equipment, Skiwear, and Accessories, ed. Tanler 144 pp. $11.95
Ski Tech's Guide to Maintenance and Repair, ed. Tanler 160 pp. $11.95
A Traveler's Guide to Asian Culture, Chambers 224 pp. $13.95
Traveler's Guide to Healing Centers and Retreats in North America, Rudee and Blease 240 pp. $11.95
Understanding Europeans, Miller 272 pp. $14.95
Undiscovered Islands of the Caribbean, 3nd ed., Willes 264 pp. $14.95
Undiscovered Islands of the Mediterranean, 2nd ed., Moyer and Willes 256 pp. $13.95
Undiscovered Islands of the U.S. and Canadian West Coast, Moyer and Willes 208 pp. $12.95
A Viewer's Guide to Art: A Glossary of Gods, People, and Creatures, Shaw and Warren 144 pp. $10.95
The Visitor's Guide to the Birds of the Eastern National Parks: United States and Canada, Wauer 400 pp. $15.95

2 to 22 Days Series
Each title offers 22 flexible daily itineraries that can be used to get the most out of vacations of any length. Included are not only "must see" attractions but also little-known villages and hidden "jewels" as well as valuable general information.
22 Days Around the World, 1993 ed., Rapoport and Willes 264 pp. $13.95
2 to 22 Days Around the Great Lakes, 1993 ed., Schuchter 192 pp. $10.95

22 Days in Alaska, Lanier 128 pp. $7.95
2 to 22 Days in the American Southwest, 1993 ed., Harris 176 pp. $10.95
2 to 22 Days in Asia, 1993 ed., Rapoport and Willes 176 pp. $10.95
2 to 22 Days in Australia, 1993 ed., Gottberg 192 pp. $10.95
2 to 22 Days in California, 1993 ed., Rapoport 192 pp. $10.95
22 Days in China, Duke and Victor 144 pp. $7.95
2 to 22 Days in Europe, 1993 ed., Steves 288 pp. $13.95
2 to 22 Days in Florida, 1993 ed., Harris 192 pp. $10.95
2 to 22 Days in France, 1993 ed., Steves 192 pp. $10.95
2 to 22 Days in Germany, Austria, & Switzerland, 1993 ed., Steves 224 pp. $10.95
2 to 22 Days in Great Britain, 1993 ed., Steves 192 pp. $10.95
2 to 22 Days in Hawaii, 1993 ed., Schuchter 176 pp. $10.95
22 Days in India, Mathur 136 pp. $7.95
22 Days in Japan, Old 136 pp. $7.95
22 Days in Mexico, 2nd ed., Rogers and Rosa 128 pp. $7.95
2 to 22 Days in New England, 1993 ed., Wright 192 pp. $10.95
2 to 22 Days in New Zealand, 1993 ed., Schuchter 192 pp. $10.95
2 to 22 Days in Norway, Sweden, & Denmark, 1993 ed., Steves 192 pp. $10.95
2 to 22 Days in the Pacific Northwest, 1993 ed., Harris 192 pp. $10.95
2 to 22 Days in the Rockies, 1993 ed., Rapoport 192 pp. $10.95
2 to 22 Days in Spain & Portugal, 1992 ed., Steves 192 pp. $9.95
2 to 22 Days in Texas, 1993 ed., Harris 192 pp. $10.95
2 to 22 Days in Thailand, 1993 ed., Richardson 180 pp. $10.95
22 Days in the West Indies, Morreale and Morreale 136 pp. $7.95

Parenting Series

Being a Father: Family, Work, and Self, *Mothering* Magazine 176 pp. $12.95
Preconception: A Woman's Guide to Preparing for Pregnancy and Parenthood, Aikey-Keller 232 pp. $14.95
Schooling at Home: Parents, Kids, and Learning, *Mothering* Magazine 264 pp. $14.95
Teens: A Fresh Look, *Mothering* Magazine 240 pp. $14.95

"Kidding Around" Travel Guides for Young Readers

Written for kids eight years of age and older.

Kidding Around Atlanta, Pedersen 64 pp. $9.95
Kidding Around Boston, 2nd ed., Byers 64 pp. $9.95
Kidding Around Chicago, 2nd ed., Davis 64 pp. $9.95
Kidding Around the Hawaiian Islands, Lovett 64 pp. $9.95
Kidding Around London, Lovett 64 pp. $9.95
Kidding Around Los Angeles, Cash 64 pp. $9.95
Kidding Around the National Parks of the Southwest, Lovett 108 pp. $12.95
Kidding Around New York City, 2nd ed., Lovett 64 pp. $9.95
Kidding Around Paris, Clay 64 pp. $9.95
Kidding Around Philadelphia, Clay 64 pp. $9.95
Kidding Around San Diego, Luhrs 64 pp. $9.95
Kidding Around San Francisco, Zibart 64 pp. $9.95
Kidding Around Santa Fe, York 64 pp. $9.95
Kidding Around Seattle, Steves 64 pp. $9.95
Kidding Around Spain, Biggs 108 pp. $12.95
Kidding Around Washington, D.C., 2nd ed., Pedersen 64 pp. $9.95

"Extremely Weird" Series for Young Readers

Written for kids eight years of age and older.

Extremely Weird Bats, Lovett 48 pp. $9.95
Extremely Weird Birds, Lovett 48 pp. $9.95
Extremely Weird Endangered Species, Lovett 48 pp. $9.95
Extremely Weird Fishes, Lovett 48 pp. $9.95
Extremely Weird Frogs, Lovett 48 pp. $9.95
Extremely Weird Insects, Lovett 48 pp. $9.95
Extremely Weird Primates, Lovett 48 pp. $9.95
Extremely Weird Reptiles, Lovett 48 pp. $9.95
Extremely Weird Sea Creatures, Lovett 48 pp. $9.95
Extremely Weird Spiders, Lovett 48 pp. $9.95

Masters of Motion Series
For kids eight years and older.

How to Drive an Indy Race Car, Rubel 48 pages $9.95
How to Fly a 747, Paulson 48 pages $9.95
How to Fly the Space Shuttle, Shorto 48 pages $9.95

Quill Hedgehog Adventures Series
Green fiction for kids. Written for kids eight years of age and older.

Quill's Adventures in the Great Beyond. Waddington-Feather 96 pp. $5.95
Quill's Adventures in Wasteland, Waddington-Feather 132 pp. $5.95
Quill's Adventures in Grozzieland, Waddington-Feather 132 pp. $5.95

X-ray Vision Series
For kids eight years and older.

Looking Inside Cartoon Animation, Schultz 48 pages $9.95
Looking Inside Sports Aerodynamics, Schultz 48 pages $9.95
Looking Inside Sunken Treasure, Schultz 48 pp. $9.95
Looking Inside Telescopes and the Night Sky, Schultz 48 pp. $9.95
Looking Inside the Brain, Schultz 48 pages $9.95

Other Young Readers Titles

Habitats: Where the Wild Things Live, Hacker & Kaufman 48 pp. $9.95
The Indian Way: Learning to Communicate with Mother Earth, McLain 114 pp. $9.95
The Kids' Environment Book: What's Awry and Why, Pedersen 192 pp. $13.95
Kids Explore America's African-American Heritage, Westridge Young Writers Workshop 112 pp. $8.95
Kids Explore America's Hispanic Heritage, Westridge Young Writers Workshop 112 pp. $7.95
Rads, Ergs, and Cheeseburgers: The Kids' Guide to Energy and the Environment, Yanda 108 pp. $12.95

Automotive Titles

How to Keep Your VW Alive, 15th ed., 464 pp. $21.95
How to Keep Your Subaru Alive 480 pp. $21.95
How to Keep Your Toyota Pickup Alive 392 pp. $21.95
How to Keep Your Datsun/Nissan Alive 544 pp. $21.95
The Greaseless Guide to Car Care Confidence: Take the Terror Out of Talking to Your Mechanic, Jackson 224 pp. $14.95
Off-Road Emergency Repair & Survival, Ristow 160 pp. $9.95

Ordering Information
If you cannot find our books in your local bookstore, you can order directly from us. If you send us money for a book not yet available, we will hold your money until we can ship you the book. Your books will be sent to you via UPS (for U.S. destinations). UPS will not deliver to a P.O. Box; please give us a street address. Include $3.75 for the first item ordered and $.50 for each additional item to cover shipping and handling costs. For airmail within the U.S., enclose $4.00. All foreign orders will be shipped surface rate; please enclose $3.00 for the first item and $1.00 for each additional item. Please inquire about foreign airmail rates.

Method of Payment
Your order may be paid by check, money order, or credit card. We cannot be responsible for cash sent through the mail. All payments must be made in U.S. dollars drawn on a U.S. bank. Canadian postal money orders in U.S. dollars are acceptable. For VISA, MasterCard, or American Express orders, include your card number, expiration date, and your signature, or call (800) 888-7504. Books ordered on American Express cards can be shipped only to the billing address of the cardholder. Sorry, no C.O.D.'s. Residents of sunny New Mexico, add 5.875% tax to the total.

Address all orders and inquiries to:

John Muir Publications
P.O. Box 613
Santa Fe, NM 87504
(505) 982-4078
(800) 888-7504